# First Aid for House Plants

# First Aid for House Plants

## BY SHIRLEY ROSS

### ILLUSTRATIONS BY BETH CANNON

McGRAW-HILL BOOK COMPANY

New York   St. Louis   San Francisco
Toronto   Montreal   Mexico   Düsseldorf

Book design by Ingrid Beckman.

5678910 MUMU 98


**Library of Congress Cataloging in Publication Data**

Ross, Shirley.
    First aid for house plants.

    Includes index.
    1. House plants—Diseases and pests.    I. Title.
SB608.H84R67        635.9′65        75-37763
ISBN 0-07-053869-7
ISBN 0-07-053868-9 pbk.

*To my sister Peggy*

# Contents

# Buying a Plant

Technically, there is no such thing as a house plant. Most plants commonly grown in the home are tropical plants that have managed to adapt themselves to an indoor environment. They have been domesticated. Of course, the more closely your environment matches that of your plant's natural habitat, the easier it will be for the plant to flourish. Hybrids, the result of the crossbreeding of two different species of plants, usually of the same genus, adapt especially well to indoor environments. The offspring are stronger and more vigorous than their pure parents and therefore easier to grow.

When shopping for plants for your house or apartment, there are several things to watch for in order to determine what kind of treatment the plant has been given, how healthy it is, and whether the plant you have selected is a sensible purchase:

1. The plant you select should have leaves approximately the same size, shape, and color as described in the Dictionary (see page 29).
2. Avoid a plant that has brown edges. It has been overheated or overfertilized.
3. If the lower leaves are yellow or pale in color, the plant has been improperly watered.
4. Buy bushy plants. If the new leaves on a plant are far apart, this is a sign of overwatering or overfertilizing, a common method of speeding the growth of a plant for selling purposes.
5. Read the chapter on pests and diseases (page 22) and check the plant carefully for signs of either. Examine the tips of new branches, the leaf nodes (where the leaf joins the stem) and the underside of the leaves.
6. Plants are not a sensible purchase if they are extremely root-bound. If the roots of a plant are visible above the surface of the soil, or poking through the drainage holes, the plant is definitely root-bound. If the leaves are wilted, and new leaves are smaller than older leaves, this too is evidence that the plant has become overcrowded in its pot.
7. It is wise to buy young plants, provided they have a sufficient root system. Young plants are more able to withstand the shock of moving from the greenhouse to the home.

As an initiation, give your newly purchased plants a bath when you bring them home. Besides being good for a plant in general, it is also an added precaution against any undetected insects which might be present on the plant.

Fill a sink with warm water and a small amount of nondetergent soap flakes. Cover the top of the pot with a piece of aluminum foil. Place your hand over the foil and invert the pot. Immerse the foliage in the water and gently swish it back and forth. Rinse it with clean, warm water.

Overdosing a plant with fertilizer can create an accumulation of salts in the soil that can be injurious to the roots of a plant. After bathing your plant's foliage, you can also, in a sense, clean the soil by giving it a thorough watering from the top. Let it drain for an hour and then water it thoroughly again. This well help dissolve the salts and lessen any buildup that might be present.

When a plant is moving to a new environment, it will naturally go through a period of adjustment. Don't be upset if your plant begins to drop some of its older leaves. Let this process happen organically—don't pick the leaves off before they are ready to fall. When a leaf falls, it seals the point of attachment to the stem and thus leaves no open wound for insects or disease to attack.

# Dormancy

The day-to-day rhythm of most plants, which finds them working during the daylight hours and eating and resting at night, is broken by a periodic interval of rest called dormancy. It can be likened to hibernation in animals. Activity in the plant slows down to the point where growth is imperceptible. There are no new foliage, flowers or buds.

The assumption that cold weather causes dormancy in plants is not true. In the north, terminal growth on the branches of trees and shrubs subsides in August, before the arrival of 40 degree temperatures (the temperature at which physiological activity stops in many plants). And there is evidence of swellings in the twigs, a sign that the starches essential for new growth in spring are being stored by the plant.

Dormancy is now believed to be triggered either by a change in the quality of light or a change in the length of daylight. As the fall season arrives, a chemical called Dormin, or abscissic acid, accumulates in trees and shrubs and other woody plants until physiological activity slows to a virtual standstill. As winter progresses, this chemical is gradually destroyed, and by spring, when plants begin to grow again, traces of Dormin have disappeared.

Plants usually enter a dormant period shortly after they have bloomed. Typical signs of the onset of this phase in a plant's life cycle are a slowdown or complete halting of new growth, a slight discoloring in the leaves, and a drooping of the foliage.

Length of dormancy varies greatly, depending upon the plant. Some plants, African violets for example, will bloom all year long if they are in the proper environment. Some plants are dormant for a few weeks only. Geraniums will slow down only very slightly and for a short period of time. Other plants spend six months or more in a dormant state.

When a plant is dormant, it needs little or no sun. A dormant plant should not be fertilized. Watering should be greatly curtailed. Never repot a plant that is dormant; this will disturb the plant by upsetting the root system unnecessarily.

Dormancy in plants is a natural phase of their seasonal cycle and has to be accepted and tolerated. Many plants are inadvertently thrown away, or treated for all kinds of ailments and diseases, when all the plant is doing is taking a break. Dormancy is, in fact, a good sign that the plant is healthy, and there is no reason to want to prevent it. Be patient with your plant even if it looks like it has had it. The aftereffects make it worthwhile.

# Grooming

Regular grooming is an important part of caring for house plants. You will probably have to spend an hour each week in a routine grooming procedure for a large collection of house plants:

1. Remove yellowed leaves and any marred foliage.
2. Scrub off fertilizer salts or mold that has accumulated on the outside of clay pots, or on the rims of pots, with a stiff brush and warm water.
3. Remove the top layer of soil and replace

it with fresh medium if excess fertilizing has formed a crust on the surface of the soil.

4. Misting your plants every few days will help keep the leaves clean. For very large-leaved plants, use a soft sponge and warm water to wash them at least once a month. Never use any waxy substances to give the leaves an artificial shine. Wax will clog the stomata of the leaves, the pores through which the plant transpires.

5. Check your plants for any evidence of disease or insects. If the leaves are exceptionally sticky and dusty, this can be a sign of insects. Add mild, nondetergent soap flakes to the water, and rinse the leaves off after washing.

6. Once a month, your plants will benefit from a good washing. Rinse small plants, including hairy-leaved plants like the African violet or piggyback plants, in a sink filled with warm water and mild soap flakes (not detergent). Rinse with warm, clean water.

Larger, stronger plants can be given a shower. Cover the top of the pot with a piece of aluminum foil, and put the plant in the tub or shower stall. Shower them in a gentle stream of warm water.

# Pruning

Pruning consists of cutting a plant's branches back for the purpose of eliminating unwanted or superfluous growth. Pruning plants encourages thick and bushy plants. This grooming procedure will improve the shape of a plant if it is done properly, as well as promote the growth of strong, flower-bearing shoots. If a plant is permitted to grow wild, it will eventually begin to drop leaves, the leaves will get brown and ragged in appearance, and its branches will become entangled in each other. This unkempt appearance is not only displeasing to the eye, but also can be unhealthy for the plant.

Using a sharp knife or pruning shears, carefully snip unwanted growth evenly around the plant to achieve a desired shape. Make all pruning cuts directly above a leaf which has a bud in its axil, growing in the direction in which you want the plant to develop. Where a single stem exists, a pruning cut will encourage two new shoots to develop. Similarly, if an entire branch is removed, two new branches will take its place. To avoid unattractive stubs, make your pruning cuts very close to the parent branch or trunk from which the shoot grows.

Plants that grow from crowns (African violets, for instance), plants that spring from growing points close to the soil, and plants that grow directly from soil level (ferns and *Spathiphyllum*) should not be pruned. Succulents exhibit scars where they have been pruned. Palms and dracaena and other single-stemmed plants are usually ruined in appearance for so long after they have been pruned that it makes it an unhelpful grooming procedure.

## PINCHING

Pinching is a method of pruning which will promote a compact and bushy plant by removing the tips of growing shoots. This checks the growth of strong shoots and causes shoot buds to grow which would have otherwise remained dormant. It encourages budding and flowering, and controls the height of a plant.

The term is quite literal. Using your thumb and forefinger, "pinch" off a growing shoot immediately above the node, the point where the leaf is attached. Pinches made here will force branching below the cut, except in succulents whose stems have become woody. Philodendrons, coleuses, begonias, geraniums and most other soft-stemmed plants will benefit in growth and appearance from pinching.

## DISBUDDING

Disbudding is a method used to prevent a plant from blooming until desired, by pinching off the flower buds. If the side buds growing beneath a terminal bud are pinched off, this will cause the terminal bud to produce a better-shaped flower.

## TRAINING

Training is a method used along with proper pruning and pinching to achieve a desired shape in a plant by attaching the shoots of the plant to supports by tying or using special tacks. The supports can be improvised from pieces of wire coat hanger, or other materials. It is best to train a plant this way when it is fairly young.

## ROOT PRUNING

If a plant outgrows its pot and you don't wish to repot it into a larger pot, root pruning can be done to solve the problem of the plant becoming harmfully pot-bound. Root pruning should be done in the spring when the plant shows signs of new growth. During this time, the root wound will be able to heal more quickly.

Place your hand over the soil surface and tip the pot over. Give it a firm knock against a hard surface. This should dislodge the root ball from the pot, and it should slip out quite easily. Make sure the soil is damp before removing the root ball from the pot. If the soil is too dry, it will fall away from the roots and make root pruning more difficult.

Place the root ball on a piece of newspaper on a tabletop or other hard surface. Using a sharp, sterilized knife, carefully shave down the sides of the root ball. The root ball should be pared down so that there is an inch of space between the root mass and the sides of the pot when it is repotted. Be careful not to disturb the heart of the root ball in any way; your plant will recover more quickly. Reshape the root ball so that it will conform to the shape of the pot, that is, wider at the top and narrowing at the base.

If old drainage material and roots are stuck to the bottom of the root ball, remove them with a stick, and then repot the plant. (See *Potting.*)

It is a good idea to remove some of the new top growth on a plant that has been root pruned. This will help the shocked roots recover more quickly by cutting down the loss of moisture by evaporation through the leaves.

Cover repotted smaller plants with a plastic bag and keep them out of the sun for about two weeks. The plastic will raise the heat and humidity and keep the foliage in good condition. When signs of new growth are evident, remove the plastic and return the plant to proper light and normal environmental conditions.

# Propagation

## ROOTING MEDIUMS

Although sand and peat moss are traditional rooting mediums for starting new plants, vermiculite and perlite have become very popular.

Vermiculite is mica ore that has been exposed to intense heat which causes the layers of mica to separate. The resulting material is ideal for root cuttings because its spongy texture holds water, and it is also sterile and free of any organisms which might attack the new plants. Vermiculite contains small amounts of potassium, calcium, and magnesium, which are elements that are beneficial to the growth of new plants. Vermiculite has a special ability to hold water and nutrients in reserve within the platelike structure of the particles and to release them to the root hairs later. This will allow you to use more fertilizer than is normally allowed with soil, without damaging the plants.

Perlite is volcanic ash that is also a very good

medium for rooting new plants. It will not decay or deteriorate and retains water. Unlike vermiculite, perlite does not contain minerals, nor does it have vermiculite's special ability to hold water and nutrients in reserve.

Vermiculite and perlite can be used alone or in a mixture with sand or peat moss.

## STEM CUTTINGS

For the propagation of long-stemmed plants, the stem cuttings should be vigorous, well-growing shoots, 3 to 4 inches in length, containing four to six leaves. Using a sharp, sterilized knife, make your cuttings about ¼ inch below the leaf node, the point where the leaf is attached to the stem.

Root formation will be structurally stronger if the cuttings are placed in a moist growing medium, rather than water. The only plants that root well in water are philodendrons, water ivy, *Ficus* and some species of begonias. The rooting medium can be vermiculite, perlite, peat moss or sharp sand, either used singularly or in a combination of two or more of them.

Fill a pot (clay or plastic) to within an inch of the rim with the rooting medium you have selected and water it thoroughly. Using a pencil or stick, make holes in the soil and insert the cuttings, spacing them well to avoid crowding. Be sure to remove any leaves that are below the soil, because they will eventually decay. Water the soil a second time to eliminate air pockets. With your fingertips, gently pack the medium around each cutting to secure it. Let the pot drain.

It is normal for leaves to lose moisture quite rapidly through transpiration. Without a root system to replace this moisture, the leaves on the cuttings will soon wilt. To prevent this, cover the pot with a plastic bag and secure it with tape or a rubber band. The plastic will create the humidity and heat necessary for the cuttings until roots have been formed. (Plastic covering is not necessary if the cuttings are kept in a basement or greenhouse where the humidity is 50 percent or more. Succulents, rhizome sections and thick-leaved cuttings do not require covering if the humidity of the environment is 50 percent or more, but the rooting medium should be kept moist at all times. Cuttings rooted in water need not be covered.)

Cuttings should be placed in bright light, but avoid direct sunlight. Succulents are the only cuttings that will endure the direct rays of the sun without wilting.

Check the root formation of your cuttings after a period of ten to fourteen days. Give each one a gentle tug. If the roots are well formed, the cutting will hold to the medium. If the cutting slips out in your hand, reinsert it in the soil and check it again in another week.

Repot the cuttings in very small pots once the roots have formed (see *Potting*) and give them the appropriate light and watering required by that particular species.

## LEAF CUTTINGS

A leaf, in order to be propagated, should be mature and should have at least ½ inch of leaf stem (petiole) attached to it.

Fill a pot to within an inch of the rim with a moist growing medium (vermiculite, perlite, peat moss, sharp sand or a combination). Insert the stem of the leaf into the medium and secure it by packing the soil gently around the stem. Cover the pot with a plastic bag and place it in bright light, avoiding direct sunlight. Succulent leaf cuttings can stand direct sunlight and do not require plastic covering, but the medium should be kept moist at all times.

Within four to eight weeks, small plantlets will begin to grow at the base of the leaf cuttings. Using a sharp razor blade, cut the plantlet from the leaf and pot it in a thumb pot with the appropriate soil mixture. The plantlets can now be placed in sunlight and watered according to the plant's requirements.

## REX BEGONIA LEAF CUTTINGS

Another form of leaf propagation is using the leaf of a rex begonia. A growing medium of sand and peat moss is the best mixture for leaf cuttings from rex begonia.

After placing the leaf flat down (underside down) on top of the moistened soil, pin the leaf down at the veins with hairpins. This will keep the leaf in contact with the soil. Then, with a razor blade, make several small slits in the major veins of the leaf. These points are where the new plants will begin to develop.

Cover the pot securely with plastic. When new plantlets begin to appear, pot each one separately in thumb pots. Use begonia soil and give the plantlets the correct light and water required by that particular species.

## RUNNERS

Many plants propagate by sending out from the base long, trailing stems, at the tips of which small plantlets form. These runners, or stolons, are very easy to root. Simply pin the plantlet down in the soil of the pot the mother plant is growing in. The plantlet will begin to develop its own root system, and when it is sufficient enough you will be able to repot it in a small pot.

An alternative method to propagate runners is to cut the plantlet off the runner and root it the same way you would a stem cutting.

## SUCKERS OR OFFSHOOTS

These are small complete plants that grow using the same root system as the mother plant. They can be found either growing at the base of the larger plant or some distance away from the plant. In the latter case, the offshoot is connected by underground runners to the main root system, as well as having a root system of its own.

Suckers or offshoots will not grow well if separated from the mother plant unless their root system is sufficiently developed. Wait until they are at least 3 or 4 inches tall before taking any action.

To separate them from the main plant, tip the plant over and knock out the root ball from the pot. Shake off the soil. Then, using a sharp, sterilized knife, cut the suckers away from the mother plant. Cut as close to the main stem as possible. Repot the mother plant and pot each sucker separately in smaller pots.

## DIVISION

Division is an ideal method of propagation for plants that increase their size by sending up more than one stem or grow in clusters or irregular masses. African violets, spider plants and ferns are several plants that can be propagated by division. The best time to divide a plant is in the spring, when there has been new growth.

Division entails separating a plant into two or more smaller plants and transplanting them. Each smaller plant retains a portion of the original root system, crown, and top growth, and only requires a few days of readjustment.

Invert the plant to be divided and remove the root ball from the pot by tapping it against a hard surface. You should be able to pull the stems apart gently, making sure that each separate stem keeps a share of the root system. If this is difficult, remove enough soil from the roots so that you can see how they are organized. Using a sharp, sterilized knife, separate the stems by cutting through the crown of the plant (the point where the top growth and roots are joined). Because this process is somewhat hard on a plant, it is best not to make your divisions too small. If the divided sections are substantial, the plant will recover more quickly.

After you have repotted the new plants, water each one thoroughly. Overwatering is often the reason why divided plants fail, so let the top soil dry out between waterings. Cover the plants with plastic if the leaves look wilted. Support the plastic with sticks so that it doesn't come in contact with the foliage. And keep the plants out of direct sunlight for approximately one week.

There might be some leaf loss. If there is yellowing of leaves on the outer edges of the plant, remove those leaves.

Return the plants to normal light, temperature and watering when they appear to be well reestablished.

## AIR LAYERING

What to do with a house plant—a *Ficus* or dieffenbachia or dracaena, for example—that has grown too tall? Air layering is an excellent solution to this problem. It is a method of propagation by which roots are induced to grow "in air" at a point on the stem of the mother plant. This section of the stem is then removed from the main plant and grown separately, as a new plant.

About one-third of the way down from the growing tip of your plant, make a slit with a razor blade or sharp knife. Cut halfway through the main stem, and insert a small piece of toothpick or wooden match into the slit to keep it slightly open. Wrap thoroughly dampened sphagnum moss around the stem where the cut has been made. Wrap a piece of plastic around the moss, tying it securely with string, and leaving an open space at the top where water can be sprinkled in to keep the moss damp.

Continue to care for the plant as before. Depending on the species of plant, it will take several weeks to several months for roots to form inside the moss. When you are able to see roots through the plastic, make a cut all the way through the stem, just below the plastic, severing the plantlet from the mother plant.

Pot the plantlet in proper soil in a small pot and cover it with plastic to give it sufficient heat and humidity until the roots have established themselves in the medium.

## SEEDS

Seeds are the result of the fertilization of an egg cell in the pistil of a flower by pollen from the stamen of a flower. Both pistil and stamen can be in the same flower or in different flowers. Each seed is unique and has its own individual heredity.

Milled sphagnum moss (or unmilled sphagnum moss run through a wire strainer) is a very good medium for starting seedlings. Vermiculite and perlite can also be used.

Refrigerator food-storage containers, glass jars, or pots and plastic bags can be used for starting seeds. The important thing is that the container should be able to be well covered in order for the seeds to germinate, and it must have drainage holes in the bottom through which the seeds will receive moisture.

Fill the container to the top with the growing medium you have chosen and pack it down until it is about ½ to ¾ inch below the rim. Moisten it thoroughly and let it drain.

If you are planting small seeds, sprinkle them on top of the medium. They will sift down into the soil by themselves. If you are planting larger seeds, cover them with a layer of damp sphagnum moss or a fine vermiculite. This layer should be about twice the size of the seeds in depth. It will be important in keeping the seeds damp while they are germinating.

Make sure the seeds are well placed so that they will not be overcrowded when they start to grow.

Place the container in warm water and let it sit until the medium has absorbed enough water to be moist on the surface. Never water the seeds from the top—the water will wash the seeds too deeply into the soil.

Cover the seeds in their container and place it in a bright spot (no direct sun) where the temperature is 70 to 80 degrees. It is best not to uncover the seeds until they have germinated.

When germination has occurred, uncover the seeds and put them in an environment appropriate for the species of plant you are growing. Water them in the morning just enough so that the soil will begin to dry out by night. If the soil is too wet, the young plants will be susceptible to a fungus disease called "damping off," which attacks the cells at the soil level and can kill the plants.

The first leaves you see on your seedlings will be used to nourish the young plant. True leaves begin with the second pair of leaves. When the seedlings have four to five leaves, it is a good time to transplant them.

Use a fork to carefully pry the seedling out of the soil. Pot each one in a thumb pot in the correct growing medium for the plant. Be sure to secure the seedling in the soil by pressing the soil against the sides of the stem. Avoid touching the plant itself. This is important because it forces the root system into contact with the soil and encourages strong growth.

Rapid-growth seedling plants (begonias, geraniums, coleuses, etc.) if pinched when transplanted will send up side shoots and develop into lush, bushy plants.

As the seedlings become pot-bound, repot them into the next size pot. There is no need to disturb the root ball when repotting. (See *Potting.*)

## RHIZOMES

Rhizomes are the thick, creeping stems that grow along the surface of the soil. One method to propagate rhizomes is to break each one into two or three sections. Sprinkle them with a low-strength hormone powder, and plant them the way you would large seeds.

Another method is to prepare a moist growing medium and shave the rhizomes into scales, so that the scales fall onto the top of the soil. Cover them with pure milled sphagnum moss or with the grow-

ing medium. This layer should be about twice the size (depth) of the scales. Using this method, a 1-inch rhizome can yield over twenty new plants. Treat them like seedlings.

Gesneriads with rhizomes will double the number of rhizomes per pot per season. (Gesneriads are cultivated ornamentals. They include many tropical and subtropical perennial herbs and shrubs with showy blossoms such as African violets, gloxinia and the lipstick plant.)

---

# Pots

---

House plants can be successfully grown in most any type of container, but you must keep in mind the fact that different kinds of pots will require different watering schedules and procedures.

## CLAY POTS

The red clay, or earthenware, pot has been the standard house plant pot for years, and for good reason. The clay pot has many advantages over pots manufactured from plastic or other materials. Because clay is porous, any excess moisture in the soil is permitted to seep through the sides of the pot as well as down through the drainage holes. This porosity also allows oxygen to get to the roots of the plant.

It is easy to tell if a plant in a clay pot has been overwatered. The pot is dark in color and damp and may have a slimy feel. A clay pot that has a green slime to it should be cleaned thoroughly with warm water and a stiff brush.

If you use a decorated or glazed clay pot without a drainage hole, you will have to be careful about watering. It is easy to overwater a plant in this type of pot without knowing it.

If you are interested in growing orchids, rhizomes, begonias or bulbs, you can buy clay pots that are especially designed for the fast drainage that these plants require.

## PLASTIC POTS

Plastic pots are not porous, therefore neither water nor air can pass through the sides of the pot. The roots can not breathe as well as they can in a clay pot, and soil will not dry out as fast. If your plant is in a plastic pot, it will not require watering as frequently as it would otherwise. This is important to remember because if a plant is overwatered, the water will accumulate and eventually cause the roots to rot. Evidence of this will be yellow leaves and dropping of buds; if the condition is not corrected, the plant will die.

It is possible to buy clear plastic pots through which the roots are visible and can be checked for any signs of overwatering or decay. The exposure of the roots to light in transparent pots does not seem to impede growth of the plant in any way.

Avoid using pots made of flexible plastic or rubberlike plastic. If you purchase a plant growing in this type of pot, repot it. Flexible pots damage the plant's roots and also seem to contain a toxic substance which is harmful to plants.

## POT SIZE

How large a pot should a plant have? This is determined by a plant's growth habits. If a plant grows very slowly (cactus, for example), it will not need a large pot or frequent repotting.

Plants that have rapid growth patterns (begonias, for example) can be repotted from a 4-inch to a 6-inch pot when they are pot-bound.

Most plants, though, will only require one size larger when repotted. A plant growing in a 4-inch pot should be repotted in a 5-inch pot. If you put your plant in a pot that is too large for the root ball, the plant will be forced to sacrifice leaf and top growth while the roots are busy spreading and growing in the soil area.

All used pots must be thoroughly scrubbed before using again with detergent and rinsed in boiling water to kill any source of plant disease that might be present.

Do not repot a plant that has been growing in a plastic pot into a clay pot, and vice versa. The interiors of the clay and plastic pots are different. A clay pot is smooth, and the root ball that has been growing in it will conform to these lines. Plastic pots have inside rims, and the root mass that has become pot-bound here will have roots tangled along the rim as well as in the pot itself. To transfer a root ball of this shape into a clay pot will require a pot that is several sizes larger.

## WHEN TO REPOT

Normally, the best time to repot a plant is in the spring, when the plant has started new growth. There are several ways to tell if a plant is in need of repotting:

1. The plant wilts several hours after watering.
2. Bottom leaves turn yellow and drop off.
3. New growth on the plant fails to reach normal size or seems stunted.
4. Roots can be seen growing out of the drainage hole of the pot and/or growing out of the surface of the top soil. These wandering roots are searching for food, and when they reach this point of exposure, the delicate root hairs at the tips are likely to be damaged, unprotected by soil or the pot.

If you observe any one or more of these conditions in a plant, it is time to take a careful look at the root ball of the plant.

Place one hand over the surface of the pot and turn the plant upside down. Gently tap the rim of the pot on a hard surface to dislodge the root ball. It should drop out easily if it is firm. In case it is stuck, poke the end of a pencil through the drainage hole to dislodge it.

A plant has outgrown its pot or is "pot-bound" if its roots are found to be thickly twined and matted around the outside of the root ball. Although a certain degree of pot-boundness is good for a plant in that it encourages the plant to bloom, when it reaches an extreme stage, and the root system has actually outgrown the pot, the plant will begin to show adverse effects. The soil area is no longer large enough to hold water long enough for the roots to absorb it. The plant can not get enough water to survive. In an attempt to compensate, the plant will put its energies into new growth and consequently lose older growth; or it might produce new growth that is stunted. Eventually, no matter how much water it is given, the plant will wilt repeatedly, and this wilting will weaken the entire structure of the plant.

All potting soils will gradually lose their richness over a certain period of time. To prevent this, as well as any accumulation of chemicals in the soil, house plants should be given new growing mediums every two to two and a half years.

Plants also get old. If a plant has long, tired-looking stems and few leaves, it might be time to replace it with another plant. If the older plant is healthy, use it to produce new plants.

Care must be taken to watch plants that are growing well in order to gauge when it is time to repot them, before they get harmfully pot-bound.

# Soil

The soil in which your house plants grow performs several important life-sustaining functions. It supports the plant physically. It acts as protection for the roots. And it is the medium through which the plant receives water, air and food essential for healthy growth. Soil is also the source of certain nutrients and minerals which the plant can utilize for growth.

Sand, clay and humus are the three main ingredients in a good soil mixture for house plants, and each has a special job to do. Sand is disintegrated rock. Its loose granules create air pockets in the soil which permit excess water to drain off and prevent the soil from becoming waterlogged. Vermiculite and perlite can be substituted for sand in a soil mixture. Clay is made up of very fine particles that stick together and pack hard when water is added to it. Clay acts like glue to hold the soil firmly together and give it solidity. Humus is the organic part of the soil, formed from partially decomposed plant and animal matter. It provides nourishment for the plants, and its spongy quality enables the soil to retain moisture. (It would also cause the soil to become waterlogged unless sand were added.)

Premixed soil which has already been pasteurized and sterilized to kill any harmful bacteria is safest to use. You can buy it prepacked in plastic bags and specially mixed for different plants. Or you can buy separate ingredients—peat moss, perlite, vermiculite, whole or milled sphagnum, and all-purpose soil—in separate packages and blend soil mixtures yourself.

Sphagnum moss is very good for seedlings because it has antibiotic properties which protect them from disease. Sphagnum moss originates in bogs where it has been forming and building up for centuries. There are two varieties available. One is the light brown peat moss, which is coarse in texture and is in a lesser degree of decay than darker peat moss. It is best suited for plants that require humus. The darker brown, velvety, sphagnum peat moss has a high acid content and is good for acid-loving plants, gardenias and most gesneriads.

If the soil is too acid or alkaline for a plant, its vital elements (phosphorus, magnesium, potash, etc.) will not be properly assimilated by the plant's root hairs. The plant will consequently be deprived of essential nutrition. Plants must be grown in their proper medium to thrive.

A recent development of agricultural research are the soilless mixes. They are sterile, contain the proper elements for a growing medium and are lightweight for easy shipping of plants to retailers. These mixtures are especially good for plants growing under artificial light.

It is not wise to use soil for your house plants which has been scooped up from outside in its natural state. First of all, it should be pasteurized before using to kill off any microorganisms that could later cause extensive damage to your plant collection. To do this, add water to the soil and bake it in a 180°F. oven for thirty minutes.

Secondly, it is likely that the soil you find outside is going to be too heavy and too dense in its natural state to allow for good drainage when used for house plants.

If you would like to mix up a batch of houseplant soil that will be very good for your plants, use the following recipe:

1 part garden loam (or all-purpose soil)
1 part sand (vermiculite or perlite can be substituted)
1 part peat moss (compost)
Small amount of charcoal (soil conditioner and purifier)

If a plant likes acid, use an extra measure of peat moss, and be sure to include vermiculite or perlite for good drainage.

# Potting

Equipment:

1. Clean pot (clay, plastic)
2. Soil mixture
3. Small stones, pebbles, pieces of broken pot
4. Netting—can be a piece of old stocking
5. Wooden ice tongs for handling spiny plants

In order for a potted plant to thrive, it must have proper drainage. If you are using a clay pot, place several pieces of broken pot or small stones over the drainage holes. This will allow any excess water to drain out through the bottom of the pot and at the same time prevent soil from clogging up the drainage hole.

If you are using a plastic pot, you will have to take extra steps to ensure the plant has proper drainage. In a plastic pot, water can only evaporate through the top soil, or drain out through the bottom—plastic is nonporous. To provide for proper drainage, layer the bottom of the pot with about ½ to 1 inch of small stones or pebbles. Cover the stones with a piece of nylon netting. This will act as a filter to keep soil from clogging the spaces in between the pebbles and to allow the water to run through.

If you are using a pot without a drainage hole, you must provide a sufficient space below the bottom of the soil where excess water can collect without harming the roots. Put at least 1 to 1½ inches of small stones or pebbles in the bottom of the pot and cover with a piece of nylon netting. This drainage layer should not pack down or become dense. And the soil used in such a pot should have the proper amount of sand, vermiculite or perlite in it to facilitate drainage. Be very careful about watering a plant that is in a pot like this.

When removing a plant from a pot for repotting, the soil should not be too dry or it will fall away from the roots. Put one hand over the top of the pot, invert it, and tap the pot against a firm surface. The root ball should slip out easily. If there is sticking, use the end of a pencil to poke the root ball through the drainage hole and gently push it out.

If you are repotting a very large plant, the safest way to remove it from its old pot without harming the plant is to break the pot with a hammer. Save the pieces for drainage material.

Once the root ball has been removed, keep it intact and gently clean up any drainage matter that is stuck to the bottom of it, including old roots that have become entwined in the pebbles.

If you desire to remove all the soil from the roots, either to exterminate insects or to prune the roots, shake as much soil off the roots as will come easily, and then wash the remaining soil off under a stream of warm water, being careful not to damage or break off any roots.

For root pruning, use a very sharp sterilized knife, and make your cuts at the point where the root originates or at the joint of the root. Be sure to remove all roots that are not healthy or are broken or overly long. If the removal of root tips, which are the means by which a plant absorbs water and nutrients, is overdone, the plant will enter a state of shock.

For repotting, the soil mixture should be damp but not soggy or it will pack too hard. The pot should be clean and dry.

If you have removed all the soil from the roots, you must first pour a handful of loose potting soil into the bottom of the pot (after you have provided for drainage). Then hold the plant erect in the pot, by the stem, with its base about half an inch below the rim of the pot. Pour in the soil around the roots until the pot is filled to the rim.

Press the soil down with your thumbs around the *rim* of the pot *only*. Do not pack the soil down close to the stem or try to force the root ball down into the pot. This would damage the roots. When you are finished, the plant should stand about half an inch below the rim of the pot for proper watering.

The easiest way to repot a plant with the root ball intact is to make a mold in the new soil in which to drop the root ball. To do this, fill the pot three-fourths full of potting soil. Press the old pot firmly down into the soil. This will create a hole slightly larger than the root ball. Then place the root ball in the cavity, making sure that the base of the plant is about half an inch below the rim of the pot. Still holding the plant steady, rap the edges of the pot. The soil will gently settle around the root ball. Add more soil if necessary with a funnel or a spoon, and be careful not to bury the old soil surface with new soil.

It is important that you preserve the *same soil line* when you repot a plant. If you have removed all the soil from the roots, you will be able to distinguish the soil line by the coloring of the stem: it will be lighter above the soil line and darker below. If you have repotted the plant with the root ball intact, do not cover the surface of the root ball with new soil, but fill in new soil around the edges. Why? If the old soil surface or line is buried by new soil, the roots will deteriorate because the plant adjusts to a certain depth in the soil and will not adjust to a change. If the old soil line is above the new soil surface, the plant could fall over and the tips of the roots would be exposed and die. (An exception to this rule are philodendrons, which have active roots above ground.)

After you have repotted a plant, it will need high humidity and thorough watering. If the roots have been extensively pruned, cover the plant with a plastic bag to prevent wilting until the root hairs have had time to grow back.

Very large plants need never be repotted. They can be properly maintained if the top layer of soil is changed every few years. Being careful not to damage the roots which might lie beneath the surface of the soil, scrape away 2 to 3 inches of top soil and replace it with fresh growing medium. Water it thoroughly.

# Watering

There is only one correct time to water a plant and that is when it needs it. Different plants have varying water requirements: some prefer a drier soil, others like their soil to be continually damp, some can go for weeks without watering, and so on. It is not simply a matter of deciding that you will give your plants a certain amount of water every Monday at 8 A.M. The schedule of watering will be determined not only by the kind of plant, but also by other factors which you will have to take into consideration, such as outside weather conditions, air temperature, ventilation and type of pot the plant is growing in. These factors are never the same in any home or apartment, and so a plant's need for water will always be subject to change.

It is important to give your plants daily attention to determine whether to water or not.

In general, it is a sound practice for most house plants to let the soil dry out somewhat between waterings. When the soil is allowed to dry, the soil particles shrink, allowing oxygen to enter and aerate the soil and, importantly, the roots and root hairs. The root hairs, located at the ends of the roots, absorb nutrients and moisture that support the plant life. Root hairs require oxygen to stimulate their growth and carry out their functions. Active root hairs are the key to optimum plant growth. When the soil dries out a bit, the root hairs become active, pushing out in all directions in search of moisture. If the soil is in a constant state of wetness, the root hairs are deprived of oxygen and won't be able to function properly and the plant will eventually die.

To determine if a plant needs water, test the soil by poking your finger about half an inch down into it—you will be able to feel how dry or moist it is. Also, look at the soil—it will be lighter in color when it is dry.

You will be able to tell by the pot, if it is clay, if a plant is being overwatered. The pot will give you clues—it will be very dark in color and have a slimy feel to it. If a plant looks unhealthy and you think the reason might be overwatering, it is a good idea to check the roots of the plant in order to see if they are healthy. When you remove the root ball from the pot, it should be firm and hold together. The roots should be white in color. If they are soft, brownish in color and have a sour smell, the plant is suffering from root rot and cannot be saved.

A plant can appear to be suffering from overwatering and the problem might not be as drastic as root rot. It might be that the drainage system in the pot is clogged with soil particles that have been worked into the spaces between the pebbles or around the drainage hole itself, thus blocking the passage of surplus water. To check the drainage system of a pot, poke a stick into the drainage hole—if it goes inside the pot with no resistance, then it is likely that the drainage system is clogged. Repot the plant (see *Potting*).

If a plant has been underwatered and is drooped and withered, the best way to revive it, rather than dousing it with water from the top, is to let the pot stand in a pan of warm water for one hour. This way, the plant will soak up a new supply of moisture that will go directly to the roots.

Transpiration, the process by which plants throw off waste products in the form of moisture, and the interaction of root and top growth in a plant, takes place at a much higher rate during daylight hours than at night. As a result, a plant requires more water during this period of the day, so it is best to water a plant in the morning, when temperatures are rising. Toward night, when temperatures begin to drop, the soil will begin to dry out somewhat, which is desirable. (This, of course, does not mean that if a plant needs water it shouldn't be watered at night.)

When plants are growing in a natural environment, they are "watered" from above. The water enters the soil through the surface and gradually seeps down to the roots, where it is absorbed. Use the same method for your house plants. Water each plant thoroughly from the top, using warm water—warm water is more readily absorbed than cold water, which can shock the roots and cause a plant to wilt. When water seeps out through the drainage hole into the saucer, this is an indication that the soil has been saturated. Don't let a plant stand in a saucer full of water for more than an hour.

If the water seems to run through the soil very quickly, the soil may have been allowed to become too dry and shrunk away from the sides of the pot. In this condition, the soil can not hold water efficiently and the water washes right through the soil before the roots will have a chance to absorb it. To correct this, immerse the plant *and* pot in a deep sink filled with water (or a bucket). The water level should be 2 inches above the soil line of the pot. You will notice air bubbles escaping out of the soil when you do this. Keep the plant immersed until the air bubbles stop rising. Remove the plant from the water and let it drain. If the soil is a very dry peatlike medium, it will probably require thirty minutes to drain, to allow the soil to absorb enough moisture. When the plant has finished draining, remove the remaining water.

While clay pots are excellent for growing house plants, there is a tendency for the soil to dry out very quickly. To slow this down, put the clay pot into a larger pot, and fill the space between the two pots with moist sphagnum moss, peat moss, vermiculite or perlite. If you use a plastic or glazed pot as the larger pot, this will slow the evaporation process down even further. In this case, fill the bottom of the plastic or glazed pot with about 2 inches of small stones or pebbles to allow for drainage if the larger pot does not have a drainage hole.

Hard water contains lots of calcium and magnesium. When it is processed through a water softener, the calcium, which is not especially harmful to plants, is exchanged for sodium. Sodium is absorbed by plants and becomes a toxic substance. It is therefore preferable to use water that has not been mechanically softened.

In general, it is a good idea to allow tap water to run for a few minutes before filling the watering container. The chlorine present in the water will disappear as it is aerated. If you live in an area where there is heavy chlorination, gather water for plants the night before you water them in order to let the chlorine evaporate.

## WATERING PLANTS WHILE AWAY

Water your plants thoroughly two days before going away and place them in a slightly darker area than usual. The day after watering, cover each plant loosely with a plastic bag. Use sticks or pieces of wire coat hanger to keep the plastic off the foliage. If a plant requires a lot of moisture, secure the plastic bag tightly under the pot. It is best for your plants if, while you are away, the temperature of the environment can be maintained at 65 degrees. These measures should keep your plants supplied with adequate moisture for a period of two weeks. Naturally, some plants will not react well to the extra moisture, but it is well worth trying.

An alternate method to the plastic bags is to put your plants in the tub on top of bricks. Fill the tub with about half an inch of water. This should keep your plants going for two weeks.

# Humidity

House plants, for the most part, originated in tropical regions where the climate provided abundant rainfall and high humidity.

Humidity is an important factor in transpiration, the process by which plants give off waste matter in the form of moisture through their stomata (pores), which then evaporates into the air. Plants are designed to work best when a balance is maintained between the water they take in through their roots and the water they give off through transpiration.

If the air is dry, evaporation speeds up. The surfaces of the leaves dry up quickly, and transpiration speeds up. If the air is extremely dry, the plant's rate of transpiration will become too high and the leaves and stems will eventually dehydrate, lose turgidity and wilt. One would think that an obvious solution to this problem would be to water the plant more—but this, in itself, is not enough. The moisture in the air must also be increased to create a balance for the plant.

The percentage of humidity in homes and apartments is often as low as 12 percent—proper humidity is 30 to 40 percent. This 12 percent is much too dry for plant (or human) comfort. Plants prefer a humidity of 80 to 90 percent. In a greenhouse the humidity is always 60 percent or more—no wonder, then, that plants start to turn brown, drop leaves, flowers and buds soon after being moved into an apartment!

Succulents are the only plants that are designed to withstand an almost complete lack of moisture both in the air and at the roots for long periods of time. Like camels, these plants can store water in their leaves and stems. And their leaves have specially designed structures that help to slow down the process of transpiration.

How can you increase the percentage of humidity in the air for the benefit of your plants? There are several ways to do this:

1. Simply grouping plants together will increase humidity in the air as each plant transpires, throwing off moisture.

2. Fill a tray with a solid layer of pebbles and group plants together on it, with the bottom of the pots resting on the pebbles. Keep the pebbles wet—but make sure the water level is below the top of the pebbles or the plants will be constantly soggy and eventually suffer for it. The water in the tray will slowly evaporate, resulting in an increase in the humidity in the air.

3. Mist plants every few days (or daily if the air is extremely dry). Misters with a fine spray are preferable as plants don't like to be drenched with water. Plants growing under artificial lights without sun will not require misting often (but they will need more watering).

4. Buy a humidifier. This will help your plants, and you might find that you like what it does to dry city air yourself.

# Light

When plants are exposed to light, the chlorophyll-containing tissues produce carbohydrates (sugars, starches and cellulose) which serve as the plant's food source. This process, called photosynthesis, can not take place without light.

Natural daylight is composed of color bands. When we see a rainbow, we are seeing light broken down into its separate color components. Research indicates that the important color bands in the light spectrum for plant survival are the violet/blue and orange/red properties. The violet/blue bands determine the direction of a plant's growth and are responsible for the production of sugars and starches by the chlorophyll in the plant. The orange/red bands are necessary for germination of seeds, vegetative growth and flowering, as well as food production.

Practically all flowering plants require sunlight to produce blooms, although some, called "short-day" plants, require less daylight than others. Photoperiodism is the effect upon the growth of plants of the length of alternating periods of darkness and light. By influencing day length, greenhouse gardeners have induced chrysanthemums, normally a fall-blooming plant, to produce flowers all year long.

House plants, particularly in winter, can be starved for light. There are several ways in which you can improve the quantity of light your plants receive in the home. White, or light, walls will increase the intensity of the light that is reflected off them, whereas dark walls absorb the light. It is important that you keep your plants' leaves very clean by washing them regularly with warm water and mild soap. Clean leaves can absorb more light, which means that they will be able to manufacture more food, look better, and be generally healthier. Plants placed in or near windows should be given a quarter turn each time they are watered to ensure even distribution of light on all sides of the plant. Light concentrated on one area of a plant will cause it to grow unevenly. Turning them systematically will result in symmetrical growth.

The best windows for house plants are those that face east, because the most beneficial light is that produced from sunrise to 11 A.M. South windows are for plants that like intense light and high temperatures.

A plant that has survived a winter of relatively weak light will not be able to withstand the intensity of the summer sun and should be protected from direct sunlight. Sheer curtains, or semiclosed blinds will prevent the soil from heating up and scorching the roots.

Most plants can do quite well with twelve to fourteen hours of light a day. When darkness falls, they enter a cyclic state of rest which continues until daybreak.

# Artificial Lights

Sometimes it is difficult to place a plant in a house or apartment so that it receives the proper amount of natural light it requires for healthy growth. Although plants only use 1 percent of the total light energy received on earth for photosynthesizing, this 1 percent is vital to life. If plants are deprived of light, their natural development is altered. They ap-

pear bleached, because the chlorophyll, which gives plants their green color, is not being manufactured. The leaves and stems can become elongated (etiolation), and on a succulent plant tissue will be soft.

It is now possible to solve the problem of light for plants through the use of artificial lights, used either as a supplement for natural light or as the sole source of light for plants.

An ordinary light bulb can be used as a supplement to natural light to aid plant growth. It is also possible to grow plants successfully using only artificial lights. Even cacti and geraniums, which like full sunlight, can now grow and flower using the special plant lights that have been developed.

The best kind of artificial light is that which most closely resembles natural light. The red and blue radiant energy found at opposite ends of the spectrum are the important light waves. Plants use twice as much red light as blue. Red light stimulates vegetative growth, blue light regulates the respiratory system.

The fluorescent lights developed for growing plants are especially designed for use indoors. The lights produce a high intensity of light at both the red and blue ends of the spectrum. For best results these tubes should be used exclusively, but for plants that need a lower intensity of light, using them in combination with the standard fluorescent tubes will be successful.

Gro-Lux Spectrum and Duro-Test lamps produce a white glow. Gro-Lux and Plant-Gro tubes produce a warm red-violet light that enhances colors. Also available are the sunlight-colored Duro-Test lamps, or Gro-Lux Wide Spectrum, as well as standard white fluorescent tubes. The color of the light is your choice; they all give good results. The best light for plants that require high energy, like cacti, succulents and orchids, is the Gro-Lux Wide Spectrum light, which combines a nearly natural color with a good plant-growth spectrum.

Preheated tubes are better than rapid-start ones.

The following chart is an artificial-lighting footcandle guide. There is usually more than one option to achieving the correct footcandle of light. Spotlights, floodlights, or fluorescent tubes can be used. The chart provides the correct wattage and distance between light and plant for the appropriate footcandle.

*150 footcandles*
1) 150-watt reflector floodlight: 2½ feet from center of light.
2) 150-watt reflector spotlight: 2 feet from center and 2 feet to the side or 7 feet from center of light.
3) Two 40-watt fluorescent tubes: 30 inches beneath the center of tubes.

*400 footcandles*
1) 150-watt reflector floodlight: 1 foot beneath the center of light.
2) 150-watt reflector spotlight: 4½ feet beneath the center of light.
3) Two 40-watt fluorescent tubes: 12 inches beneath and 6 inches to the side of the center of tubes.

*500 footcandles*
1) 150-watt reflector spotlight: 4 feet beneath the center of light.
2) Two 40-watt fluorescent tubes: 12 inches beneath the center of tubes.

*650 footcandles*
1) 150-watt reflector spotlight: 3½ feet beneath the center of light.
2) Two 40-watt fluorescent tubes: 9 inches beneath the center of tubes.

*800 footcandles*
1) 150-watt reflector spotlight: 3 feet beneath the center of light.
2) Two 40-watt fluorescent tubes: 6 inches beneath the center of tubes.

*1,000 footcandles*
1) 150-watt reflector spotlight: 2 feet beneath the center of light.
2) Two 40-watt fluorescent tubes: 4 to 5 inches beneath the center of tubes. Adding more tubes or using higher-wattage tubes will increase the wattage to allow more distance between the plant and the tubes.

They are less expensive and last longer—seven thousand hours with a fourteen-hour day average. When you notice black rings at the ends of tubes, this is a sign that the tubes are old and should be replaced. Plants do not grow well under light produced by worn-out tubes. They usually require changing every eight to ten months.

If plants have a low light requirement, you can mount incandescent reflector floodlights or spotlights for plants on the wall or ceiling. A floodlight of 150 watts will produce 50 footcandles at a distance of 5 feet in a wide beam. A spotlight of 150 watts will produce 300 footcandles at a distance of 5 feet in a narrow, concentrated beam.

Tube lengths range from 24 to 96 inches. Light intensity is diminished at the ends of the tubes, so longer tubes are better to use. Tubes which have 40 watts and are 46 inches long are the most practical.

To increase the efficiency of artificial lights and prevent light dissipation, back up lights with a reflective surface—either a reflector which can be fitted over the fixture or a painted surface like a shelf.

Check the Dictionary charts to find the proper distances at which to place the lights for specific plants.

Lights should be between 8 to 15 inches from flowering plants. As the intensity of light declines with the distance from the tubes, the maximum distance is 3 feet—any more and the light will be insufficient, and you will find you have to use more tubes or incandescent lamps.

If artificial light is the only source of light for plants, they should be left on for twelve to sixteen hours a day. This length of time is necessary to compensate for the fact that artificial light is not as intense as sunlight. A clock timer set to turn the lights on and off every day at a certain hour will eliminate variation in length of light and dark.

It has been found that plants do not necessarily need a period of darkness. The vegetative growth of plants can be speeded by constant illumination; however, it does interfere with some flowering plants. The control of periods of darkness for flowering plants can force them to bloom.

If it is necessary for you to leave your plants for several days, it is best to keep the lights turned off. This will prevent the soil from drying out while you are away.

It is interesting to note that, with the exception of whiteflies and aphids, insects almost never infest plants that are growing under artificial lights.

# Air

Both a good air supply and good air circulation are important for healthy plants. Plants need air for photosynthesis—the process by which they take in carbon dioxide and give off oxygen. Air circulation facilitates transpiration—the means by which plants give off waste products through the leaves. Good air circulation keeps the air clean and keeps air from stagnating or becoming concentrated with poisonous fumes, especially in a city environment where air pollution is a factor to be considered.

It is important that your plants are located in a place where there is good air circulation. But it is just as important to keep them out of direct drafts, which are harmful to most plants, causing them to drop leaves.

If your plants are grouped together, make sure there is enough space among them to allow the air to circulate.

If you live in an air-conditioned apartment, your plant will benefit from the filtered, cooled air, but you must make up for the loss of moisture in the air caused by air conditioning.

If you wish to improve air circulation, you can buy small, low-wattage fans and place them at short distances from your plants. Never place a fan so that it is blowing directly on your plants. This will cause moisture to evaporate from the leaves too quickly for the roots to replace it, and the plant will eventually dry up.

# Temperature

Proper temperature is important for healthy house plants. It has been found through research and experimentation that plants need the temperature change that normally occurs between day and night. During the daylight hours, plants work producing and storing food. Photosynthesis takes place, and it cannot happen without warmth. When darkness falls and the temperature drops, plants cease this activity in order to assimilate the stored food and grow. This drop in temperature is an essential factor in the plants' change of activity.

If plants are kept in an environment in which the temperature remains constant, they are not able to assimilate food very well, nor do they grow or bloom to their normal capacity. An exception to this rule are African violets, which grow very well in an environment that has a constant temperature.

The average temperature range in most homes and apartments is between 68 and 72 degrees. Logically, plants that enjoy this temperature range will grow best in the home. Plants die if exposed to frost or freezing temperature, but some tropical plants are so delicate and sensitive to temperature that they will suffer damage at temperatures below 50 degrees.

The temperature in your home or apartment should be 10 to 15 degrees lower at night for optimum growing conditions for your plants. In winter, when apartments tend to get overheated, the night temperature near windows will be low. This micro climate can be useful to help geraniums, orchids, succulents and other plants that like a cool climate to grow well in overheated rooms.

Never put plants near radiators or directly over heat: they will dry up. You can place plants on a radiator if you insulate them with a thick piece of wood or asbestos. The small amount of bottom warmth the plants will get is perfectly fine.

When plants are placed near windows in winter, it is a good idea to give them some protection from the cold. Pull your shades at night, and use plastic insulation on the windows to stop drafts if necessary.

Check the Dictionary for the temperature requirements of various plants. Some are very delicate and precise in the kind of temperature they require for healthy growth.

# Fertilizing

There are three main ingredients essential for plant growth, without which a plant would gradually waste away and die.

1. Nitrogen (ammonium nitrate): Aids the plant's growth in general. It is responsible for the deep green color of the foliage. If a plant is suffering from a lack of nitrogen, it will lose foliage, and leaves will gradually turn pale green or weak yellow.

2. Phosphorus: Important for a good, strong root system and strong stems. It promotes the maturation of the plant—budding and blooming. If a plant has insufficient phosphorus, its roots will grow and develop slowly, and the plant will be stunted.

3. Potassium (potash): Helps flowering, growth in general, and is an important factor in the plant's ability to resist disease. A lack of potassium will result in loss of stems and terminal branches, and the plant will have few or no blossoms.

Most fertilizers contain the above three main elements, as well as the following elements in small amounts: boron, calcium, copper, iron, manganese, molybdenum, sulfur and zinc.

When you shop for fertilizer, you will notice that the percentage of each major nutrient is listed on the package as 5-10-5, or 20-20-20, or 10-20-5, and so forth. The first number in the series represents the percentage of nitrogen (N) in the mixture, the second phosphorus (P) and the third potassium (K).

Buy water-soluble fertilizers. They are preferable for house plants because they dissolve in water and are made immediately available for absorption by plant's roots. You also avoid the risk of burning a plant's roots, which often happens when dry fertilizers are used.

For strong leaf growth on foliage plants, buy a fertilizer which contains a high percentage of nitrogen. For blooming, or for slowing down a plant's activities before dormancy, buy a low-nitrogen formula. If desired, it is possible to buy fertilizers that are especially formulated for specific plant varieties (roses, African violets, orchids, cacti, etc.)

Read the labels on fertilizers carefully, and follow directions. Fertilizers are sold under a variety of different trade names, and the formulas and the instructions for dilution are different.

Organic fertilizers are of no value to house plants. They need bacterial action to render them usable by plants. Either because the soil lacks the necessary bacteria, or because the temperature is too low (70°F. is considered to be the minimum temperature for bacterial activity), they are useless. Even if the conditions are correct, the process is very slow. Most likely, the nutrients will get washed out through the drainage hole before the plant has a chance to assimilate them.

Don't overfertilize your plants. This will do more harm than good. Plants normally absorb small amounts of nutrients over a long period of time. If too much fertilizer is present, it will force the plants to speed up their growth and you will then have to cut them back or throw them away.

If a plant is potted in a plastic, glazed or other nonporous container, it is a good idea to cut the amount of fertilizer recommended and the frequency of feeding in half. There are two reasons for this. Plants growing in this type of container don't need to be watered as frequently as plants in clay pots, so less nutrients are washed away. Secondly, because of the nonporous nature of these containers, the water holding the nutrients is not permitted to escape and evaporate through the sides of the pot. There will be a buildup eventually of excess fertilizer salts in the soil. These salts will cause the roots to lose moisture, and root tissues will be "burned." Overfertilizing is especially harmful to plants growing in dim light and can kill them by burning away the roots.

In clay pots, the excess fertilizer will escape through the sides of the pot and form deposits. Excess fertilizer will also accumulate on the rims of plastic pots, or build up a crust on the top soil. When you notice signs of this, you should take the appropriate steps to remove the buildup, either by scrubbing the pot or removing and replacing the top soil.

For a newly purchased plant, no fertilizing should be necessary for at least the first four months in your home, except in special cases. Most plants benefit from regular feeding during the spring, summer and fall months, when plants are especially active and there is strong sunlight. Flowering plants will require extra fertilizer, administered in small amounts, particularly when buds are forming and prior to blooming. Slow-growth plants, cacti and bromeliads, thrive with very little fertilizing. The Chinese evergreen doesn't need anything but air and water for long stretches of time. Cut back on feeding semidormant plants, and discontinue feeding plants in a full state of dormancy.

In general, for most house plants, the correct fertilizer, administered properly, will mean the difference between the plant merely surviving and thriving.

# Pests

House plants can be the victims of damage or disease caused by an infestation of insects. Often new plants will harbor insects in the foliage or in the soil which are undetected by the buyer. The first rule is to shop carefully and to buy healthy plants, and to get rid of any plants that are suffering from an infestation that can not be brought under control. The second rule is to give your plants regular preventive care whether they show any signs of pests or not. Frequent misting of the foliage and regular washing of plants will keep them free of insects, insect eggs, mites and dust. It is wise to bathe plants once a month in warm, soapy water.

Mild cases of aphids, mealybugs and scales can be successfully controlled by washing the plant with 2 teaspoons of mild detergent added to a gallon of water. Spraying plants with warm water is also effective in washing away insects. A Q-Tip dipped in alcohol applied directly to the insects is also an efficient way of ridding a plant of a mild infestation.

Naturally, washing is not always possible for several reasons. Some plants are just too large to bathe. If your plant collection is very large, washing each individual plant is impractical. And some insects will resist washing. You must be able to identify the specific insect that is present on your plant and know what kind of insecticide or pesticide is most effective for control in order to give plants the proper cure.

## INSECTICIDES AND PESTICIDES

The most effective control of insects is usually achieved through the use of insecticide sprays and dips. They are not prone to drifting to nearby objects when applied as dusts, and they do not leave heavy residues.

Combinations of two or more pesticides are available and control a wider variety of pests than pesticides containing only one active ingredient. Carefully follow directions on the label when mixing.

Malathion, and rotenone in water-spray forms don't require the use of protective clothing. Chlordane and lindane should not be allowed to come in contact with your skin. They can be absorbed through the skin, and this is harmful.

Push-button sprays, available in hardware or garden-supply stores, are ready to use. Read the label on the can to make sure the spray does not contain oil or other substances that can kill plants or burn foliage. They are most effective when used to kill insects which can be hit directly with the spray (aphids and adult whiteflies on foliage, and fungus gnats swarming in windows).

If you use a hand atomizer, the most efficient kind produces a continuous spray and has an adjustable nozzle so that the spray can be directed up and down. Always empty the atomizer after using, wash it out thoroughly, and set the tank aside to drain. Keep the cap or pump off the atomizer when not in use.

For the most effective results, use the proper insecticide at the first sign of an infestation. If this initial treatment does not exterminate the insects, repeat it in a week or ten days, unless otherwise noted.

The addition of ½ teaspoon of mild household detergent to a gallon of spray or dip will increase the wetting power of the mixture and reduce residue.

Dipping the plant into the insecticide and water mixture is often easier than spraying. In this case, put the mixture into a sink or pail deep enough to accommodate the top of the plant. Cover the soil with cardboard or paper to prevent spilling, and invert the plant. Immerse the foliage and stems in the liquid for several seconds. Be sure to wear rubber gloves to protect your skin.

Insecticides have to be used with caution and care. They can be harmful to you, to animals and to plants if used carelessly and allowed to drift. Prolonged inhalation of pesticide spray can be dangerous and should be avoided. Wear protective clothing and wash well after treating plants.

# Pest Chart (Pest/damage/cure)

| PEST | DAMAGE | CURE |
| --- | --- | --- |

*ANTS* Several different kinds, they can be black, brown, yellow, red. From 1/16-1/2 inch long, with tiny neck and waist. They live in the pots of plants.

Carry away newly planted seeds or dig up new seedlings. Burrowing activities can damage roots. Attracted to and feed upon honeydew excretions left by aphids, mealybugs.

If plant exhibits signs of honeydew excretions from other insects, treat plant for these. If ants are still present, use diluted malathion or chlordane as a drench, soaking infested soil, pots and shelves in the solution.

*APHIDS* Several different kinds, green, pink, red, black. From 1/16 to 1/18 inch long. Bodies soft rounded or pear shaped, long legs and antennae. Wingless species are more common. Winged species when at rest hold wings rooflike. May appear powdery or wooly because of waxy covering. Found in clusters on undersides of leaves, on young growing tips, stems, flower buds. Some feed on roots. One of the most common plant pests, but easy to eradicate.

Feed on plants by sucking juices. Causes poor growth, distorted leaves (curled) and buds. Excrete honeydew substance which encourages growth of sooty mold, attracts ants. Can migrate from plant to plant.

For mild case, wash plant in warm, soapy water, rinse with clean water. If case is severe, use Malathion, lindane or rotenone as dip or spray. After insecticide dries, wash leaves with clean water.

| PEST | DAMAGE | CURE |
| --- | --- | --- |

*COCKROACHES* Brown beetlelike insect. Invade houses in cool, wet weather.

Plants will look chewed up.

Spray around plant area with roach sprays or pine-oil-based cleaners. Don't allow spray to come in contact with plants. Use Malathion spray on leaves to control roaches.

*CRICKETS* Large insect, related to grasshopper. Brown or black. Makes clicking sound. During day hides under pots, saucers, baseboards, in trash. Active at night.

Feed at night on new plant growth.

Poison bait for control. If heavy infestation, eggs might be present in soil. Drench with Malathion solution.

*CUTWORMS AND OTHER CATERPILLARS* Several species. Barely visible when newly hatched. Solid color, striped or mottled. Usually green, brown, but also can be yellow, gray, black, red. Sometimes hairy. Develop from eggs laid by night-flying moths that come in through windows. Cutworms hardest to detect because they burrow deep into soil.

Can eat away leaves, buds and flowers overnight. Some cut off young plants at soil line or eat through branches or flowers of larger plants. Leave excrement of dark pellets.

If infestation mild, hand picking will be adequate. Otherwise, spray using Malathion or rotenone. Drench soil surface as well with diluted Malathion to control cutworms in soil.

*CYCLAMEN MITES* Adult mites oval, amber or tan, semi-

Infested leaves are brittle, twisted and curled. Flowers are de-

Immerse plant and pot in water at temperature of 110 degrees

| PEST | DAMAGE | CURE |
|---|---|---|

transparent and glistening. Need a magnifying glass to see adults. Young are milky white, smaller than adults. Found on young leaves, stem ends, buds and flowers. Crawl from plant to plant if leaves touch, and can be spread by hands, clothing.

formed, striped with darker colors. Most deformed foliage becomes blackened.

for 15 minutes. Success of this treatment depends on control of water temperature. Or spray with dicofol, two or three times at 10-day intervals.

*EARWIGS* Beetlelike insect. Dark brown and has forcep-like attachment at end of body. Common mostly in coastal states.

Young earwigs chew young shoots. Adults eat holes in leaves, flowers, fruit.

Hand-pick if only a few. If infestation severe, spray with Malathion, and aerosol roach sprays can be used around growing area (not on foliage).

*FALSE SPIDER MITES* Flat, oval, dark red mites. Need magnifying glass to see them. Eggs and young are bright red. Found generally along veins and undersides of leaves in all stages.

Veins or entire leaves will be striped with bronze or rusty-brown color. Edges of leaves may die, drop off. Plants become stunted, leaves lose color, and entire plant is weakened.

Use Malathion in dip or spray, being careful to wet undersides of leaves. Add ½ teaspoon of mild household detergent to spray to increase wetting action.

*FUNGUS GNATS* Adults 1/8 inch long, gray or dark gray flying insects. Adults seldom feed on plants, but are attracted to light and can be seen swarming around windows. Eggs laid in soil. Young are whitish maggots, 1/4 inch long. Burrow through soil rich in decaying vegetable

Young maggots feed on roots and crowns of plants. Severely infested plants have yellowing leaves, drop foliage, little new growth. Possible root rot.

Kill adults using any push-button plant spray. For maggots in soil, flood soil with Malathion solution and use it as dip or spray for maggots on crowns of plants.

24 §

matter, embed themselves in root tissue.

*LEAF MINERS* Larvae of flies, moths, sowflies, beetles.

Winding trails, tunnels, blisters throughout leaf, eat tissue between upper and lower leaf surface. Some roll tips of leaves, placing themselves inside in order to spin cocoon and feed off leaves.

Remove all damaged and rolled leaves. Isolate plant, keep growing conditions on dry side, until no more signs remain. If many plants infested, spray with a systematic insecticide repeatedly.

*MEALYBUGS* Soft bodied, have waxy covering that makes them look flourdusted. 3/10 inch long. Some have waxy filaments extending from rear. Eggs laid in clusters enclosed in white, waxy, cottony, fuzzy material. Found moving or at rest along stems, where stems and leaves join, along veins and underside of leaves.

In soil, mealy bugs feed on roots, sucking out juices and stunting plant's growth, possibly killing it.

Strong measures are necessary. Mealybugs are persistent and destructive. If one plant only is infested, try hosing with spray, or use cotton swab dipped in alcohol to touch each white cluster or speck, rinse afterward with water. Do this every 5 days to kill eggs. Dip or spray badly infested plants in Malathion every 5 days until no more sign of bugs. If soil infested, immerse in diluted solution of Malathion. Do not spray or dip ferns or succulents with an insecticide. Use nicotine sulfate.

*MILLIPEDES* Slow-moving, wormlike insects, many short legs along body. Hard bodies, brown, tan, gray. Can grow to 1½ inches long. Found in moist places where there is organic material, under flowerpots. Active at night. If disturbed, coil up.

Feed on seeds, roots, fleshy stems, but mostly eat decaying organic material. Can be a nuisance.

Drench soil surface and hiding places with lindane spray or Malathion solution.

§ 25

| PEST | DAMAGE | CURE |
|---|---|---|

*(Not visible to the naked eye)*

*NEMATODES* Microscopic wormlike insects. So numerous and destructive that a zoological science called nematology is devoted to their study.

Produce galls, knots on plant roots, feed on root systems. Unnoticed until in advanced stages. Plant becomes weak, stunted, develops root rot. Plant susceptible, as result, to fungi and bacterial infections in roots.

Good sterilized soil will usually protect plant from nematode infestation. Only cure: destroy plant.

*PSOCIDS* Soft, oval bodies, pale yellowish white to gray. Some have wings. 1/16 inch long, cluster together in groups of 100 or more. Quick moving, hide in damp places. Feed on dead vegetable and animal matter and fungi.

Found on foliage. Do not feed on plants, but can be nuisance.

Spray soil, pots, shelves with chlordane.

*RED SPIDER MITES* (See "Spider mites.")

*SCALES* About 20 different species, all common on house plants. Shell-like or scale covering, oval, hemispherical, oyster-shell shape. Soft scales don't have shell, retain larvae legs and are mobile, others are stationary. 1/16 to 1/8 inch long to four times larger in size. Color range

Some attack leaves only, others stems and leaves, other stems. Scales insert needlelike mouth parts into outer-leaf or stem tissue and suck juices of plant. Leaves develop yellow spots, will turn completely yellow and fall off. Plant's growth stunted. Scales leave honeydew excre-

Insects may be controlled by washing. Scales will cling to leaves even after they are dead (dead scale will become dry and chaffy; live scale if squashed will be juicy). Use Malathion and 1/2 teaspoon of mild household detergent to increase wetting power as dip or spray. Spray

| PEST | DAMAGE | CURE |
|---|---|---|

from white to black (browns, grays most common). Some lay eggs in a whitish sac and can be mistaken for mealybugs.

tion attractive to ants, sooty mold.

every 3–4 weeks to get rid of scales. Do not mistake fern spores for scales. Do not spray ferns with Malathion; use nicotine sulfate.

*SOWBUGS, PILL BUGS* Segmented shell-like bodies, oval in shape, 1/4 to 1/2 inch long. Found in places of high humidity. Active at night. When disturbed, pill bugs coil up, sowbugs run for cover. Hide in loose soil, any place with a cover. They are terrestrial crustaceans (crabs, lobsters are marine crustaceans).

Found clustered on crowns of plants, over tops of pots. Will usually feed only on organic decaying matter, but sometimes eat tender stems, roots, seedlings.

Hand-pick and destroy any you see. Eliminate hiding places. Spray soil surfaces with lindane or Malathion.

*SPIDER MITES, RED SPIDER MITES* Several species. Abundant in dry, warm conditions. Barely visible. Oval shape, green yellow or red. Found at first on undersides of leaves, then spread over plant. When infestation heavy, form silky webbing from leaf to leaf. Can see mites crawling along webbing.

Suck plant juices and leave white or speckled areas on tops of leaves; tiny white flecks underneath leaves are shed skins. Leaves will turn bronze, gray or yellow and may fall. Plant may die if infestation is heavy. Flowers are faded. Webs are first sign of infestation.

Difficult to get rid of, because usually unnoticed until damage advanced. Easily spread with hands. Wash plant with forceful spray to break down webs and dislodge mites. Two days later use Malathion or dicofol as spray or dip. Will require several applications at weekly intervals.

*SPRINGTAILS* Some have globular bodies, other segmented, slender bodies. White to black, some tinted purple,

Chew seedlings, tender parts of plant, especially at soil level, leaving small round holes. Provoked usually by overwatering.

Use chlordane or Malathion to spray or drench soil, pots, saucers, parts of plant. Check and correct watering habits.

blue. Size: microscopic to 1/5 inch. Wingless, propelled by tail-like appendages. Most can jump. Like moist organic material. Usually are found on surface of soil.

Heavy watering drives them to surface where they can be seen as bright, dark colors.

*THRIPS* Several small species, small and flealike. Tan, brown, black with light markings. Young yellow or orange. Adults fly or jump away when disturbed. Young less active.

Penetrate plants with mouth and suck juices. Leaf surfaces when injured streaked silver, white, and speckled with black dots of excrement. Tips of new leaves curled, foliage may drop. Flowers deformed, discolored, streaked, won't open.

Treat mild case with strong spray of lukewarm, soapy water. Dip with Malathion (or spray) at several weekly intervals for most effective treatment.

*WHITEFLIES* Adults 1/16 inch long, with white, wedge-shaped wings. Young are oval, flat on top. Scalelike and pale green to yellow or white. Immature stage looks like sesame seeds attached to leaves, especially underside. If infested plant is moved, adults take flight and look like small snowflakes.

Young and adults suck plant juices. Infested leaves become pale, turn yellow, die, drop off. Their honeydew excretion attracts ants and sooty molds.

Hard to kill since they can fly around. Cover plants with plastic bag or cardboard carton and spray into bag or carton using Malathion, rotenone or lindane. Be sure to wet undersides of leaves. Leave cover on plant for couple of hours to ensure fumigation of insects. Several applications at weekly intervals necessary.

# Part Two:
# First Aid and General-Care Plant Dictionary

The failure of plants to grow well in the home is more often the result of careless or neglectful tending, and a lack of knowledge of the basic cultural requirements of the plant, than more exotic troubles such as diseases caused by pest infestation or fungi. Extreme temperatures, improper light, improper watering, excessive fertilizing, the use of water containing calcium, repotting at the wrong time or repotting a plant incorrectly are some of the most common reasons why house plants do not flourish. It is important, therefore, to concentrate on the proper day-to-day care of your plants in order to maintain them at their optimum level.

There are several conditions that make plants vulnerable to bacterial and fungal infections. Extreme temperatures, overwatering, lack of sufficient light, excessive fertilizing, open wounds where a branch or leaf has been cut off, air pollution and high humidity are the most common causes of plant disease. Fungi, related to bread molds, mushrooms and penicillin, look like spongy growth of plant tissue. Fungi reproduce from spores, visible only under a microscope, that germinate in conditions of excessive moisture and humidity.

Bacteria are single-celled organisms that reproduce and feed on organic material, living or dead. Bacteria are spread by insects, water, dirty tools and hands. Some bacteria are, of course, beneficial and in fact, vital to the natural processes of plant life. Other forms of bacteria act as parasites feeding off the living plant tissue and causing it to degenerate.

If plant ailments are allowed to persist, unchecked, they will eventually produce rather dramatic symptoms, such as total withering or extreme defoliation. Whatever the symptom a plant exhibits, this symptom will be the clue to the ailment. Some, such as yellowing of leaves, can be caused by several different ailments. You will have to evaluate the symptom in relationship to other conditions to determine the correct cause of the problem and take the proper corrective measure. Applying the wrong therapy to a plant can be just as harmful as no therapy at all, and it might prove fatal if the plant is in a very weakened condition.

Indoor gardeners should therefore concentrate on proper day-to-day care in order to maintain healthy, beautiful plants and to catch any potentially severe diseases early.

In the following section, plants are arranged in alphabetical order—common name first, followed by Latin name. Use this section in conjunction with the Introduction. For instance, references are made about specific plants (i.e., watering, repotting, artificial lighting, etc.) that deal with areas of information comprehensively described in the Introduction. Also, if you cannot find the problem with your plant, please refer to Part Three: Quick-Reference First Aid Charts.

# AFRICAN HEMP— SPARMANNIA

A very sturdy plant from Africa with downy, lime-colored leaves. The white flowers with dark red and yellow stamens bloom in late spring and summer. It quickly develops into a very large plant despite pruning and pinching, and new plants should be propagated to replace the old one.

Sparmannia must have a rest period in the spring in order to produce abundant blooms. In April or May, reduce watering and remove the plant from the sun. In four to six weeks, repot and prune back the longest stems to stimulate new growth. Return it to its original place in the sun and give it proper watering.

## Location

Needs full sun during the winter but must be protected from the hot noon sun of summer. Likes average room temperatures in the summer and temperatures not below 55 degrees during the winter.

## Soil

Needs alkaline soil. Two parts all-purpose loam, one part perlite or vermiculite and only a small amount of peat moss to keep the soil from drying too quickly.

## Watering

Keep soil moist at all times during the growing period. Water sparingly during the winter but don't let the plant wilt too often. Needs to be mist-sprayed daily.

## Fertilizer

Once a month from March to September. No feeding during the winter.

## Propagation

Cutting from firm top growth in the spring.

## Artificial light

800 footcandles.

## First Aid

Red spider mites. (See *Pests*.)

*Yellowing and dropping of leaves.* This is due to insufficient fertilizer. Fertilize more frequently, especially during the growth period.

*Yellowing leaves.* This is caused by an atmosphere which is too hot and too dry. Plant should be placed on a bed of wet pebbles without the bottom of the pot touching any water. Spray-mist daily and use a humidifier during the winter.

This is probably the easiest flowering house plant to grow. Actually, it's not a true violet but a gesneriad (members of the Gesneriaceae family, mostly tropical and subtropical perennial herbs and shrubs with showy blossoms; they are cultivated ornamentals). They originate in tropical East Africa. The plants have a very wide range of shape and leaf form and come in trailers and miniatures, but the most popular are the thick, oval, succulent, downy, petiolate leaves that grow in rosettes. Rarer forms have white or gold variegated leaves, but most are green-leaved. The flowers grow in loose clusters of two to six. They can be blue, white, pink, lavender or purple and in single and double blooms, with the double blooms lasting longer than the single. They have no dormant period, and with proper treatment they will flower year round. Sometimes in the winter the flowers will disappear, but they will reemerge once again in the early spring. The ideal-looking plant has a single crown. Thus, all side shoots that appear should be removed by using tweezers. The leaves should be brushed weekly with a soft brush to keep the foliage clean.

## AFRICAN VIOLET— SAINTPAULIA

### Location

They respond to direct sun in the winter with constant blooming. In the summer they need filtered sun or a bright north window. They enjoy average room temperatures with temperatures not below 60 degrees during the winter.

### Soil

One part all-purpose loam, one part peat moss, one part sharp sand, perlite or vermiculite, or you can use the prepackaged soil for African violets with sharp sand added to improve the drainage. (Peat moss is the basic ingredient of this soil, so adding peat moss will give you improper soil combinations.)

Use plastic pots when repotting, as the leaves can be injured by touching the edges of clay pots. If you do use clay pots, wax-coat the rims of the pots or cover them with tape. As plants age, they have a stalky neck which when repotted can be buried below the soil. They do not resent the change in the growing level. Do not water for at least a week after repotting.

### Watering

During the heavy blooming period, allow the surface soil to become dry between thorough waterings from the top. Do not allow water to get on the leaves. Water less as the blooming slows down. Spray-mist no more than twice a week and very lightly to prevent water from remaining on the leaves.

## Fertilizer

Use commercially packaged brands that are available for African violets. Follow the directions carefully to have continual flowering.

## Propagation

Leaf cuttings.

## Artificial Light

500 footcandles. Watch their reaction; sometimes they need to be placed either closer or farther away from the tubes.

## First Aid

*Mealybugs, nematodes, thrips, cyclamen mites, springtails. (See Pests.)

*Scorching and yellowing of leaf edges. This is the result of too much direct sun during the summer. Filter the area with a curtain or move to a less bright location.

*Yellowing foliage. This is usually due to too much fertilizer or lack of humidity. If using clay pots, salts build up on the pots, and the plant should be drenched twice thoroughly to wash away as many salts as possible. Fertilize less often with half the amount indicated on the label. To raise the humidity, keep the plant on a bed of wet pebbles without the bottom of the pot touching any water. African

violets can be successfully sprayed with warm water occasionally.

*Irregular, yellow mottling on the leaves; new growth can be malformed with leaf edges turning brown or white. This is a disease called chlorosis caused from soil that is too alkaline. Use an acid-rich plant food or feed plant regularly with African violet fertilizer.

*Spots, colored markings, yellowing leaves. These are signs of underwatering. Remove any damaged foliage and water over the entire soil surface slowly until excess water drains out of the drainage holes. Don't allow the plant to sit in a saucer of water for more than an hour. Allow plant to become just dry before another thorough watering.

*Brown spots on leaves. This is usually caused by using cold water and thus chilling the plant. Make it a practice with all plants to use warm water for watering and spraying.

*Ring spots on leaves. These are caused by water that is too warm and by sun burning wet foliage. Use room-temperature water and move plant farther away from its present light source or filter it from the bright sun.

*Browned centers of the plant. This is caused by overfertilizing. Fertilize less often, using half the amount recommended on the label. Water the plant thoroughly twice to remove the salt build-up in the soil and, if using clay pots, scrub any salt residue off the pots with warm water and a stiff brush. Giving the plant a little more light will usually help.

Allowing water to settle in the crown of the plant will also turn it brown. Water directly on the soil, avoiding the leaves by using a water can with a long, thin stem.

*A wilting plant and rotting main stem.* This is a fungus disease called crown and stem rot or root rot. It is caused by overwatering, excessive humidity or extremes in temperature. This is a difficult condition to treat, but you can try to repot. Before repotting, cut off all damaged foliage and wash the root system in warm water. Spray the wounds with a fungicide. Repot and give proper environmental conditions.

*Jellylike leaves which droop over the rims of the pot.* This is the result of too much fertilizing. Flush out salts by drenching the soil twice with water and allowing it to drain well. If white salts have accumulated on the pots, wash them off with warm water and a stiff brush. This plant grows best in a plastic pot. Repot in fresh soil and use a plastic pot. Fertilize less often with half the recommended amount on the label.

*Flower buds that dry up.* This is the result of lack of humidity or a sudden shift in the plant's location. Place on a bed of moist pebbles without the bottom of the pot touching the water. If the humidity is correct, the plant will adjust to a new location.

*Flower buds will not bloom.* The problem is low humidity or a location which is too cool. Place plants on a bed of wet pebbles without the bottom of the pot touching the water and move away from the window or any drafts.

*Flower buds that get dark, do not flower and fall prematurely, accompanied by yellowing of foliage.* This is a result of a gas pollution or street pollution. Circulate the air better in the growing area and avoid allowing excessive moisture to remain on the leaves, until the plant is cured.

*Leaves grouped together in small bunches rather than laying in a flat rosette.* This is the result of overexposure to artificial lights or a location which is too cool. Move plant farther away from the artificial lights. Prevent any drafts or move plant to a warmer location.

*Gray or white feltlike coating on foliage is powdery mildew. It blocks out light and forces the leaves to curl and shrivel up.* This is caused by an overabundance of humidity. Good ventilation will be necessary to control this problem. Rinse the mildew off the leaves with warm, soapy water. Lower the humidity. If badly mildewed, the affected leaves will have to be removed.

# ALOE

There are many varieties of aloes, but the most popular are shaped like rosettes. They have spiny, succulent leaves which store water, allowing them to withstand severe drought (because evaporation is so slight). The leaves are very thick, with few pores. Most have flushed or speckled foliage and are soft-colored. Flower spikes are born between the leaves and produce orange and red bell-shaped blooms. Flowers rarely appear on young plants raised in the house but will bloom on mature plants during the winter. Here are a few varieties: *Candelabra*, which is rather treelike and has thorny branches that reach upward. *Aloe variegata tiger* can grow 6 inches across and 12 inches high and forms a mound. Its leaves have bands of white and are sometimes accented by a bronze tint. *Aloe vera* has a sap in its white-spotted, light green, narrow leaves which can be used on the skin, especially on burns and bad complexions.

## Location

They prefer direct sun during the summer but need slight protection from the hot noon sun of a south window. They will grow well with partial sun and fairly well in bright indirect light. They prefer dry air with warm days and cool nights in summer and a general drop in temperature in the winter, but the temperature should never be below 50 degrees.

## Soil

One part all-purpose soil, one part sharp sand, one handful peat moss or add a handful of peat moss to the packaged sand/soil mixture. Repot at several-year intervals. Repot in July or August after flowering has ceased for older plants and in any season for young plants. When repotting, don't set the plant in the soil any deeper than it was previously.

## Fertilizer

Newly purchased plants need not be fed for the first year; after this, once each fall at half the recommended strength on the label of the fertilizer.

## Watering

The soil should be allowed to become thoroughly dry between waterings. In the winter, water only enough to keep leaves from shriveling up.

## Propagation

Suckers or offsets usually don't have their own root system but do root easily. Allow the cut end of the new shoot to dry for a day or two before planting.

## Artificial Light

1,000 footcandles.

## First Aid

*Scales, mealybugs. (See Pests.)

*Shriveled leaves.* This indicates either a location that is too warm or underwatering. Remove damaged foliage and move plant away from hot radiators to a cooler location. Water more often. Plant's soil should be allowed to dry well between waterings but not so much that the leaves shrivel.

*Variegata's *leaves lose their green coloring.* This is caused by too much sun. Move plant farther away away from its light source or keep it shaded or filtered.

*Black spots on foliage.* This is caused by hot sun during the summer. Shade or filter the plant from hot sun or move to a less bright location.

*Weak growth with misshapen and elongated foliage.* This is due to lack of light. Move the plant to a brighter exposure or move closer to its artificial light source.

*The stems of the plant turn soft and mushy.* This indicates a fungus disease called stem rot which spreads quickly. This fungus is promoted by too much humidity, overwatering and changes in temperatures. First try immersing plant in hot water for twenty to forty minutes and allow the plant to dry thoroughly between waterings. If this does not solve the problem, infected areas must be removed and sprayed with a fungicide. Repotting in fresh soil is a good idea, and you should pay special attention to the plant's proper growing requirements. *Variegata* is affected more than others.

*Shriveling, yellowing of lower leaves with stems turning soft and dark.* This is a fungus called root rot which prevents the root system from absorbing water. Remove plant from pot (see *Potting*). Remove all soil and wash the roots in warm water and repot in fresh soil. Remove damaged foliage and drench the soil with a fungicide. Water very little until plant has resumed normal growth.

*Yellowing foliage.* This can be due to too little water, too much water or too much heat. The plant probably needs a cooler location, and you will have to experiment with your watering until the problem is solved.

*Rotting, wilting, bleaching of foliage and usually a mass yellowing of leaves. Tips of leaves turn brown and die back with new growth weak, and soil is constantly wet.* This is caused by overwatering. The plant must be removed from the pot (see *Potting*) and a root check must be made. At the same time, make sure there is not anything blocking the drainage holes and that there is enough drainage material over the drainage holes and proper soil. If roots are white and healthy, repot in fresh soil and allow the soil to dry thoroughly between waterings. Partially decayed roots can be cut off and the plant repotted in fresh soil. If all roots look dead and mushy, the plant will have to be discarded.

# ALUMINUM PLANT—PILEA

## Location

Can tolerate sun during the winter, but a bright location away from direct sunlight is most suitable for healthy summer growth. Keep away from cold windows during the winter.

## Soil

Two parts peat moss, one part sharp sand, one part all-purpose loam. They grow best in 3- to 4-inch pots. This size allows space for a good balance between root and top growth.

## Watering

Keep the soil moist but never soggy. Allow the soil to dry once every two weeks between waterings. Spray-mist daily.

## Fertilizer

Feed once a month while growing.

## Propagation

Stem cuttings. Break off a leaf-tipped branch and plant in a 4-inch pot. Division.

## Artificial Light

400 foot-candles.

## First Aid

*Mealybugs. (See Pests.)

*Older plants become straggly and leggy. This is natural for Pilea, and healthy cuttings should be propagated.

*The leaves tend to lengthen, turn black and drop during the cold months of winter. This is natural.

There are many species of *Pilea* from tropical Southeast Asia. The most popular is the aluminum plant. Silvery-gray markings on the green, quilted leaves appear to be aluminum but are in fact air spaces between the tissues of the leaves. The leaves are oval-shaped and pointed. They are glossy, leathery and grow in pairs alternating up the stem. The plant grows up to 10 inches tall and fits easily into small spaces. Older plants send out pendants that stream over the sides of the pot. These should be cut back every spring in order to maintain compact plants. Brown flowers appear occasionally on the tips of the stems.

*Microphylla* is a very unusual variety because of its tiny globular-shaped leaves that resemble a fern. When touched, the plant discharges ripe pollen into the air. When grown in bright light, it has a reddish appearance.

In March or April prune back drastically and it will soon regain its shrubby form.

*Shedding of leaves, pale or discolored leaves. A mass of yellowing foliage, tips of leaves and margins turn brown and die. Older plants shed leaves from the bottom up. During winter the growth is soft and discolored.* This indicates too little light. Needs bright light in a sunny room away from any direct sun.

*Shedding of leaves.* This can be caused from improper soil. Repot if necessary.

*Rotting, wilting and bleaching of foliage. A mass yellowing and dropping of leaves. New growth is weak, flowers will blight, and soil is constantly wet.* The problem is overwatering. The plant must be removed from the pot (see *Potting*) and the roots checked. Also check for proper soil and proper drainage material over the drainage holes. If the roots are white and healthy, repot in fresh soil, remove damaged foliage and water properly. If roots are partly brown, cut them away and repot in fresh soil. If all the roots are brown and mushy, the plant is beyond help and must be discarded.

---

A stiff succulent plant from South Africa. The leaves are arranged in tight, firm rosettes with leaves that curve upward. The leaves are brown, green or purple-brown in color. All varieties are covered with white spots called tubercles. The small, bell-shaped, whitish flowers appear in spring on long, thin, flower stems. The haworthia is one of the few succulent plants that will grow in the shade.

## Location

They do best in sunlight facing south; however, they will grow in filtered sunlight, bright indirect light and shade. The temperature in winter should not get any lower than 53 degrees, and summer temperatures suit them fine.

## Soil

One part all-purpose soil, one part sharp sand or use a prepackaged cactus soil mixture. They prefer to be slightly pot-bound; however, they have a tendency to have dry roots that rot during the summer, so annual repotting may be necessary.

# ARISTOCRAT PLANT— HAWORTHIA

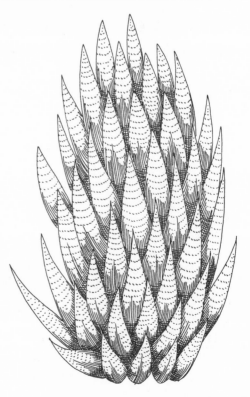

## Watering

The soil must become dry between thorough waterings. Water less in winter.

## Fertilizer

After the first year of purchase, feed only once every spring.

## Propagation

Leaf cuttings, seeds, suckers and offsets.

## Artificial Light

400 footcandles.

## First Aid

*Mealybugs. (See *Pests*)

*Rotting, wilting and bleaching of foliage.* This is the result of overwatering. The plant must be removed from the pot (see *Potting*), and a root check must take place. At the same time, check to make sure that the drainage holes are not clogged, the proper drainage material is being used and the plant has the proper soil. If the roots are white and healthy looking, either repot or place plant back into the same pot and aerate the soil, by stirring it with a fork, gently, to promote drying. Remove damaged foliage and allow soil to dry out thoroughly between waterings. Keep the plant in a well-ventilated location until new growth appears, then move back to proper location. If a few roots are damaged, remove them and repot in fresh soil. If all the roots are soft and mushy, the plant cannot be saved.

*Yellowing of foliage.* This is due to too much water (see above), too little water or too much heat. Underwatering is usually only improper watering.

Water slowly over the entire soil surface until excess water runs out of the drainage hole in the bottom. Do not let the plant sit in the water-filled saucer for more than an hour. Before rewatering, allow the plant to dry out thoroughly. The plant needs to be moved away from hot radiators and into a slightly cooler location.

*Plant becomes elongated, misshapen with underdeveloped leaves.* This is from insufficient light. The plant must be moved to a brighter exposure or closer to artificial lights.

*Growth is soft and discolored almost as though it has been overwatered.* This is caused by too much humidity. Cut down on the humidity in the growing area and ventilate the area better while avoiding drafts. Don't grow haworthias near plants that thrive on high humidity.

*Top growth yellows, stems become soft and dark in color, and new growth dies back.* This happens when the plant suffers from a fungus called root-rot disease. This fungus prevents the root system from absorbing water. These signs are usually mistaken for underwatering, but treating it for underwatering intensifies the problem. Plant must be removed from its pot (see *Potting*). All soil has to be removed and the roots washed in warm water and repotted in fresh soil. Remove damaged foliage and water plant only enough to keep it from wilting. Once normal growth resumes, water properly. Drench soil with a fungicide.

*Stems of plant turns soft and mushy, especially at its base.* This is caused from a fungus called crown and stem-rot disease. This disorder is promoted by too much humidity, overwatering and too high or low temperatures. First try dipping the plant in a hot bath for twenty to forty minutes. If this does not solve the problem, remove all infected areas and spray the plant with a fungicide. Give the plant its proper growing environment.

An easy-to-grow vine from Central America that has many varieties. The leaves are arrow-shaped and range from solid green to variegated. They usually need supports by which their stems will wind round and produce a large number of aerial roots which should never be removed. These aerial roots are a sign of a very healthy plant. An unusual characteristic of nephthytis is that the leaves change dramatically as it ages. The young leaves are simple, 3-inch-long leaves and become quite large. Stems can be pinched at any season to increase branching and foliage markings. If the stems get too tall, the tips can be cut off and parts of the stem can be used as cuttings.

## Location

Will grow very well in limited light exposures but prefers bright light. Must be protected from direct sun during the summer. Needs a warm location. Don't allow the plant to grow on a cold windowsill. A young plant will thrive on a corner of a warm mantelpiece.

## Soil

One part all-purpose soil, one part peat moss, one part sharp sand, perlite or vermiculite. Needs to be transplanted every year in February so that growth will not be retarded.

## Watering

Keep the soil moist at all times. Spray-mist daily.

## Fertilizer

Feed once a month in spring and summer. No feeding during the winter.

## Propagation

Stem cuttings.

# ARROWHEAD VINE— NEPHTHYTIS, SYNGONIUM

## Artificial Light

400 footcandles.

## First Aid

*Red spider mites are the plant's worst enemy. (See *Pests*).

*Annual repotting seems to prevent major problems.

*Soft, discolored foliage with curled leaves, brown edges. Stems can rot from the top down. This is from too cool temperatures and drafts. Temperatures should never be below 60 degrees. Never attempt to grow this plant on a cold windowsill.

*Occasional yellowing of leaves. This is old age and is natural for the plant.

# ASPARAGUS FERN— ASPARAGUS

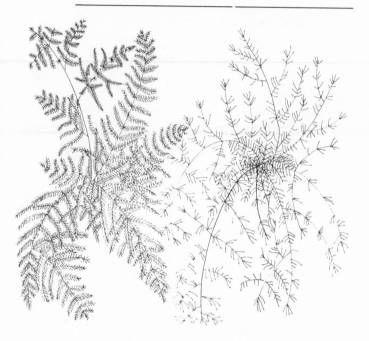

*Asparagus sprengeri* is a South African plant that has no relation to ferns at all. It has a feathery appearance which is due to its deeply arching branchlets that grow 18 to 24 inches long. The leaves are narrow, flat needles an inch long, and older plants develop thorns. The sprays are a bright green and tiny pink flowers will appear if growing conditions are ideal. If you have both sexes of the plant, it will bear small red fruit which contain the seeds for new plants. They are ideal for hanging baskets. In order for the plant to remain healthy, old shoots need to be cut away. If you like ferns but haven't the humidity for them, the asparagus would be a good choice as it needs far less humidity than a true fern.

The *plumosus* is another variety of the asparagus. It has a ferny foliage and is found mostly in florist shops used in floral arrangements, corsages and sprays. It will develop red berries if you have both sexes of the plant. When pruned, fresh shoots will always appear.

## Location

It prefers filtered sunlight or very strong light. It can survive a sunny place but must be protected from the hot noon sun during the summer and will not survive in shade or dark rooms. Needs average room temperatures without reaching below 50 degrees during the winter.

## Soil

Likes acid soil. One part all-purpose loam, one part peat moss, one part sharp sand, perlite or vermiculite. Do not allow the plant to become pot-bound. Its roots are flat and fleshy, needing a lot of space. The plant needs to be repotted every spring and sometimes twice a year. Repot it in a container at least two or three times larger than the old one.

## Watering

The surface soil should feel dry between thorough waterings. Never allow the soil to remain soggy. Water less frequently during the winter as the plant has small tuberous roots that protect it from drying out in the winter.

## Fertilizer

To avoid overfertilizing, do not feed after the first six months of purchase. Afterward feed every other month with a fertilizer for acid-loving plants.

## Propagation

Division of roots. Seeds kept very warm will take thirty to thirty-five days to germinate.

## Artificial Light

400 footcandles.

## First Aid

*Spider mites. (See *Pests*.) Nicotine insecticides will scorch the plant.

*Yellowing of top leaves or yellow margins and retarded growth.* This problem is from no root development which is from an iron or magnesium deficiency. The plant needs to be fed an acid fertilizer. If you have more than one acid-loving plant, investing in a home soil tester will prevent problems of this kind.

*Yellowish green coloring.* This is due to a lack of nitrogen in the soil. Make sure the nitrogen content of your fertilizer is high if you suspect this problem.

*Shedding needles and glossy, translucent foliage.* This is the result of fluctuating temperatures. Keep plant away from drafts, radiators or air conditioners. If the damage is severe, the plant should be knocked out of its pot (see *Potting*) and the roots checked. If the roots are firm and white, prune back the roots to help the surviving foliage and repot the plant. If the roots look unhealthy, discard the plant.

*Shedding needles, masses of yellow foliage, no new growth or new growth that shrivels and dies. Winter growth that is soft and discolored.* These are symptoms of too little light. Move the plant to a brighter exposure. If growing under artificial light, it needs to be moved closer to the light source.

*Shedding needles, grayish scorch marks on leaves, and a general bleached-out appearance.* This is from too much sun. Move plant farther from the light source or shield the plant with a thin curtain.

*Shedding needles, weak, limp and wilted stems, brown crisp spots and scorched edges on the foliage.* This is the result of letting the plant dry out too often. The soil must never dry out completely. When the surface soil feels dry, then watering is necessary.

*Yellowing of lower leaves, stems that are soft and dark in color, top growth usually is wilted, and new growth dies back.* This is a fungus called root-rot disease which prevents the root system from absorbing water and is caused by improper watering. Plant must be removed from its pot (see *Potting*) and all soil removed. Wash the roots under warm water and repot in fresh soil in a large enough pot. Remove damaged foliage and water plant only enough to keep the plant from wilting. Once the plant has normal growth, water properly. The soil must be drenched with a fungicide along with its first watering.

§ 41

# AUSTRALIAN UMBRELLA TREE, UMBRELLA TREE— SCHEFFLERA, BRASSAIA

An Australian plant with an upright growth that has horizontal tiers of long-stalked leaves that stretch outward like the ribs of an umbrella. Young plants have only three to five tiny leaflets with leaves no larger than 2 to 3 inches. Mature plants change dramatically and develop leaves 12 inches long and 1½ inches wide with seven to sixteen large leaflets. The naturally silky leaves are light green in color. Scheffleras can grow up to 6 feet tall at a strong and rapid rate. To keep the plant under control, snip off the tips of the stems just above a leaf.

## Location

A west window with bright light, semishade or filtered sun. Will tolerate direct sun but has to be protected from the hot sun of summer. Likes normal room temperatures and doesn't mind dry air.

## Soil

One part all-purpose loam, one part peat moss, one part sharp sand, perlite or vermiculite. Repot overcrowded plants at any season.

## Watering

Allow soil to become completely dry between thorough waterings. Spray-mist frequently to keep dust off plants and pests away.

## Fertilizer

Feed monthly.

## Propagation

Cuttings from the top or tips. Seeds, and suckers that cluster around the main stem.

## Artificial Light

800 footcandles.

## First Aid

*Spider mites, mealybugs, scales. (See *Pests*.)

*After watering, water stands on the soil. Wilting, slow growth, yellowing and rapid loss of lower leaves.*   This is the result of improper soil. The soil becomes so compressed that oxygen cannot circulate around the roots, the drying process happens too quickly, and the soil never gets enough water. Cut off any damaged foliage and repot in soil required for scheffleras.

*Mass yellowing and dropping of leaves. Leaves curl, tips turn brown and die back, plant has a general rotting, wilting look. New growth is weak.* The problem is overwatering. The plant must be removed from the pot (see *Potting*) and a root check must take place. While checking, make sure the plant has proper soil and the drainage holes are not clogged and there is enough drainage material covering the drainage holes. If the roots are white and healthy, put the plant back in its pot or repot in fresh soil. Remove all damaged foliage and keep the plant in a warm, well-ventilated location until new growth appears. Allow the soil to dry out thoroughly before rewatering.

The avocado is started from an avocado pit in the home and rarely purchased. The plant can eventually grow to the ceiling and a branch spread as much as 6 feet. If you don't want a large tree, its size can be controlled by pruning and pinching. The leaves are either oval or elliptical and grow from 4 to 15 inches long. They are a dark green color with a glossy effect if kept clean by washing gently with a sponge and some warm water.

There are avocados available from many parts of the world, but the most popular are from Florida and California. The Florida fruit pit grows more rapidly and produces larger plants than the green, smooth-skinned species from California.

The first step in growing a pit is recognizing which side of the seed is up and which is down. Many are tapered with the broader end being the bottom. Many seeds are perfectly round and oval and the bottom end has a folded dimple. Clean the seed well in warm water, removing as much skin as possible. If you should have a pit that is split and has a root mass starting, be careful not to break the seed in two, for if you do, it won't grow. Place toothpicks at intervals around the pit about a third of the way from the bottom. These are to support the pit when placed in a glass of water. When put in the water, make sure water covers half an inch of the seed. Maintain this water level by adding water, never changing the water. As long as the water is clear, the pit is not rotting. If the pit does rot, you must discard it and start a new seed. Place the glass in a warm, shaded place and watch for signs of growth.

# AVOCADO—PERSEA

First, small roots force their way out of the bottom, then it cracks and you can see light tendrils ready to shoot outward. There may be more than one stem, and these should always be left alone, even when growing in soil. The main stem will be obvious. Tiny leaves are curled tightly at the tip of the green stem. Some have red, speckled stems with bronze-colored leaves. When roots and stem are both developing, the seed is actively growing and preference must now be given to promoting strong roots. When the stem reaches 6 inches, cut it back to 3 inches; this will also induce a bushy, leafy plant. Don't wait more than three weeks after cutting it to plant it, taking care not to injure roots. The new pot should be clay and large—from 8 to 11 inches in diameter. Roots need plenty of room and excellent drainage. Remove the toothpicks or break them off. The upper part of the seed must be exposed to allow any new stems to grow. (See Potting.)

The plant will probably show no signs of growth for a while. Place the plant in strong light and new growth will appear more quickly. Keep the plant constantly moist.

When new growth appears, place the plant in sunlight or artificial light. As the plant reaches 18 inches, some sort of support will have to be employed. Place the support an inch or two away from the seed and push it to the bottom carefully so as not to injure too many delicate roots.

To encourage growth of young branches that grow out from the bottom of the main stem, cut off stems that grow on the next upper set of branches. Always work down from the top of the plant. Young stems and shoots that give the plant a lopsided appearance should be removed. Single leaves and crowns can be removed by pinching with your fingers.

## Location

Prefers sunlight but will survive in bright light. Likes normal room temperatures but not below 40 degrees during the winter.

## Soil

One part all-purpose loam, one part peat moss, one part sharp sand, perlite or vermiculite.

## Watering

A persea must be kept moist at all times. Leaving water in its saucer will not harm the plant. Spray-mist it daily to give it proper humidity and to keep the leaves free from dust.

## Fertilizer

Monthly, even if no growth is evident.

## Artificial Light

400 footcandles.

## First Aid

*Scales, thrips, red spider mites, aphids. (See Pests.)

*A black coating on leaves. This is black sooty mold developed from very humid conditions, and the mold is attracted to honeydew secretions of insects. It is not a disease and can be removed by washing leaves with soapy water and having the air circulating well around the infected plant. Also check for insects if the leaves feel at all sticky from their honeydew secretions.

*A mass of yellow foliage, tips of leaves and margins turn brown and die. Older plants shed their leaves from the bottom up, and new growth shrivels and dies. These symptoms indicate insufficient light. Remove damaged foliage and move plant to a brighter exposure.

*Scorch marks on leaves turning grayish where scorched, spots and a general bleached appearance. This is the result of too much sun. They like sunlight but the hot noon sun of summer may be too bright. Move farther away from its light source.

*Drying edges that curl under, drying foliage from the base upward, dropping older leaves, soft and discolored foliage and lower leaves that turn yellow with brown spots.* This is from too warm temperatures. Move out of the bright, hot sun and away from hot radiators. Remove damaged foliage. If this does not solve the problem, the roots will have to be checked. If they are brown and mushy, the plant is dead.

*Brown crisp spots, scorched edges on leaves, the leaves curl under and lower leaves turn yellow with brown spots and fall. Dark undersized leaves with loss of lower ones. New growth dies back and the whole plant can wilt and look limp.* These symptoms indicate underwatering. The avocado must always be kept moist, and even one drying out can injure the plant. When watering, water slowly over the entire soil surface until excess water runs out of the drainage hole in the bottom. This plant does not mind wet feet and water can be left in its saucer.

---

# AZTEC LILY— STAPELIA

There are many species, but this one is a hanging succulent of the milkweed family originally from South Africa. It has upright shoots about ½ inch thick that grow 4 to 6 inches and can also trail over the rim of its pot. From its soft, flexible spines small, green balloons emerge. The balloons increase in size daily, having geometric designs and shapes. The largest balloon will open first, petal by petal, and unfold into a five-cornered, star-shaped flower. They are a light brown color with darker brown patterns. The flower has a smell that attracts flies. They lay their eggs on the plant, and larvae pollinate the flowers.

## Location

Needs full sunlight to flower but will grow without direct sun. Needs normal room temperature in the summer and not below 45 degrees during the winter.

## Soil

One part all-purpose loam, one part peat moss, one part sharp sand. Use prepackaged cactus soil mixed with added sharp sand and peat moss to have im-

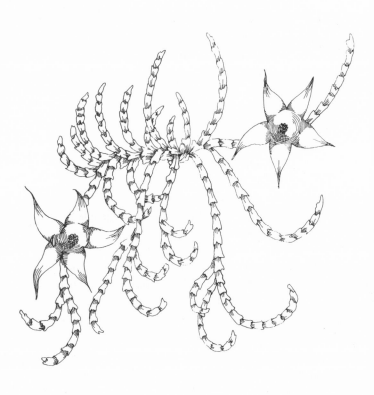

proved drainage. Stapelias like to be pot-bound, and repotting is seldom necessary.

## Watering

The soil must be allowed to become dry between thorough waterings with less watering during the winter; but if the plant is allowed to become limp from underwatering more than a few times, it will not recover. While the plant is flowering, mist-spray lightly daily.

## Fertilizer

Feed monthly March through July and withhold feeding the rest of the year.

## Propagation

Stem cuttings in the spring will flower within a year.

## Artificial Light

800 footcandles.

## First Aid

Pests don't attack this plant.

*The flower buds curl up soon after they appear.* This indicates lack of humidity. If you are growing this plant around other succulents and cacti, you don't want to raise the humidity in the air too much or you will have trouble with the other plants. Cover the plant with a plastic bag until the stem with the bud grows at least 6 inches. You can then remove the plastic as the extra humidity is no longer necessary.

*Spiny stems go limp and turn yellow.* This is the result of underwatering. If this has happened often,

the plant may not survive. However, if this is the first time, water slowly over the entire soil surface until excess water runs out of the drainage hole in the bottom. Do not let the plant sit in the water-filled saucer for more than an hour. Before rewatering again, allow the plant to dry out enough to meet its normal requirements for watering.

*Rotting, wilting and bleaching of foliage, and the soil is constantly wet.* This is caused by overwatering. Plant must be removed from the pot (see *Potting*) and the roots checked. Also check the drainage material over the drainage holes to make sure it is not clogged and make sure the plant has the proper soil. If the roots are still white and healthy looking, repot in fresh soil and be careful with your watering. If roots are partially brown, remove them and repot in fresh soil. If the roots are all brown and mushy, the plant can not be saved but there may be cuttings that can be taken to start new plants.

*Plants become leggy and elongated with soft and discolored foliage.* This is from temperatures that are too warm. The plant will have to be moved to a cooler location with good air circulation.

*Plants get elongated and misshapen with pale or discolored foliage. New growth shrivels and dies.* These symptoms indicate lack of light. The plant needs sun or a very bright location. Move into a brighter position or move closer to its light source.

*Black, brown or yellow damp or blistered spots, usually with yellow margins.* This is a fungal or bacterial invasion called leaf spot and is caused by high humidity, overwatering, chilling or low light. Repot plant in fresh soil and check the environmental conditions for stapelias. Infected areas should be removed and sprayed with a fungicide.

*Top growth wilts and yellowing of foliage, with stems becoming soft and dark in color.* This is a fungus called root-rot disease which prevents the roots from absorbing water. This is the result of improper watering and bad drainage. Plant must be removed from its pot (see *Potting*). All soil has to be removed and the roots washed in warm water and repotted in fresh soil. In the first watering, the soil must be drenched with a fungicide. Allow the soil to dry thoroughly between waterings.

*Base and stem of plant turn soft and mushy.* This is the result of a fungus called stem-rot disease. The disease is promoted by too much humidity, overwatering and changes of temperature. First try dipping plant in a hot bath for twenty to forty minutes, then repot in fresh soil. If this does not solve the problem, remove infected areas and spray with a fungicide.

A low and spreading succulent plant from the islands of Corsica and Sardinia. The moss has Kelly-green leaves the size of a pinhead, and the plant has a green-carpet effect when the leaves are bunched together with the intertwining stems.

About May or June little green flowers appear and will bear orange berries in August if a paintbrush is passed over the flowers daily to self-pollinate for the setting of the fruit. The plant sheds all its foliage annually. It will turn brown, dry up and drop off. It will look terribly unattractive but within a short time it will be covered with tiny, new, green leaves. This plant is very good for covering the ground of a terrarium.

### Location

Prefers filtered sun or bright light but will also thrive in semishade. East or west exposures are the most suitable, but the plant cannot sit in direct sun. It needs warmth, and cool window sills are detrimental. *Helxine* can withstand dry air very well but prefers not to. While the plant is bearing fruit, a temperature of 50 degrees will give the best results.

### Soil

One part all-purpose loam, one part peat moss, one part sharp sand, perlite or vermiculite.

# BABY TEARS
# IRISH MOSS—HELXINE

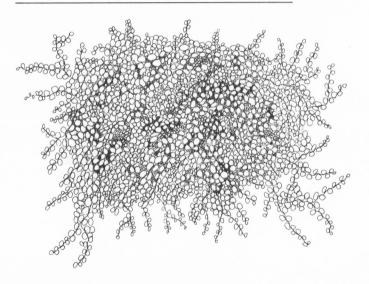

### Watering

Humidity and moisture are vital to its health. Soil needs to be kept moist but not too soggy. Water more in the summer and less in winter during dormancy. During summer, weekly dunks in a sink of water are beneficial. Winter or summer the plant must never dry out. The delicate leaves under the visible foliage are easily damaged if not watered carefully.

## Fertilizer

Fertilize monthly during its growing period but don't allow any fertilizer to get on the very sensitive leaves.

## Propagation

Division or root cuttings. The easiest way is by removing clusters of the brown stalks during the dormant period. Press them into moist soil and keep them moist.

## Artificial Lights

500 footcandles.

## First Aid

It is virtually pest-free.

*Drying out of the foliage of both center and outer portion of leaves during the winter.   This indicates the dormancy period, which usually lasts a month. Continue to keep the plant moist, and soon new growth will appear.

*Scorch marks on leaves with a general bleached-out appearance. Plant becomes limp and shrivels up.   This is the result of too much sun. The plant must be filtered from sunlight, watered well, and soon new growth will appear.

*Weak, limp and wilted. Brown crisp spots, scorched edges with older leaves turning yellow.   This is underwatering. Soil must be kept moist at all times. If thorough watering doesn't revive it, the plant will have to be discarded.

There are more than six thousand species of begonias, mostly from Africa and Brazil. Many forms of begonias do well as houseplants; they are categorized into three groups according to their root systems: fibrous rooted, rhizomatous and tuberous. All except the tuberous have fine fibrous roots. Their foliage is very diverse, with many textures and colors. All begonias except tuberous ones eventually need pruning to prevent them from looking too straggly. Because the foliage will grow toward the light, to maintain symmetrical growth, turn pots occasionally. When the leaves of begonias feel warm to the touch, no matter what location they're growing in, they are not happy.

There is such a wide range of care needed for particular plants that you should buy your plants from a good plant store and get all the information for the care of that individual plant. I will describe and help you grow the most popular.

The most popular of the fibrous-rooted variety of begonias is *Semperflorens*, the common wax plant. They have shiny, round, waxen leaves with leaf colors ranging from light green to dark green, brownish red and variegated. The flowers are borne in small clusters, and the brilliant colors of white, pinks and reds are very attractive. It will bloom all year round if conditions are good. It seldom reaches 12 inches in height. The plant has to be pruned back severely after each peak flowering. This keeps the plant bushy and helps new growth prosper.

*Angel wing* is another popular fibrous-rooted variety with its lopsided leaves which resemble an angel's wings. They are easy to grow. Pinching and pruning is a must or they will grow out of bounds. The leaves come in several shades of green and also a deep maroon. The leaves are spotted with silver specks. The clusters of white, pink, orange to bright red flowers bloom at the ends of the stems. They are also referred to as cane-stemmed begonias, because their stems can be thick and woody, unlike other begonias.

# BEGONIA

*Rhizomatous* begonias grow from thick stems that creep along the surface of the soil and come in a variety of colors and forms. They endure hardships better than other begonias because their rhizomes store food and moisture. Many of the rhizomatous plants have a habit of sprawling growth, and the rhizomes grow over the side of the pot. This can be corrected only when the plant is repotted by centering the growing point. This spillover growth does not harm the plant in any way and this growth can reach more than 2 feet long. There are low, wide pots sold especially for rhizomatous begonias, but don't make a mistake and overpot because you don't want the rhizomes growing over the pot.

The *beefsteak* is a rhizomatous begonia that grows very quickly. The leaves are glossy green with undersides of a deep red. The 5-inch leaves have the shape of rounded lily pads and the stems are covered with fuzz. The plant can spread more than 2 feet across and up to 1 foot tall. The flowers develop on the end of long stems and are pale pink. The rhizomes grow out of the pot quickly. There are not pots large enough to constantly keep the rhizomes in soil. Either let them spread out of the pot, which won't hurt them, or use parts of the rhizome for propagation.

The *hirsiites* are very durable, hairy-leaved begonias, the most popular being the Iron Cross. The leaves have a slightly gold coloring combined with the light green. They are ruffled and frilled with jagged edges. The center of each leaf is strikingly marked with a German "iron cross" colored in a dark brown.

*Begonia rex* is very popular because of its beautifully colored leaves. It has tiny pink or red flowers which are usually removed to keep the plant strong. Not all of the rexes will flower in the house. Many have fibrous roots without a noticeable rhizome. Rex begonias go into dormancy. When you're sure you have been giving your plant all the proper requirements but it looks like it's collapsing and losing leaves, then it's probably dormant. It is usually older plants or those that are in a cool location or one with low humidity that are affected. Dormancy usually occurs in mid-winter for two months. Eventually new growth will appear growing from the rhizome. If the plant loses its leaves, put it in a dim location until there are signs of new growth. Until plants are growing strongly, keep them just barely dry at the roots. Rexes grown under artificial light usually keep growing but will slow down.

Tuberous begonias are summer bloomers. The stems grow from tubers in the soil. Tuberous plants are best grown out of doors. Twelve hours of light a day will make them flower. The plant must be pinched back by removing three or four sturdy stems as they sprout, leaving only the largest stems to grow. The resulting flowers will be larger. If you are happy with many smaller flowers, let all the stems develop. When the stems are 6 to 8 inches tall, they will need to be supported with stakes. As the winter approaches and the days become shorter, growth slows down. This slowdown encourages the formation of tubers in preparation for dormancy to build up energy for next year's growth. As the foliage dies, hold off water. When all the foliage has died, prune foliage back until it's only a couple of inches tall. Place the tubers in their pots or remove from the pots and place in paper bags filled with unmilled sphagnum moss and put in a cool place (45 to 50 degrees). In the spring, plant tubers in proper soil and water sparingly and don't give them too much light. Once new growth appears, restore to proper environment for tuberous begonias.

## Location

All begonias need to be turned every few days so the growth is uniform and light is given to all the leaves. In winter all begonias like sun. Avoid sudden changes of temperatures, but a 5- to 10-degree temperature drop at night will give you sturdier plants.

*Fibrous*   The wax begonia needs a sunny, warm position. A location that provides 55- to 60-degree temperatures at night and 70 degrees during the day will help the plant to flower better. The wax begonia should be protected from hot, noon, summer sun.

Angel wing begonias remain more compact and bloom better if they receive bright light, but will tolerate lesser intensities. Give it as much light as it can stand but watch for burn spots or yellowing of leaves, which shows that it is getting too much.

*Rhizomatous*   They like several hours of sun a day but must be protected from the hot summer sun.

Rex prefers light but not direct sunlight. A north or northeast window is best but an east or west window will suit it as long as it is shaded from sun.

*Tuberous* Needs filtered sun, east or west window protected from hot noon sun in summer. The temperature needs to be under 75 degrees during the summer or the flowers will be short and dried.

## Soil

One part all-purpose loam, one part peat moss, one part sharp sand or perlite. They like to be root-bound, but overcrowded begonias can be repotted. You can repot at any season, but spring is best because new growth is strongest. Because roots are shallow and spread, they grow best in clay pots one-half to three-fourths as tall as they are wide. Tall, growing plants also have shallow roots and do well in these squat pots. When potting, pot loosely; they will not grow if the soil is compacted. Rhizomatous begonias need careful planting. The rhizome must remain on top of the soil; do not cover it with soil or you risk the problem of rot.

## Watering

All begonias need high humidity.

*Fibrous* Wax begonias need plenty of water. Keep the plant moist when growth is strong. Water less when not flowering much. Needs a moist atmosphere in the winter or the leaves will drop.

Angel wing must not be kept constantly moist or leaves will fall. Make sure you use clay pots and guard against overwatering. Let dry between thorough waterings.

*Rhizomatous* These plants hold lots of moisture. The soil should not be kept constantly moist. A slight drying on the surface soil between waterings will maintain healthy roots.

Rex begonia's dormancy period must be watched for. When the plant is dormant, water sparingly.

*Tuberous* The soil needs to be kept moist, but not soggy, at all times.

## Fertilizer

Feed monthly during strong growing periods without feeding during the colder winter months.

## Propagation

*Fibrous*
Stem cuttings root very easily.

*Rhizomatous*
Thick leafed plants by leaf cuttings or parts of the rhizomes.

*Tuberous*
Seed or tubers.

## Artificial Light

They do very well under artificial lights. 400 foot-candles.

## First Aid

*White flies, leaf rollers, thrips, mealybugs, aphids, spider mites, root nematodes. (See Pests.)*

*Slowly dying plant with bumps on the stem.* This is root knot. The plant must be destroyed. There is no cure for this disease.

*Wax begonias get leggy and fail to branch.* They

must have regular pinching back to encourage side shoots to form. After a strong flowering they should be pruned back severely. Turn plants regularly so that all sides are exposed to full light and water a little less.

*Leafstalks become long and leggy. Pale or discolored leaves. A mass of yellow foliage appears, tips of leaves and margins turn brown and die. Older plants shed leaves from the bottom up.* The problem is too little light. Move plant to a brighter light source or closer to the present source.

*Scorch marks on leaves, turning grayish where scorched, with a general bleached-out appearance.* This indicates too much light. Move farther away from the light source or shield the plant with other plants or a curtain.

*Rex begonias drop leaves in the fall.* The plant is going into dormancy. Water less, remove rotted leaves and flowers because they can attract bugs. Soon new growth will appear and you can resume proper environment.

*Drying foliage from the base upward, dropping older leaves, dry edges curl under, soft and discolored foliage.* The temperatures are too warm. Move plant into a well-aerated location without any cold drafts. If problem continues, a root check will have to be made. If roots are brown and soft, they have rotted and you must discard the plant. If roots are white and healthy, prune the roots back to keep them in balance with the surviving top growth and repot in fresh soil.

*Leaf tips turn brown, yellow leaf margins, stunted or no new growth, wilting, shriveling and dropping buds.* The humidity is too low. Spray-mist plant daily, water properly and place pot on a bed of wet pebbles without the bottom of the pot touching any water.

*Brown crisp spots, scorched edges on leaves and flowers. Flower buds drop, leaves curl under and lower leaves turn yellow with brown spots. Plant stems look weak and limp.* The problem is underwatering. Water slowly over the entire soil surface until excess water runs out of the drainage hole in the bottom. Do not let the plant sit in the water-filled saucer for more than an hour. Before rewatering, allow the plant to dry out enough to meet its normal requirements for water.

*Rotting, wilting and bleaching of foliage. A mass yellowing and dropping of leaves. Flowers will blight and soil is constantly wet.* These symptoms indicate overwatering. The plant must be removed from the pot (see *Potting*) and a root check must take place. While checking the roots, make sure nothing is blocking the drainage holes, that there is enough drainage material over the drainage holes and that the plant has the proper soil. If the roots are white and healthy looking, put the plant back into its pot or repot in fresh soil and allow to dry according to watering requirements for the particular begonia. Remove all damaged foliage. If roots are only partially damaged, remove the damaged roots and repot. If all roots are brown and soft, the plant is dead, but if there are any healthy stems, cuttings can be used to start new plants.

*Black, brown or yellow damp or blistered spots, usually with yellow margins.* This is a fungal or bacterial invasion called leaf-spot disease. It is caused by overwatering, chilling, low light and high humidity. Temperature, light, ventilation need to be increased, and soil must dry out before rewatering. Damaged foliage must be removed. Spray remaining leaves with a fungicide.

*Graying mold on leaves and flowers.* This is Botrytis, a fungus that spreads rapidly when plants live with high humidity, poor light and not enough ventilation. Remove infected parts, avoid syringing until cured and make sure you are giving the plant its proper growing requirements. If the problem is not cured, the infected plant must be destroyed before the fungus spreads.

*Pale spots on leaves of rex and tuberous begonias.* This is mildew which is caused by high humidity and cold temperatures. Improve ventilation and lower the humidity. Damaged leaves should be pinched off.

*Top growth shows signs of underwatering, wilting, and new growth dies back.* This is a fungus which prevents the root system from absorbing water. It is called root-rot disease, and if treated for underwatering the problem is usually intensified. Plant must be removed from its pot (see *Potting*). All soil has to be removed and the roots washed in warm water. Repot in fresh soil. The soil must be drenched with a fungicide. Remove damaged foliage and water plant only enough to keep the plant from wilting until normal growth is resumed.

*Bases and stems of plant turn soft and mushy.* This is a fungus disease called stem rot and is promoted by too much humidity, overwatering and too high or low temperatures. Infected areas must be removed and sprayed with a fungicide. Repotting is a good idea, and be sure to give the plant a proper environment for its species.

*Deformed buds and flowers, new buds dry up.* This is either from pests or low humidity. Spray-mist daily, place plant on wet pebbles without letting the bottom of the pot touch any water and use a humidifier during the winter.

*Failure to bloom.* This is from lack of light or too much nitrogen. Move the plant closer to a window or closer to artificial lighting. If the lighting is correct, then fertilize with a food with less nitrogen and fertilize less often using half the amount on the label.

# BLOODLEAF
# CHICKEN GIZZARD—IRESINE

A low-growing plant that trails and climbs. The foliage and the fleshy branches are both brilliantly colored deep crimson red. The sun shining through the leaves reflects red through the whole room. Some plants have leaves that are round, others are pointed. The plant needs to have the points of shoots pinched frequently to induce bushy growth and pruned often to prevent the plant from becoming straggly and leggy. There is a variety that is solid green without any red coloring.

## Location

Needs a full sun exposure, preferring south windows. Bloodleaf does not mind direct, hot sun. Average room temperatures are necessary.

## Soil

One part all-purpose loam, one part peat moss, one part sharp sand, perlite or vermiculite. Repot overcrowded plants in early spring. If the plant has become straggly, it should be cut back severely at this time.

## Watering

Allow the soil to become dry between waterings, but because it likes hot sun, daily checking is necessary to guard against drying out. Spray-mist daily.

## Fertilizer

Feed once a month.

## Propagation

Cuttings. Regular propagation will ensure healthy-looking plants, since older plants become so straggly and should be discarded.

## Artificial Light

1,000 footcandles.

## First Aid

*Mealybugs, aphids. (See Pests.)*

*Poor growth during the winter, pale leaves, dropping of foliage.* These symptoms are all due to insufficient light. Bloodleaf needs full sun. Some of the poor light symptoms can be from lack of humidity. If you're sure the plant has plenty of sun, place it on a bed of wet pebbles without the pot touching the water and spray-mist daily. Sun will not injure the wet leaves.

A succulent tree from Texas and Mexico with thin, graceful straplike leaves. The plant has a bulbous swelling of the trunk at soil level. The bark has a wrinkled texture and has a grayish brown color. The swollen trunk serves as a water tank, enabling it to survive drought. A young plant has the leaves coming directly from the bulb, but as leaves grow a trunk will develop. A carefree plant which grows slowly, it can be classified as a small plant but under the right circumstances it will grow very large. In the desert it reaches 30 feet.

## Location

They do best in direct sunlight but will survive in filtered sunlight or bright light. They can withstand a temperature range from 40 to 90 degrees.

## Soil

One part all-purpose loam, one part peat moss, one part sharp sand, perlite or vermiculite. Plants like to be pot-bound and can live for years in small containers. When they become overly pot-bound, repot in early spring before new growth begins.

## Watering

Soil should become dry between thorough waterings. Spray-mist foliage daily.

## Fertilizer

Do not feed for one year after purchasing, then feed once a year in the spring.

## Propagation

Seeds at any season.

# BOTTLE PLANT
# PONY TAIL
# ELEPHANT FOOT—
# BEAUCARNEA

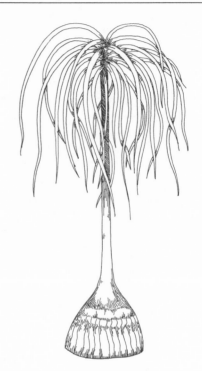

## Artificial Light

800 footcandles.

## First Aid

*Mealybugs. (See Pests.)*

*The bulbous trunk gets soft and mushy.* This is a fungus disease called stem-rot disease and is promoted by overwatering, too much humidity and changes in temperatures. Dip the plant in a hot bath for twenty to forty minutes. If this doesn't solve the problem the plant must be destroyed.

*Rotting, wilting and bleaching of foliage. A mass yellowing and dropping of leaves. Leaves curl, tips turn brown and die back.* This is overwatering. The plant must be removed from the pot (see *Potting*) and the roots checked. At the same time, check to make sure the drainage holes have not been blocked and that the plant has the proper soil. If the roots are white and healthy, repot and water well. Allow to dry according to watering requirements. Remove damaged foliage. If only a few roots are damaged, remove them and repot. If all the roots are damaged, the plant can not be saved.

*Leaves yellow and the trunk looks wrinkled.* This is from lack of water. Water slowly over the entire soil surface until excess water runs out of the drainage hole in the bottom. Do not let the plant sit in the water-filled saucer for more than an hour. Before rewatering, allow the plant to dry out thoroughly. Underwatering is the safest watering method with any succulent. Remove all damaged foliage.

*Lower leaves turn yellow with brown spots, dry edges curl under, drying foliage from the base upward, dropping older leaves.* These symptoms indicate temperatures that are too warm. Move into a well-ventilated area away from cold drafts and away from hot radiators.

# BOXWOOD—BUXUS

A small-leaved indoor shrub from North Africa and southern Europe. It has compact, dense foliage and grows only 2 to 4 inches a year. Has smooth firm, 1-inch, oval leaves that are a rich green. The boxwood grows to 4 feet but responds to pruning and pinching to keep it compact, round and bushy.

## Location

Likes sun but will survive in bright light. Likes cool temperatures and can withstand drafty places.

## Soil

One part all-purpose loam, one part peat moss, one part sharp sand, perlite or vermiculite. Do not repot until roots are growing on the surface of the soil and through the drainage holes.

## Watering

Allow the surface soil to dry between thorough waterings and every few weeks let the soil dry thoroughly between waterings. Spray-mist daily.

### Fertilizer

Feed once every six months.

### Propagation

Stem cuttings in late summer or early fall.

### Artificial Lights

800 footcandles.

### First Aid

*A practically problemless plant in the home.

*Black, brown or yellow spots, damp or blistered, and leaves usually have yellow margins.   This is a fungal or bacterial invasion called leaf-spot disease caused by high humidity, overwatering and low light. Infected areas should be removed and sprayed with a fungicide. Temperature, light, ventilation need to be increased, and soil must dry out before rewatering.

*A general decline or dieback. Branches in the middle or top of the boxwood first become gray-green, then bronze and finally yellow.   This is caused by poor care during the winter. This problem usually only affects outdoor plants but sometimes attacks a houseplant that has been neglected. Start with repotting, removing all damaged foliage and give the plant a better environment.

---

# BROMELIAD

There are over eighteen hundred species of bromeliads from many parts of the world's tropical regions. Some have grasslike leaves, and others broad leaves. They have magnificently marked foliage in colors of white, pink and green, and many are variegated. They grow in many forms, but the popular ones we see in plant stores are the vase or bowl types. New leaves are formed from the center and form rosettes. On some, the rosette forms a tall vase, while others are much flatter and have small rosettes. As the plant forms new leaves from the center, the lower outer leaves eventually dry out. In some varieties as they age, the foliage will change its colors to much brighter and vivid shades. These dying outer leaves can be removed to improve the appearance of the plant. The rosette blooms only once and the plant dies. Young plants can take from one to three years to bloom. Blooms appear either in clusters on tall spikes or low clusters in the heart of the plant and last as long as six months. The blooming season varies from year to year and depends on the variety. One can place plastic bags over the plant with an apple inside to force the plant to bloom. The apple gives off ethylene gas which initiates flower buds.

§ 57

There are two kinds of bromeliads: epiphytes, which receive nourishment and moisture from the air and debris on tree limbs and grow clinging to trees by their roots, and terrestrials, which grow in the soil and receive their nourishment there.

Bromeliads are very simple to grow, will survive some neglect and adapt well to home environments. They have small root systems and should be in small clay pots. Their soil should never be allowed to become soggy.

Once the plant has flowered, it will die, but no matter how badly it looks or how bad a smell it has, water should still be kept in its rosette in order for new plantlets to appear. At early stages the new plants do not have their own vases and moisture is supplied by the dying plant. When rosettes have formed on the new plants, these can be potted up individually and will bloom in one to three years and begin another cycle.

*Earth stars* are stemless bromeliads that are extremely easy to grow. They have rosettes with small, narrow, flat leaves with very brightly colored markings. They have a very poorly developed root system and should be kept in small pots or on a small tree trunk.

The ordinary pineapple is a common bromeliad, and starting your own pineapple plant is easy to do, though some refuse to take root. Slice the top off of a fresh pineapple from your grocery store, leaving an inch of fruit attached. Remove the outer part of the fruit, leaving the stringy center intact. Allow to dry out for two or three days to prevent rotting. On potting day, remove the lower leaves and plant it in a bromeliad soil mixture using a 5-inch pot. They grow quickly and need planty of space to grow. Do not allow the soil ever to become too wet but spray-mist daily. Give it the proper growing conditions for bromeliads. If you are lucky, a large spike will grow from the center with a small pineapple at its peak. This happens rarely indoors but it is possible. The pineapple plant can grow large with leaves up to 3 feet long. The leaves have sharp teethlike edges and the color of the leaves is a dull gray-green. There are varieties with reddish pink leaves and those with ivory and green stripes.

## Location

Bromeliads need plenty of light and will grow in direct sun, but to prevent burning of foliage and flowers, shade them from hot summer sun. Earth stars like more sun than most to intensify their leaf colors; however, they must be protected from hot, noon, summer sun. The harder, stiffer and more sharp the teethlike leaf edges, the more light is needed. Softer and more pliable leaves need less light. Temperatures between 50 and 70 degrees are the best. They need good circulation but cold drafts must be avoided. The pineapple thrives in full sun.

## Soil

Most species do not have extensive root systems and should have shallow containers with a very porous, well-drained soil. Osmunda fiber, roots of the osmunda fern, purchased at a plant store, can be used for epiphytes. Epiphytes can also be secured to a piece of a tree and sprayed daily and fed by spraying fertilizer in solution on the root ball twice a year. The following mixtures can be used for both types of plants: One part peat moss, one part perlite, one part fir bark (chips of the fir tree) or one part peat moss, one part bark chips, one part all-purpose loam, one part sharp sand. You can use prepackaged orchid potting mix.

## Watering

Water sparingly when the soil is dry. The soil should never be too wet. The vases formed by the rosettes must be kept continuously full of water. Spray-mist the leaves daily to keep them clean. If any of your plants are fastened to a tree or bark, the root ball should be wrapped in moist sphagnum and kept damp.

## Fertilizer

Twice a year feed half the amount of fertilizer recommended on the bottle. Do not pour fertilizer into the rosettes, as this can be disastrous for the plant.

## Propagation

Offshoots from the base. Some varieties send shoots from the axils of the leaves at the top of the cup. When large enough these can be pinched off and potted like offshoots.

## Artificial Light

From 400 to 1,000 footcandles depending on the species.

## First Aid

*Spider mites, mealybugs, scales, hard black scales. (See *Pests.*) Insecticides can be used, but if they get into the rosette the plant can be damaged, so first try getting rid of pests without using sprays.

*No flowering.* The problem might simply be time. It can take from two to three years to flower. Moving it to a brighter location can encourage blooming.

*Rotting plant.* This is natural. As the old plant dies after flowering it will bear new young shoots at its base.

*Brown tips on leaves.* This is due to dry air, dry soil or improper soil. Knock the plant out of its pot (see *Potting*) and check to make sure the drainage holes are not blocked and that there is proper drainage material over the drainage holes. Repot in proper soil and give the plant its proper environment.

# CACTUS SUCCULENTS

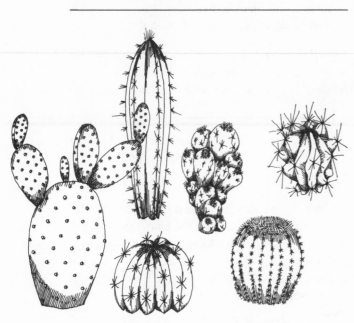

There are over two thousand known species of cacti in all shapes and sizes from 1 inch to 50 feet tall. Cacti are part of a large group of plants whose traits include succulent or fleshy stems that serve to store water. They have thorns, prickly or hairy coverings and few if any leaves.

Cacti are New World plants indigenous only to northern, central and southern America and their neighboring islands. Cacti had leaves at one time in history and in their seedling stages they still do. There are species that have small leaves on new growth for a short time in spring and there are a few that have leaves throughout the year. As climatic changes occurred and the native habitats became deserts, most cacti lost their leaves because of dry air and scarcity of water. Their stems thickened and became fat and round in order to store what moisture there was against the drought periods.

*True cacti are succulents, but not all succulent plants are cacti.* There are over sixty-five hundred species of water-storing plants that are succulents but not cacti. The cacti are from the Cactaceae family, and the others belong to forty-four different botanical families that are spread around the world. Included are relatives of poinsettias, geraniums, lilies and the grape. Most of these succulents have leaves, but they are thick and fat due to their water-storing abilities. Most have waxy tissue that reduces evaporation from the surfaces. For simplicity those with spines can be referred to as cacti and other fleshy plants as succulents.

To encourage any cactus or succulent to bloom it needs to be left pot-bound. The roots pressed tightly together force blooms. To thrive, all cacti and succulents need a resting period or dormant period. With cacti this should coincide with the cold weather, usually November through February. The globe or barrel cactus fits into this category. Succulents vary their length of dormancy depending on the particular plant. Aloes, agaves and kalanchoes need very little, if any, rest.

## Location

You must learn the requirements of your particular plant. Globe cacti and many succulents require a minimum of six hours of direct sun in order to bloom abundantly, while some succulents need shade and the more tender varieties have to be protected from the hot noon sun of summer. The plants need to be turned every few days so the light reaches all areas of the plant. However, if the plant is beginning to bud, turning the plant can cause these buds to drop off. Cacti require warm temperatures, the warmer the better, with a minimum of 60 degrees at night. Succulents like temperatures of 75 to 85 degrees during the day with a 10-degree drop at night.

## Soil

Cacti do not grow in pure sand in their natural environment. They grow among other desert plants where the roots can absorb nutrition from decaying organic matter. In arid regions where cacti usually grow, the soil is high in minerals and limes.

Use one part all-purpose loam, one part sharp sand, one part peat moss with a small amount of perlite, or use one part prepackaged cactus mix with a handful of sharp sand and perlite or vermiculite added to improve drainage.

Small plants need to be repotted every two years. Larger plants not for three or four years. Use small clay containers. Round plants need a pot an inch wider than the diameter of the plant. Tall, growing plants should have a pot half as wide as the plant is tall. When repotting use bamboo tongs to handle spiny cacti. On most plants the root systems are small, and it will be necessary to anchor the plant to the pot until it is rooted securely in its new soil. Stake large plants and tie to the stake with string. For small plants use rubber bands vertically around the pot and plant. It is a good idea to spread sand or gravel on the surface of the soil and also under the plant between the small stem (neck) and plant. This prevents root rot and protects the plant from being discolored from water splashing on them during watering.

## Watering

Though cacti and succulents can store water, this doesn't mean they don't enjoy a good drink like any other plant. Many problems are associated with underwatering. The soil should be dry half an inch into the soil between thorough waterings (scratch into the soil gently with a matchstick to check). They will need to be watered more often while in bloom. This watering applies to cactus.

Many succulents need more watering and must be carefully checked when purchased. When the weather starts to cool, water only enough to keep from shriveling. When the plants are dormant (usually March or April) water less until new growth appears. Water sparingly at first, increasing the moisture as warm weather arrives. The dormant period is necessary in order to have a blooming plant. High humidity is not necessary. It is sufficient to have 10 to 20 percent humidity. On especially hot days give them a very light spray mist of water.

## Fertilizer

Neither cacti nor succulents need a lot of feeding. During the first year it is not necessary to feed at all. Afterward feed once a month with a 5-2-2 fertilizer. Don't feed in winter or on cloudy or rainy days.

## Propagation

It is very easy to propagate cactus or succulents with cuttings or seeds. The barrel cacti are easy to grow from seeds and these are plentiful at most plant stores. Leaf cuttings of succulents can also be propagated. To have a successful cutting to root you must let the end of the cutting dry. This is a crucial step in the vegetative propagation of succulents. Fresh cuttings are likely to rot if planted. Let large cuttings dry for two to three weeks and small cuttings only two to three days in a warm, shady spot. Leaf cuttings need to be dried out for only a few days. Cuttings from the ends of branches will grow and root without any shriveling of the old leaves. As new plants form at the base of a leaf cutting, the old leaf will die.

## Artificial Light

Cacti and succulents can be grown from seed to maturity under artificial lights. 1,000 footcandles.

## First Aid

*Mealybugs, scales, slugs, snails, sow bugs, nematodes, red spider mites. (See Pests.)* Malathion or insecticides may injure tissues. Use nicotine sulfate.

*Rot at the point where the roots join the trunk of the plant.* This is the main problem with cacti. Water settles in this area and rots the plant. Leave 1/2 inch of space at the joint of the body and roots and fill with a coarse gritty material. The roots will tolerate more water as long as this area is protected. Dip the injured plant in a hot water bath for twenty to forty minutes and repot in fresh soil. If soft black rot appears near the base, remove the plant from the pot and very gently cut away infected tissue and let the wounds dry in air until hardened. Repot in fresh soil.

*Decay starting around wounds or depressed areas.* This, once again, is rot. Cut out infected parts and water from below, being careful not to overwater. When wounds are healed, resume watering from the top.

*The plant hasn't grown for a year.* You have been either over- or underwatering. See the following.

*Rotting, wilting and bleaching of foliage. A mass yellowing and dropping of leaves. Soil is constantly wet.* This is from overwatering. It is a special problem during the dormant period. Remove the plant from the pot (see Potting) and examine the roots. If these seem healthy, repot the plant and improve your watering methods. If the roots are dead or rotted and mushy looking, you may have lost it. If roots are partially brown, remove diseased parts, remove all soil and allow remaining roots to dry in the sun. Repot in fresh soil.

*Plant looks weak, limp, shriveled and can turn yellow. Leaves curl and lower leaves turn yellow with brown spots and fall.* This is from underwatering. Water slowly over the entire soil surface until excess water runs out of the drainage hole in the bottom. Do not let the plant sit in the water-filled saucer for more than an hour. Allow the plant to dry out thoroughly before rewatering. You have to watch closely at first until you are able to understand what your cactus expects, and then water accordingly.

*Black, brown or yellow spots that are damp or blistered and usually have yellow margins. These can appear anywhere on the cactus or succulent.* This is a fungal or bacterial invasion called leaf spot and it is caused by poor air circulation, high humidity, overwatering, low light. Temperature, light and ventilation need to be increased, and soil must dry out before rewatering. Infected areas should be removed. Spray with a fungicide.

*No flowering even when all correct conditions are maintained.* It may simply be a matter of time. Most cactus take four or five years to start flowering, although some flower when young if given the proper environment.

*Soft and discolored growth.* This is too much humidity. Humidity must be cut down and the growing area well ventilated. Keep cactus away from high-humidity plants.

*Plant becomes elongated and misshapen.* This is from too little light. (See "Artificial Light" for cacti and succulents.)

*Brown or black areas on leaves that look like scorch marks and general bleached-out look.* The problem is too much light. (See "Location" for cacti and succulents.)

*The plant becomes leggy and elongated.* This is from temperatures that are too warm. The plant must be moved to a cooler location with good air circulation.

A tuberous-rooted plant from the tropical regions of the Western Hemisphere. Caladiums have beautiful large leaves that grow to 2 feet long and are heart-shaped with a crepelike texture. The leaves are many colors of red, pink, green, white and silver, and some have marbled affects. Many are veined in a contrasting color. Sometimes a great variety of hues is displayed in the same leaf. The plant grows from 12 to 18 inches tall. To keep the foliage strong, the flowers should be removed. The plant grows from tubers (bulblike masses of storage tissue) and has an annual rest period of from two to five months, usually beginning in spring. As the leaves wither during the dormant period, watering should be reduced gradually. The tubers should remain completely dry in their pots for two months. About mid-August they should be repotted in proper soil and kept out of bright light. Water sparingly. When new shoots appear, put them in brighter light and keep them moist, feeding them every three weeks. Another way to handle their dormant period is, after the foliage shrivels, to allow the soil to dry. Remove the plant from the pot, shake the soil off the roots, pull away dead tops. Paint a fungicide-insecticide combination on the tubers. Store them at 55 degrees in dry peat moss, perlite or vermiculite for four months. Then start them by planting them in their proper soil mixture. Water sparingly and keep shaded. When new shoots appear, move them into brighter light. Keep soil moist and fertilize every three weeks.

## Location

They are shade lovers, so bright light or curtain-filtered sunlight is best. They are very susceptible to quick changes of temperature and need a warm room kept at even temperatures.

## Soil

Acid soil is necessary to keep the brightly colored leaves. Two parts all-purpose loam, two parts peat moss, one part sharp sand, perlite or vermiculite.

# CALADIUM

## Watering

Keep soil moist at all times but don't allow the soil to remain soggy. Daily misting is required.

## Fertilizer

Feed every three weeks, with an acid fertilizer used at every other feeding.

## Propagation

When replanting, divide the tubers. Cut large tubers into pieces, each containing one or two eyes, and dust the cut surface with ferbam. Using a medium of damp peat moss or vermiculite press them, bud side down, 1 inch deep into medium. Place near a warm stove of 80 degrees or more. The higher the temperature the better the starting results. Keep moist. When new leaves appear, pot in 5-inch pots in proper soil and place in the same environment as adult plants.

§ 63

## Artificial Light

400 footcandles.

## First Aid

*Virtually pest-free.

*The foliage becomes pale in color.* This problem is from lack of the proper fertilizer, low humidity and too little light. Needs to be fed every three weeks, with an acid fertilizer at every other feeding. Move it to a lighter location with some filtered sun. Keep the humidity high by mist spraying and placing the plant on a bed of wet pebbles without the bottom of the pot touching any water. Keep the plant warm and the color will improve.

*Scorch marks on leaves turning grayish where scorched, general bleached-out appearance. Plant becomes limp, shrivels and can die.* Too much sun causes these symptoms. Move plant farther from the light source or shield the plant with a curtain or larger plants.

*Wilting, slow growth, yellowing of leaves and rapid loss of older leaves and general deterioration of the plant.* This is from improper drainage. Remove any damaged foliage and repot in proper soil. Make sure the drainage holes are covered with enough drainage material (see *Potting*).

*Small leaves and very few new leaves.* This is the result of underwatering, low humidity and insufficient light. Water slowly over the entire soil surface until excess water runs out of the drainage hole in the bottom. Do not let the plant sit in the water-filled saucer for more than an hour. Before rewatering, allow the plant to dry out enough only to meet its normal requirements. Mist-spray once or twice daily and give the plant filtered sun or very bright light.

There are many varieties of calathea, all from tropical America. Their leaves emerge directly from the crown, making them useful as ground cover between other plants. They all have rhizomatous roots. The most popular is the *makoyana* (peacock plant); the leaves are green with purple undersides and red stalks. *Leitzer* and *louisae* come in shades of green and marked subtly with maroon. *Zebrina* has deep green, velvety-textured leaves which are large with dark stripes crossing the leaves. *Argyroea* has leaves of silver and green with thin lines where veins cross the leaves, and there is also a dwarf variety.

## Location

They need indirect or filtered sun with protection from hot sun from March to October. They will survive in bright light. Warm temperatures of 70 to 80 degrees and never below 60 degrees are necessary.

## Soil

One part peat moss, one part sharp sand, one part perlite or vermiculite, or use prepackaged African violet soil with a handful of vermiculite to help the drainage. African violet soil has a lot of peat moss in the mixture so don't add any more. Repot when necessary in the spring.

## Watering

Keep the soil moist at all times but never soggy. Spray-mist daily.

## Fertilizer

Feed every two weeks.

## Propagation

Dividing the rhizomes.

# CALATHEA

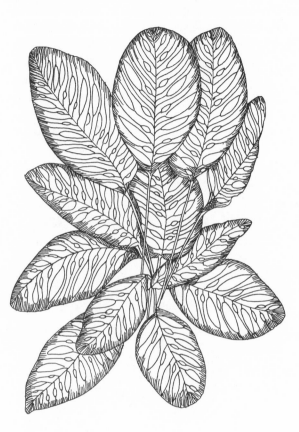

## Artificial Light

400 footcandles.

## First Aid

*Red spider mites are their worst enemy. (See Pests.)

*Shedding leaves, especially during the winter. This occurs because of low humidity. It's hard to entirely prevent, but you can keep it under control by spray misting twice a day and placing the plant on a bed of wet pebbles without the bottom of the pot touching the water. Try using a humidifier during the winter.

*Scorched leaf edges, leaves curl under and lower leaves turn yellow with brown spots and fall. Dark, undersized leaves with loss of older ones. The problem is underwatering. Water slowly over the entire soil surface until excess water runs out of the drainage hole in the bottom. Do not let the plant sit in the water-filled saucer for more than an hour. Keep the soil moist at all times but never allow it to become soggy.

*Scorch marks on leaves turning grayish where scorched, general bleached-out appearance.   This is too much sun, and the plant can become limp, shrivel and die. Move plant farther from the light source or filter it from direct sunlight.

*Leaf tips turn brown, yellowing leaf margins, wilting, shriveling.   These symptoms indicate low humidity. Spray-mist twice a day and place plant on a bed of wet pebbles without the bottom of the pot touching the water. Use a humidifier during the winter.

# CAMELLIA—THEA JAPONICA

A small evergreen shrub related to the tea plant originally from the Asiatic tropics. It flowers annually and sometimes all winter and early spring if the temperature is kept at a maximum of 60 degrees. The flowers of red, rose, pink or white are waxy, with a firm texture. Some have tints of contrasting colors. The leaves are glossy and smooth textured. Buds form easily but the conditions must be perfect to get them to bloom. The plant can grow to 3 feet tall but requires very careful attention. When purchasing the plant it is necessary to know which side was facing the light, and when taken home it must be returned to the same position. Buds will fall from a change of position.

## Location

A bright, sunny location is necessary, but the camellia must be protected from the hot sun of a south window. Cool temperatures at a maximum of 60 degrees (but no frost), must be maintained at all times to encourage the plant to bloom.

## Soil

One part all-purpose loam, two parts peat moss, one part sharp sand, perlite or vermiculite. Or use an African violet prepackaged mix with a handful of both peat moss and perlite or vermiculite added. The camellia is an acid-loving plant.

## Watering

Keep plant moist at all times but never soggy. From June to July soak the soil thoroughly, then permit it to just dry before rewatering. This will encourage formation of buds. Spray-mist daily.

## Fertilizer

Feed every three weeks with an acid fertilizer and more often when in bloom.

## Propagation

Not successful in the home. By cuttings or graftings done in nurseries.

## Artificial Light

800 footcandles.

## First Aid

*Scales, mites, mealybugs. (See *Pests.*) Camellias have great susceptibility to pests and diseases and must be constantly inspected for any uninvited guests.

*Buds and flowers fall.*   This occurs when the air is too warm or when a change of the plant's position has been made. The plant resents being moved. The buds will always turn toward the light and if constantly moved will twist themselves off. Place the plant on a bed of wet pebbles without the bottom of the pot touching the water. Spray-mist often.

*Yellowing of foliage beginning at the outer edges, usually spreading to the whole leaf and damaging roots. Yellow spots and crisp brown spots and scorched edges on leaves. Wilting and no flowers. Base of affected twigs are blackened.*   These symptoms indicate overfertilizing. Soil must be literally flooded with water twice and allowed to drain well. If fertilizer salts have accumulated on the pot, remove with warm water and a stiff brush. Remove all damaged foliage. Fertilize less often or use half the amount you have been using.

*Burning of the upper surfaces of the leaves, areas of leaves are a dark brown throughout the leaf.*   This is sunburn. Move the plant farther from the sun or filter it with a curtain. Remove all damaged foliage.

*Scabs on the underside of leaves which are brown and oval shaped.*   This is not a fungi but an imbalance within the plant. An excess of food, humidity and water make the cells of the leaves swell and burst, causing the leaves to turn brown and die. Repot the plant, remove all damaged foliage and give the plant its proper environment.

*Yellowing of leaves.*   The life expectancy of a leaf is three years, after which it will turn yellow and fall. If more than one or two leaves die, other problems are indicated.

*Leaves curl under and lower leaves turn yellow, develop brown spots and fall. Brown crisp spots, scorched edges on leaves and flowers. Stems look weak and wilted.*   The problem is a soil that is too dry. Soil must be kept moist by slowly watering over the entire soil surface until excess water runs out of the drainage hole in the bottom. Do not let the plant sit in the water-filled saucer for more than an hour. Allow to dry only to dampness, then rewater.

*A pale bleached coloring, yellowing or yellow spots on leaves, usually beginning on the outer edges and spreading to the whole leaf. Older leaves will drop.*   This is from too little fertilizer. Fertilize more often, especially during the blooming periods.

*Yellowing leaves, wilting, loss of older leaves. Water stands on the soil without filtering through quickly.* This indicates improper soil. Repot in proper soil and make sure enough drainage material is covering the drainage holes.

*Yellowing of top leaves or yellow margins with the veins remaining green.* This is an iron or magnesium deficiency. The plant must be fed with an acid fertilizer.

*Yellow, black, brown spots with damp or blistered centers that usually have yellow margins.* This is a fungal or bacterial invasion called leaf-spot disease, caused by high humidity, overwatering, chilling, low light. Increase light and temperature and allow the soil to dry before rewatering. Ventilate the growing area well. Destroy all infected leaves and spray a foliar fungicide on remaining leaves.

*Lower leaves yellow, stems become soft and dark in color. Top growth usually wilts and new growth dies back.* This is a fungus called root-rot disease which prevents the roots from absorbing water. Remove plant from its pot and wash all the old soil from the roots with warm water. Do not remove any roots unless they look badly damaged. Repot in fresh soil (see *Potting*) and water only enough to keep the plant from wilting. Once it has recovered and resumed normal growth, return to proper requirements for the plant. The soil should be drenched with a fungicide after repotting to keep the problem from recurring.

# CAST-IRON PLANT— ASPIDISTRA

A plant from China and southern Japan. The plant has long, dark leaves with an arching effect that reach a length of 15 to 30 inches and are 3 to 4 inches wide. The leaves grow from thick, fleshy root stalks in clusters at the base. The plant can grow to 3 feet tall. The small flowers grow at soil level and are globular with a violet-brown color. There is also a variety with white stripes.

## Location

Must be shaded from any sun. The bright light of a north window is best. Extremes of temperatures from 45 to 85 degrees do not seem to affect the growth of the plant.

## Soil

One part all-purpose loam, one part peat moss, one part perlite or vermiculite. Likes to be pot-bound and needs repotting only every two to three years. Repot in early spring before new growth begins.

## Watering

Keep the soil moist at all times without allowing it to get soggy. Aspidistra prefers some humidity but can withstand dry air.

## Fertilizer

Feed once a month except during the cold winter months when the plant should be left unfed.

## Propagation

The only form of propagation is by division of the roots. Each division should be cut so that it has two to three leaves. These divisions are planted together to make a large plant.

## Artificial Light

150 footcandles.

## First Aid

*Spider mites, scale. (See Pests.)

*Cracked leaves. This is from bruising. Move the plant to a location where people are less likely to brush against it.

*Yellowing leaves. This problem is usually caused from light that is too strong. This plant is a shade lover and must not be allowed to sit in direct or even filtered sun. It demands shade.

*The white strip is changed to solid green. This happens if the soil is too rich or not properly drained, or the plant receives too little light. It likes shade but not darkness. Move it closer to its light source or move it to a brighter location. Do not feed the plant during the winter, or if you have been feeding it properly, give it smaller amounts than you would normally but continue to feed it once a month unless you have repotted it. After repotting it's not necessary to feed for six months. If a drainage problem is suspected—usually the water stands on the soil with wilting foliage—repot (see Potting) and also check to make sure enough drainage material is covering the drainage holes.

*Yellow, white, black or brown spots that are damp or blistered with yellow margins. This is a fungal or bacterial invasion called leaf-spot disease. It is caused by poor air circulation, high humidity, overwatering, chilling or low light. In severe cases all foliage can be lost. Temperature, light and ventilation need to be increased and soil must dry out before rewatering. Infected areas should be removed. Spray remaining leaves with a fungicide. Resume proper care for aspidistras.

# CENTURY PLANT—AGAVE

This plant is from Mexico and Central America. The leaves are rigid and succulent and form rosettes which have no stems. The edges of the leaves are prickly and the tips have very sharp needlelike points. Their color varies from blue, blue-green, gray-green to green, and some varieties have white or yellow longitudinal stripes. The leaves have white edges that dry and split and appear like curled, threadlike fibers. The leaves can grow to 10 inches long or more. The plant takes ten to fifty years to bloom. When the bloom appears, it arises from the center of the rosette and the flower stem can rise from 6 inches to 16 feet high. After flowering, the plant dies but usually leaves small rosettes at its base which are transplanted into new pots and the cycle begins again.

70 §

## Location

They are sun lovers but will survive in bright light. The winter temperatures should not get below 40 degrees.

## Soil

They need acid soil. One part all-purpose soil, one part peat moss, one part sharp sand. Yearly repotting will give you large plants, but is not necessary to repot more than every three years.

## Watering

Allow the soil to dry between thorough waterings but water only enough to keep the leaves from shriveling in the winter. It does very well in dry air.

## Fertilizer

After the first year feed once every spring with an acid fertilizer.

## Propagation

Seeds, offshoots.

## Artificial Light

1,000 footcandles.

## First Aid

*Very rarely attacked by pests.

*No blooms. The problem is time. It takes a minimum of ten years before they will bloom.

*Rotting, wilting and bleaching of foliage. A mass yellowing of leaves. Leaves can curl, tips turn brown and die back. Soil is constantly wet. This is overwatering. The plant must be removed from the pot (see *Potting*) and a root check must take place. While checking the roots, make sure the plant has proper soil and the drainage holes are not clogged and enough drainage material is covering them. If the roots are still white and healthy, repot in the same pot with the same soil or fresh soil and allow to dry thoroughly between waterings. If a few roots are damaged, remove them and repot in fresh soil. If all the roots are soft and mushy, the plant cannot be saved.

*Leaves turn yellow, sometimes with brown crisp spots or scorched edges. The leaves look weak, limp and shriveled.* This indicates underwatering. Soil must be allowed to dry between waterings and must be given less water during the winter. When watering, water slowly over the entire soil surface until excess water runs out of the drainage hole in the bottom. Do not let the plant sit in the water-filled saucer for more than an hour. Before rewatering, allow the plant to dry thoroughly.

*Plant looks elongated, lower leaves turn yellow with brown spots, foliage becomes soft and discolored.* Symptoms indicate temperatures that are too warm. Move to a cooler location with good air circulation.

*Pale and discolored leaves, tips of leaves and margins turn brown and die.* This is from too little light. They survive in bright light but prefer sun. They will not tolerate a dark corner. Move to a brighter location or move closer to its light source.

*Soft and discolored growth.* This is from too much humidity. Humidity must be diminished. Ventilate the growing area and keep the plant away from plants that have high humidity requirements.

# CHINESE EVERGREEN—AGLAONEMA

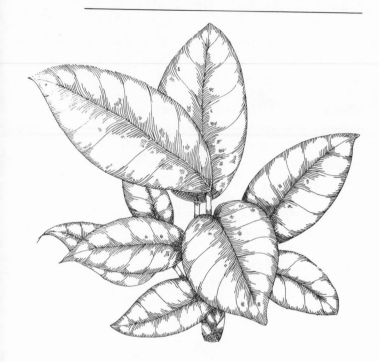

A Southeast Asian plant that comes in many varieties. Most varieties have graceful, pointed leaves, some with bluish green patterns on silver and others with light green, splotchy centers and dark green edges. Still others have dark green leaves with veins of lighter green or leaves that are completely green. Some have greenish white, lily-shaped flowers. Others, after flowering, bear beautiful red berries that last a long time. They are readily available and are among the hardiest houseplants you can buy.

## Location

Likes bright light of an east or west window but has to be protected from the hot summer sun. It will

survive in a shaded corner of a north window. Needs average room temperatures and prefers warm temperatures—not below 60 degrees—during the winter.

## Soil

One part all-purpose loam, one part peat moss, one part sharp sand, perlite or vermiculite. When repotting is necessary, the plant must be planted in wide, flat pots because its roots lie close to the surface of the soil.

## Watering

The soil should be moist at all times, and the plant won't tolerate drying out too often.

## Fertilizer

Feed every four months.

## Propagation

Division of root stalks, stem cuttings or air layering.

## Artificial Light

150 footcandles.

## First Aid

*Mealybugs, red spider mites, aphids. (See Pests.)

*Leaf tips turn brown, yellowing leaf margins, wilting and shriveling.   These symptoms indicate low humidity. Place the plant in a bed of wet pebbles without the bottom of the pot touching the water and spray-mist daily. Use a humidifier during the winter.

*Dry leaf edges, wilting, slow growth, yellowing of

leaves and rapid loss of older leaves. This is improper soil and drainage. Cut off any damaged foliage and repot (see *Potting*) in proper soil with proper drainage material over the drainage holes.

*Soft, discolored foliage with curled leaves, brown edges.* These problems are from temperatures that are too cool. Stems can rot in cold drafts. Plant needs warmth, especially during the winter. Keep away from cold windows and cold drafts.

*Rotting, wilting and bleaching of foliage. A mass yellowing and dropping of leaves. Leaves can curl, tips turn brown and die back. New growth is weak and soil is constantly wet.* The problem is overwatering. A root check will have to take place. Remove the plant from its pot (see *Potting*) and also check to make sure the plant has the proper soil

and enough drainage material over the drainage holes and that they are not clogged. If roots are white and healthy, either repot in fresh soil or return to its pot with same soil and allow the soil to dry out only until it becomes damp, then rewater. Remove all damaged foliage. If roots are partially brown, remove them and repot. If all the roots are brown and soft, the plant cannot be saved, but if there are healthy cuttings available you can propagate a new plant.

*Base and stems of plant turn soft and mushy.* This is a fungus disease called stem-rot disease and it is promoted by too much humidity, overwatering and changes of temperatures. Repot in fresh soil, remove all damaged foliage and spray remaining leaves with a fungicide. Water properly for *Aglaonema*.

# CHRISTMAS CACTUS— EPIPHYLLUM

The Christmas cactus is an epiphytic cactus, found growing on trees or on rotted leaves in the forks of trees, clinging by its roots and receiving nourishment and moisture from the air and debris. The name *Christmas cactus* has been applied to all link-type cactus. Most have upright and pendulous branches, made of pieces of flat, succulent growth. The sizes vary in length and width depending on the size of the plant and the variety. These "pieces" are called links. At the end of the branches is a growth that resembles crab claws but is not sharp. New growth has a red color and shows itself at the base, at the end of the branches or at any intersection of links.

Different varieties bloom at different times of the year. Fall bloomers have colors ranging from salmon to red. The Christmas bloomers range from white to pink to red with generally lighter tones and marginal colors. The flowers on the fall and Christmas bloomers look like bells with the petals spreading out in layers all surrounding the large bunch of stamens with a center stamen usually of a brilliant red color. Spring bloomers have flat, tiny pink flowers with the exception of the Easter cactus which has large pink flowers. In order to set the buds and have full bloom of epiphyllums, the cactus must have short days, cool temperatures and only enough water to keep the plant from shriveling, starting four months before blooms are expected. When flowers appear, begin to water more often.

## Location

Likes sun but needs to be shaded from hot summer sun. Does not like fluctuations of temperatures between the day and night and should be kept close to a window where temperatures are more constant. When the resting period begins, it must be kept cool in order to have blooms.

## Soil

One part all-purpose loam, one part peat moss, one part sharp sand, one part perlite or vermiculite. Or use osmunda fiber. This fiber is from the roots of any fern of the genus *Osmunda*. Or sphagnum can be used alone. Repot every two or three years. Too much repotting can keep the plant from flowering.

## Watering

Between April and September and also during the flowering season the plant should be kept barely moist. Needs to be kept dryer during the resting period and should be allowed to dry out between thorough waterings. While the plant is actively growing or during its flowering period, it likes humidity. Spray-mist daily.

## Propagation

In the spring or summer a fully grown stem can be treated as a cutting. Take three or four of these and pot in the same pot. This will initiate early flowering by having a strong, growing root system. Before putting the cuttings in sand, let the ends dry for several days. They root easily. After roots appear, repot in proper medium. Do not keep repotting or flowering will cease.

## Artificial Light

800 footcandles.

## Fertilizer

Monthly feeding during active growing, but no feeding the rest of the year.

## First Aid

*They are rarely bothered by pests.

*Buds drop.   This is from high temperatures or too little light. Must be cool in winter, so keep it near a window. A bright light will make it bloom, but a little sun will be better. When the plant is nearing the time for budding, it must not be moved. The buds will always face the light, and if you constantly turn the plant, the buds will twist and fall off.

*Plant becomes elongated, lower leaves turn yellow with brown spots and dry edges, foliage from the base upward drying.   The problem is temperatures that are too warm. Must be kept cool. It helps to keep it next to a window.

*Yellowing leaf margins, wilting, shriveling and dropping of buds.   This is the result of low humidity. While actively growing or during its flowering period it needs to be sprayed daily.

*Soft and discolored growth.*   This is too much humidity. Cut down on spraying and ventilate the area well, guarding against drafts.

*Yellowing of leaves, wilting, general deterioration of the plant.*   The problem is improper soil. Repot in proper soil and make sure the drainage material is not clogged and that there is enough drainage material over the drainage holes.

*Rotting, wilting and bleaching of foliage. A mass yellowing, dropping and shriveling of leaves.*

These symptoms indicate overwatering. Reduce watering, and if the problem is not solved, the plant will have to be removed from its pot (see *Potting*) and the roots checked. If they are brown and mushy, the plant is dead. If roots are partially brown, repot and water carefully. If roots are still white and healthy, repot in fresh soil and make sure the drainage material is sufficient and allow to dry according to its requirements.

*Leaves turn yellow and shrivel, the plant looks weak, limp and wilted.*   This is underwatering. Improve your watering according to the plant's requirements.

A slow-growing vine from the Malabar Coast which is very easy to grow. There are many varieties which provide us with the common condiment black and white pepper. When supported with a stake, they can grow up to 5 feet tall. They also do very well in hanging baskets. They will not bear fruit indoors. The black-pepper plant has oval leaves that look like black-green leather and are very shiny. The Celebes variety has 2½- to 5-inch heart-shaped leaves with silver-pink veins. The undersides are pale green. The pattern on the leaves has a lacy effect and its stems are red. The porphyry variety has bronze-green leaves with yellow veins bordered with clusters of pink spots. Saffron variety has 4- to 6-inch long, broad, heart-shaped leaves with light purple undersides and the red stems are accented with stiff, white hairs.

## Location

Indirect or filtered sunlight but does well in bright light of a north window. Doesn't thrive well when temperatures go below 55 degrees.

# CLIMBING PEPPER—PIPER

## Soil

One part all-purpose loam, one part peat moss, one part sharp sand, perlite or vermiculite.

## Watering

Keep the soil moist at all times without letting it get soggy. Once a month let the soil become dry to allow aeration of the roots.

## Fertilizer

Once a month March to September without feeding the rest of the year.

## Propagation

Stem cuttings.

## Artificial Light

400 footcandles.

## First Aid

*Red spider. (See *Pests*.)
*A practically disease-free and problemless plant.

*On the undersides of the leaves a white pearl-like precipitation appears. This is a natural phenomenon and not a sign of disease.

# COLEUS

This plant originates in tropical Africa and Asia. It has square, succulent stems with heart-shaped, oval leaves. Some varieties have crumpled, frilled or sawtoothed leaves, and the colors and combinations of colors are wide ranged. The plant can grow up to 3 feet high with 4-inch-long leaves. Some varieties are trailing plants.

At any season pinch the stem tips off in order to keep the plant bushy. Also remove the clusters of small, light blue flowers. These flowers take quite a bit of nourishment from the plant and when removed the plant will produce bigger and better foliage. Small-leaved varieties survive for several years but the large-leaved plants tend to get bare and straggly more rapidly and new plants should be started from cuttings.

## Location

Likes sun but needs protection from the hot noon sun of summer. Will grow in bright light, but the sun gives the foliage a brighter color. Needs a warm room with good air circulation.

## Soil

One part all-purpose loam, one part peat moss, one part sharp sand, perlite or vermiculite. It usually needs to be repotted yearly because of its rapid growth.

## Watering

Needs to be kept moist at all times, sometimes on hot summer days it may need to be watered twice a day. Do not mist-spray the foliage as it will affect the brightness of the leaf coloring.

## Fertilizer

Once a month during the summer and every two months during the winter.

## Propagation

Cuttings rooted in the sun, seeds (the tiniest seedlings usually produce the most beautifully colored foliage plants). Young plants need to be pinched constantly in order to become full and bushy.

## Artificial Light

800 footcandles.

## First Aid

*Mealybugs are its worst enemy. Whiteflies, nematodes. (See *Pests*.) Strong insecticides will damage the foliage.

*Stalks are black, waterlogged at the base. Plant wilts. This is a fungus called blackleg. Take healthy cuttings and start new plants. Damaged plants must be destroyed.

*Stem cuttings become darkened. This is a soil fungus. Little can be done; start new cuttings in fresh, sterilized soil.

*Dropping leaves. This is from insufficient water. Must be kept moist at all times; sometimes during the summer, they need to be watered twice a day.

*Sudden wilting. Yellowing of leaves and rapid loss of older leaves. Water stands on the soil, with general deterioration of the plant. This is from poor drainage. Repotting in proper soil is necessary, and you might also try a larger pot.

*Sudden wilting, discolored foliage with curled leaves, brown edges. Stems can rot from top down if there are cold drafts. This is the result of temperatures that are too low. Needs warmth and must be moved to a warmer location.

*General bleached-out appearance, with scorch marks on leaves turning grayish where scorched. This is caused by too much hot sun during the summer. Filter the sun or move the plant farther away from the light source.

*Young plants become leggy. This is from not pinching stems enough to promote a bushy plant.

*Older plants get leggy and unattractive. This is simply the nature of the plant. There's nothing that can be done about it. Start new plants from healthy cuttings.

# COLUMNEA

A gesneriad (member of the Gesneriaceae, mostly tropical and subtropical perennial herbs and shrubs, which are cultivated ornamentals) as well as an epiphyte (receives nourishment and moisture from the air and debris on tree limbs, and grows clinging to trees by its roots), from Central and South America. There are over fifty species that include both upright varieties and trailing plants that are suitable for hanging baskets. When hanging, the trails can grow up to 3 feet long and are densely covered with reddish leaves in some varieties and velvety with purple hairs on others. In all varieties the leaves grow opposite each other. The flowers range from yellow-orange to red in color and are tubular-shaped. They appear in the leaf axils from fall to spring. Occasionally, attractive red berries appear. Needs a resting period (*see Watering*) for one month. December is the best time in order to help the formation of flower buds. More flowering can be forced by adding an extra month of rest during the height of the summer.

## Location

Does best in an east window protected against the hot sun of summer but will grow in a bright or filtered-sun window. Needs temperatures about 72 degrees year round.

## Soil

One part all-purpose loam, one part sharp sand, one part peat moss or use a prepackaged African violet soil mixture with a handful of perlite added to make it more porous. Or you can use a prepackaged epiphyte mixture, or one part all-purpose loam, one part peat moss. When repotted, keep it warm and out of any sun and water sparingly at first. Once it has settled in its new pot, give it the same environment it had before.

## Watering

Keep the soil moist at all times without letting it get soggy. High humidity is necessary. Spray-mist once or twice daily, especially when flowering.

In September gradually begin to reduce watering and in December leave the soil completely dry and don't fertilize. After December resume normal care. If you intend to rest the plant during the summer, reduce watering two months before its rest, then stop watering and fertilizing for a complete month, then resume normal care. While the plant is resting, give it a cooler location but not below 50 degrees.

## Fertilizer

Once a month except during the resting periods.

## Propagation

Cuttings from stems immediately after flowering and never before. Put more than one cutting in the rooting medium to have a bushier plant. Seeds.

## Artificial Light

800 footcandles.

## First Aid

*Mealybugs, spider mites, nematodes, leaf miners. (See *Pests*.)

*Poor blooming.* This is usually due to temperatures that are too cool. The same problem, however, occurs from lack of humidity. Minimum of 70 degrees with not less than 50 degrees during the resting period. Spraying twice a day is sometimes not sufficient. A humidifier in winter will help.

*Plant looks straggly.* This is caused by not pinching back the plant when it was young. Cut out some of the woody stems and pinch and prune regularly.

*Yellow, black, brown spots, damp or blistered, and usually with yellow margins.* This is a fungal or bacterial invasion called leaf-spot disease. It is caused by chilling, low light, overwatering. Temperature, light and ventilation need to be increased, and soil must dry out before resuming normal watering. Remove infected areas and spray remaining leaves with a fungicide.

*Yellow lower leaves, stems become soft and dark in color. The plant wilts and seems to be underwatered.* This is a root-rot disease which prevents the root system from absorbing water. Remove plant from its pot (see *Potting*). Remove all soil and wash the roots in warm water, removing only roots that look badly damaged, and repot in fresh soil. Remove damaged foliage and water only enough to keep the plant from wilting. Once the plant has resumed normal growth, water properly. The soil should be drenched with a fungicide at its first watering.

*Base and stems of plant turn soft and mushy.* This is a fungus called stem-rot disease which is promoted by overwatering and temperatures that are too low. Repotting is a good idea, and infected areas must be removed and the wounds sprayed with a fungicide. Give the plant a warmer location and allow the soil to become just damp before rewatering.

# CROTON—CODIAEUM

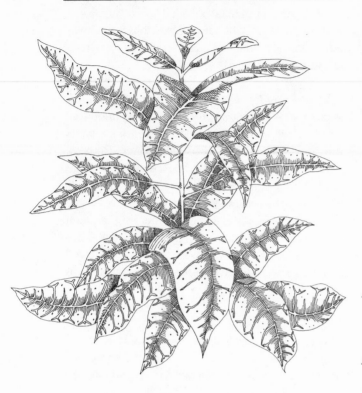

A tropical evergreen shrub from India that comes in over one hundred varieties. When new leaves first appear, they are green. With age they develop colors ranging from green, copper, yellow, pink, orange, red, ivory to brown. With some plants the color spreads over the whole leaf, on others it appears in blotches, veining or other patterns. Leaf shapes can be slender, wavy, ribbonlike and as long as 18 inches. Others are 6 inches wide and flat. Some are twisted, crinkled, corkscrew, ribbed, oval, elliptical or oak-leaf shaped. They grow very quickly up to 15 inches tall. They need to be pruned in early spring to encourage dense growth. Some plants flower, but the buds should be removed early for they retard the growth of the plant by taking energy from its growing foliage.

## Location

Needs full sunlight to keep the colors of the leaves bright but must be protected from hot noon sun in the summer. It will grow in bright light, but the colors will not be as rich. Needs warm temperatures in the low seventies.

## Soil

One part all-purpose loam, one part peat moss, one part sharp sand, perlite or vermiculite.

## Watering

Keep the soil barely moist at all times without allowing it to get soggy. Needs high humidity and needs to be sprayed daily.

## Fertilizer

Feed every two months.

## Propagation

Stem cuttings, air layering.

## Artificial Light

800 footcandles.

## First Aid

Mealybugs hide in the leaf axils and must be watched for because they can go unnoticed. Also spider mites. (See Pests.)

*Leaves drop, yellowing leaf margins, leaf tips turn brown, wilting, shriveling. This problem is low humidity. Place the plant on a bed of moist pebbles without allowing the bottom of the pot to touch the water. Spray-mist the leaves twice a day and use a humidifier in the winter.

*Leaves drop, foliage becomes soft and discolored with curled leaves, brown edges. Stems can rot from top down.* This problem results from temperatures that are too cool and from cold drafts. Remove damaged foliage and keep the plant at temperatures in the seventies, year round.

*Scorch marks on leaves, turning grayish where scorched. General bleached-out look.* This is from too much light. Croton needs sun, but the hot noon sun in summer is detrimental to the plant. Protect the plant from hot sun or move it farther away from the light source.

*Yellowing of leaves, wilting, slow growth, rapid loss of older leaves, and water stands on the soil.* This is poor drainage. Cut off any damaged foliage and repot (see *Potting*) in proper soil, making sure the drainage material over the drainage holes is sufficient.

*Base and stems of plants turn soft and mushy.* This is stem-rot disease. The problem is promoted by overwatering and temperatures that are too low. Repot plant (see *Potting*). Remove infected areas. Wounds need to be sprayed with a fungicide. Keep the plant warm and water only when the soil is barely damp.

# CROWN OF THORNS— EUPHORBIA

The branching stems are long and gray and covered with long, pointed, dark brown thorns which resemble those of a cactus, but, in fact, the plant is a succulent. The green, oval leaves are small and grow mainly toward the tips. The tiny flowers are sticky and develop between new leaves and the flower stalks. The flowers have bright red bracts, which look like flowers but are the leaflike part of the flower. The actual flower grows in the center of these bracts and unfolds in pairs at the tips of the branches. At first they are pale green, then light apricot, changing to deep pink and then deep crimson. Euphorbias can grow tall and can be pruned to any shape. All wounds of the mother plant should be brushed with powdered charcoal or white sand. The sap is poisonous, so take precautions against touching it. During the end of the year, the plant will suddenly lose all its green leaves, which will first turn yellow and drop. This is the resting period. Water infrequently and stop fertilizing. During the resting period the plant must have total darkness from 5 P.M. until 8 A.M. the next morning. A six-weeks rest works wonders and soon afterward a formation of new green buds, which will soon be small leaves, will appear. Watering and

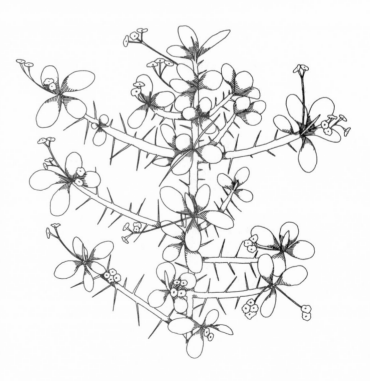

§ 81

fertilizing should be resumed as before the resting period.

## Location

Needs sun but also needs protection from the hot noon sun of summer. Will survive in bright light. Needs plenty of fresh air and does well in the dry air of a living room.

## Soil

One part all-purpose loam, one-half part sharp sand, or use a prepackaged cactus soil mix with a handful of peat moss added.

## Watering

Keep the soil barely moist during the summer and allow it to dry well before thorough waterings during the winter. Likes to be sprayed only on very hot days. It does not do well with too much humidity in the air.

## Fertilizer

Feed once a month during the growing period and only when new growth shows itself in winter.

## Propagation

Stem cuttings. Because of the sap that could be lost, treat wounded ends with powdered charcoal or white sand. The sap is poisonous, so be careful while treating the wounds.

## Artificial Light

800 footcandles.

## First Aid

Mealybugs. (See *Pests.*)

*Growth is soft and discolored.* The problem is

too much humidity. Humidity must be cut down by misting less often. Ventilate the growing area and keep the plant away from plants that demand high humidity.

*Leaf tips turn brown, leaf margins yellow, stunted or no new growth, wilting, shriveling and dropping of buds.* This can be from lack of humidity. Euphorbia needs a dry room but it needs some humidity on very hot days during the summer. Spray-mist lightly when the weather is hot and dry.

*Leaves curl under and lower leaves turn yellow with brown spots and fall or leaves turn completely yellow and drop.* The problem is underwatering. The plant needs to be kept just barely moist between thorough waterings, water less in winter (allowing the soil to dry).

*Yellow leaves that drop at the end of the year.* This is the natural preparation of the plant for its dormancy period.

*Failure to bloom.* This is from too much light at night during the dormant period. The plant must have total darkness from 5 P.M. to 8 A.M. in order to have a good blooming period. Streetlights, lamplights or car lights can be too much light and will prevent blooming.

*A mass yellowing and dropping of leaves. Rotting, wilting and bleaching of foliage. Leaves can curl, tips turn brown and die back, with soil that is constantly wet.* This is overwatering. The plant will have to be removed from its pot (see *Potting*) and the roots checked. At the same time, check to make sure the drainage holes aren't clogged and that there is enough drainage material over the drainage holes. Also check to make sure the plant has been given the proper soil. If the roots are white and healthy-looking, repot in fresh soil and allow soil to dry according to watering requirements. If partial decay of the roots has taken place, remove these roots and repot. If all the roots are soft and mushy, the plant cannot be saved, but healthy cuttings can be taken to start new plants.

# DEVIL'S IVY—POTHOS

An extremely versatile plant. Pothos has firm, glossy, heart-shaped leaves protruding at right angles to the stem with long leaf stems. The leaves are gracefully pointed with splashes of color in yellow, cream, white, pale green or silver blotches with a thin, silver line around the edges. It's a climber from eastern Asia that resembles a philodendron, but the pothos has lighter-colored leaves. Because of its demand for pot-bound roots, it never matures no matter how old the plant is and can therefore last for a very long time. It usually develops in two stages: the first has 2- to 4-inch leaves and later 6- to 10-inch leaves. The stems can be pruned or pinched to help promote a bushier plant.

## Location

They thrive in any exposure, but to assure colorful markings, bright light or curtain-filtered sunlight is necessary or the leaves will remain solid green. Needs a warm room protected from cold drafts.

## Soil

One part all-purpose loam, one part peat moss, one part sharp sand, perlite or vermiculite. Repotting is seldom necessary. You can change 2 inches of surface soil each year to ensure good nutrients.

## Fertilizer

Feed monthly.

## Watering

Allow the soil to become dry between thorough waterings. Spray-mist daily.

## Propagation

Stem cuttings from new branch ends, root in a dark place.

## Artificial Light

400 footcandles.

## First Aid

*Mealybugs, red spider mites. (See *Pests*.)

*Rotting, wilting and bleaching of foliage. A mass yellowing and dropping of leaves. Leaves can curl, tips turn brown and die back. New growth is weak.* The problem is overwatering. The plant must be removed from the pot (see *Potting*) and the roots checked. At the same time, check for proper soil and proper drainage material over the drainage hole. If the roots are white and healthy, repot in fresh soil, remove damaged foliage and allow the soil to dry between waterings. If the roots are partially brown, remove them and repot the plant in fresh soil. If all the roots are brown and mushy, the plant is dead and will have to be discarded.

*Water stands on the soil, slow growth, yellowing of leaves and rapid loss of older leaves.* This is improper soil, and the plant will have to be repotted into fresh soil.

*Leaf tips turn brown, leaf margins yellow, stunted or no new growth, wilting, shriveling. Sometimes the plant looks healthy but has no new growth.* This problem is too little humidity. Spray-mist daily and use a humidifier during the winter.

*Scorched edges, brown crisp spots, plant stems look weak, limp and wilted.* The problem is underwatering. The plant should become dry between waterings but should not remain dry for more than a couple of days.

*Leaves around the base are lost.* This is due to the age of the stem. Pinch back the tops of one or two shoots to encourage lower leaf buds to grow. If the stem has become very bare, cut back that stem to encourage new growth.

*Small new growth, leaves are all green without any colored markings, pale or discolored leaves. Older plant can shed leaves, new growth shrivels and dies.* This is the result of too little light. Move to a brighter location without direct sun or add artificial light to the plant's present source or move closer to its artificial light source.

*Only new growth is small.* This is probably due to being overly pot-bound. Repot in a larger pot with fresh soil.

*Soft, discolored foliage with curled leaves, brown edges. Stems can rot from cold drafts.* The problem is temperatures that are too cool. Move to a location where the plant has bright light but no drafts.

A slow-growing plant from tropical Africa and Asia that can survive adverse conditions. There is such a large variety of dracaenas with so much diversity in foliage that it's hard to believe they belong to one genus. Old plants need to be rejuvenated by encouraging new growth. Cut back dracaenas as close to 4 to 6 inches from the rim of the pot. This can be done at any season.

One variety of dracaena is Janet Craig (corn plant), which has arching, shiny, dark leaves 12 to 18 inches long and 2 inches wide that grow from a main stem. Leaves are dark green in color and some varieties have broad cream- or yellow-colored stripes along the margins.

Godseffiana, another variety of dracaena, has slender wiry stems with many thin shoots. The leaves are flat and oval, 3 to 4 inches long, held horizontally in tiers or spirals along the stems. The green leaves are spotted with yellow to greenish yellow colors.

Marginata is yet another variety of dracaena. It has dense terminal rosettes of narrow, deep olive leaves edged in red. The leaves are 12 to 15 inches long and 1/2 inch wide. They grow atop long slender trunks 3/4 inch in diameter. The small and medium-size plants have straight trunks, but the taller sizes, which can reach 8 feet, assume exotic proportions, twisting and bending into all shapes.

## Location

Needs bright or filtered sunlight but protection from hot sun of summer. It can survive in bright light. Normal room temperatures are adequate but not below 55 degrees during the winter.

## Soil

One part all-purpose loam, one part peat moss, one part sharp sand, perlite or vermiculite. Repot only when roots grow out of the drainage holes and on

# DRACAENA

the top of the soil, which may happen every few years. You can repot at any season.

## Watering

It resents drought and should be kept moist at all times. Allow it to become dry once a month to aerate the soil. Spray-mist daily.

## Fertilizer

Feed monthly March through October without feeding the rest of the year.

## Propagation

Stem cuttings, air layering. Godseffiana can be propagated by division or cuttings.

## Artificial Light

400 footcandles.

## First Aid

*Red spider mites, scales, aphids. (See *Pests*.)

*Marginata *loses bottom leaves.* This is due to changes of temperatures, especially when the plant is first brought home from a plant store. New leaves will grow as soon as the plant adjusts to its new environment.

*Stem rot which begins at the top and moves downward.* This is from cold drafts. Cut the plant down to 4 inches and put it in a warm location, and new growth will sprout soon.

*Soft, discolored foliage with curled leaves, brown edges.* This is caused by temperatures that are too cool. Plant must be kept warm all year round.

*Yellowing leaves.* This is due to age. The dracaena naturally loses lower leaves. A leaf will live a year or so, then yellow. When the plant becomes very bare—so that only a few leaves are left on the plant—cut it back. New growth will appear on the old stems, and the cuttings can be rooted.

*Yellowing leaf margins, leaf tips turn brown, wilting. Plant loses leaves and becomes leggy.* This is the result of low humidity. The pot needs to be put on a bed of moist pebbles. Do not allow the bottom of the pot to touch the water. Spray-mist often and use a humidifier during the winter.

*Scorch marks on leaves that turn grayish where scorched and look bleached-out in general.* This indicates too much light. The plant needs to be protected from its light source by a curtain or by moving it farther away from the light.

*Brown crisp spots, scorched edges on leaves. Plant's stems look weak, limp and wilted. Leaves curl under and lower leaves turn yellow with brown spots and fall.* These are symptoms of underwatering. Water slowly over the entire soil surface until excess water runs out of the drainage hole in the bottom. Do not allow the plant to sit in the water-filled saucer for more than an hour. Before rewatering, allow the soil to barely dry. Remove any damaged foliage.

*Rottings, wilting and bleaching of foliage. A mass yellowing and dropping of leaves. Leaves can curl, tips turn brown and die back. New growth is weak.* This is overwatering. The plant must be removed from the pot (see *Potting*), and a root check is necessary. At the same time, check to see if the soil is the right mixture, drainage holes have enough drainage material covering them and that they are not clogged. If roots are healthy and white, either repot or return it to its pot with the same soil and allow the soil to barely dry before rewatering. Remove damaged foliage. If roots are partially brown, remove them and repot. If all roots are brown and mushy, the plant cannot be saved, but healthy stem cuttings can be taken to start new plants.

*Black, brown or yellow spots that are damp or blistered, usually with yellow margins.* This is a fungal or bacterial invasion called leaf spot and is caused by overwatering, chilling, insufficient light. Temperature, light and ventilation need to be increased, and the soil must dry out before rewatering properly. Infected areas should be removed, and spray remaining foliage with a fungicide.

The original plant is from the South American tropics, but there are many hybrids, with a great variation in the distribution of colors in the leaves. The handsome, large leaves are elliptical to heart-shaped with dots and blotches in white, pale yellow or pale green markings or veined stripes on the upper surface. Some leaves are all green. They grow on a sturdy, erect trunk. When you first purchase the plant, it is usually 1 to 3 feet tall and the lower leaves cover the edge of the pot. As the plant grows, new growth appears at the tops of the stems and the older leaves gradually wither and die. Dumb cane looks like a miniature palm tree and can grow to 5 feet but usually needs to be cut back because of its loss of lower leaves. A very durable plant. The name *dumb cane* is derived from the calcium oxalate in the stems of the plant. When chewed, it has a paralyzing effect on the mouth and throat.

## Location

They like sun but need to be protected from the hot noon sun of summer. They will thrive in bright light, but the coloring of the foliage becomes dull. They need temperatures of 65 to 75 degrees and will not tolerate low temperatures.

## Soil

One part all-purpose loam, one part peat moss, one part sharp sand, perlite or vermiculite.

## Watering

Allow the soil to dry between thorough waterings. Spray-mist daily.

## Fertilizer

Once a month during the summer. Once every three months during the winter.

# DUMB CANE— DIEFFENBACHIA

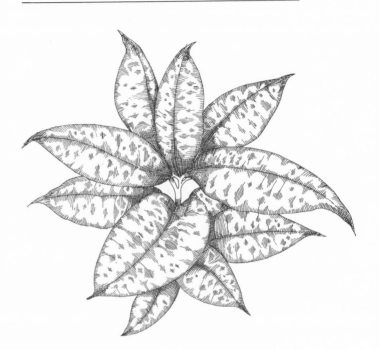

## Propagation

Stem cuttings, air layering. New growth will appear on the old plant after cuttings have been taken, so don't throw the old plant away.

## Artificial Light

400 footcandles.

## First Aid

*Aphids, mealybugs, spider mites. (See *Pests*.)

*Dark tan or black dry center spots with narrow, dark margins. The ends of the leaves can turn dark tan with darker bars crisscrossing the leaf. Tips of leaves and or leaf margins turn brown and die back. This is a fungal disease called anthracnose and is caused from sudden chilling and too much humidity. Infested leaves must be destroyed. Grow plants on the dry side and avoid mist spraying until the disease is cleared up. The area should be well ventilated to prevent recurrence of disease. The healthy leaves need to be sprayed with a foliar fungicide to ward off spread of the disease.

*The base and stems of the plant turn soft and mushy. This is a fungus disease called stem rot which is promoted by too much humidity, overwatering and too high or low temperatures. Repot in fresh soil. Infected areas must be removed and the wounds sprayed with a fungicide. Allow the soil to dry well before rewatering. Give the plant the proper growing environment.

*Soft, discolored foliage with curled leaves, brown edges. Stems can rot from top down. This is the result of temperatures that are too cold and cold drafts. All damaged foliage must be removed, and the plant needs to be kept warm all year round and must be moved into a location where this is possible.

*Yellowing leaves. One or two yellowing leaves yearly is probably due to the age of the leaf. They naturally die after they are about a year old. If more than an occasional leaf dies, a more serious problem is at hand.

*A mass yellowing and dropping of leaves. Leaves can curl, tips turn brown and die back, rotting, wilting and bleaching of foliage. New growth is weak. The problem is overwatering. The plant must be removed from the pot (see Potting), and a root check must take place. While checking roots, make sure the plant has proper soil and the drainage holes are not clogged. If the roots are white and healthy looking, put the plant back in its pot and water properly or repot in fresh soil. Remove all damaged foliage and keep the plant warm and well ventilated. If only a few roots are damaged, remove damaged roots and repot. If all the roots are soft and mushy, the plant cannot be saved. If a healthy cutting is available, start new plants.

A Mexican succulent with over one hundred fifty species. The symmetrical rosettes have ground-hugging leaves that are blue-green to gray to red in color. Leaves are waxy in some species and hairy in others. Most flower in spring and summer and a few in winter with clusters of flowers on the end of slender stalks. The flower colors can be orange, yellow, pink or red. Some species form new plantlets on the tips of the stems. The plant is small and when in bloom is no more than 4 to 6 inches high. In some species the leaves around the stem fall off easily and wherever they fall will root and develop new plants.

## ECHEVERIA

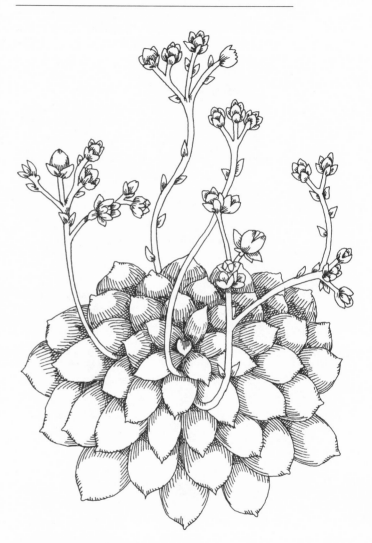

### Location

It needs as much sun as possible to keep the rosette compact. Does not need protection from hot summer sun. Needs full sun during the winter, however it will grow in bright light but will lose its compactness. Normal room temperatures in summer and winter are sufficient.

### Soil

One part all-purpose soil, one part sharp sand with a handful of peat moss added. Repot overcrowded plants after flowering.

### Watering

Allow the soil to dry between thorough waterings. In winter water only enough to keep the plant from shriveling, which is usually every two weeks.

### Fertilizer

Feed once every spring.

### Propagation

Small rosettes growing on the end of the stems potted as suckers. Leaf cuttings dried for a few hours before planting. Offshoots.

### Artificial Light

1,000 footcandles.

### First Aid

*Mealybugs. (See *Pests*.)

*Growth that is soft and discolored.*   This indicates

too much humidity. Plant must not be grown near plants that need high humidity. Never mist-spray. Ventilate the growing area well.

*Rotting, wilting and bleaching of foliage, a mass yellowing and dropping of leaves.* This is from overwatering. Remove plant from its pot (see *Potting*) and check the roots. If they are white and healthy looking, repot in fresh soil or place back into pot and allow to dry thoroughly before rewatering. If roots are partially brown, cut them off and repot. If all the roots are brown and mushy, the plant is dead. Propagate new plants with healthy growth.

*Leaves turn yellow and shrivel, plants stems look weak, limp and wilted, and scorched edges on leaves can appear.* These problems are the result of underwatering. It takes time and experimenting with succulents until you have the watering down pat. When watering, water thoroughly and water more often if you suspect the plant needs it.

*Growth is elongated and misshapen with under-developed leaves.* The problem is too little light. The plant needs more sunlight or the addition of some artificial light to its present light source.

*Legginess.* This is natural in some species. Remove the top and root it as a stem cutting.

*Soft and discolored foliage, drying foliage from the base upward, dropping older leaves. Plant becomes leggy and elongated.* This is from temperatures that are too warm. Move the plant out of hot radiator's range and closer to the window.

*Base and stems of plants turn soft and mushy.* This is stem-rot disease and is promoted by too much humidity, overwatering and temperatures that are too high. Dip the plants in a hot bath for twenty to forty minutes. Repot in fresh soil. For succulents this is usually a fatal disease, but you may be able to save it.

*Yellow lower leaves, stems become soft and dark in color.* This is a fungus which prevents the root system from absorbing water, and the affected plant usually shows signs of underwatering. Remove plant from its pot (see *Potting*), remove soil and wash root system in warm water and repot. Drench the soil with a fungicide. Water very sparingly until normal growth appears.

Episcia is a gesneriad—a member of the Gesneriaceae family of tropical and subtropical perennial herbs and shrubs with showy blossoms. They are cultivated ornamentals, from Colombia and Brazil, with thirty-five species and many varieties. They all demand careful attention. They all have downy, plush-textured leaves in many colors with decorative markings and veining. Episcia has a distinctive habit of growing vigorous laterals extending at right angles from the trailing stems. The small, clear red, orange-red, pink, yellow, blue, white and sometimes purple spotted flowers grow on these trailing stems and are produced in spring and summer. Pinching out the younger runners will help to increase the size of leaves and blooms. There is no leafless dormant period, but during the winter leaves may die and fall off. If this happens, don't throw the plant away. Cut back the runners, slow down on watering and fertilizing but maintain the high humidity, and in a month or two fresh growth will appear. Fluorescent lights and a warm room will usually eliminate this winter problem.

## Location

Needs winter sun but protection against the hot sun of summer. Needs warm temperatures all year round, and if the temperature is less than 60 degrees, the plant will literally freeze.

## Soil

Slightly acid soil. One part all-purpose loam, one part peat moss, one part sharp sand, perlite or vermiculite or two parts African violet prepackaged soil with one part perlite, vermiculite or sharp sand. The new soilless mixture (see *Soil* in Introduction) has proven successful. One part peat moss, one part perlite, one part vermiculite.

# EPISCIA

## Watering

The soil must be kept moist at all times. Needs very high humidity. It is necessary to keep the plant on a bed of wet pebbles without the bottom of the pot touching the water, and spray-mist twice a day.

## Fertilizer

Once a month with African violet fertilizer.

## Propagation

Cuttings, runners, leaves, seeds.

## Artificial Light

500 footcandles.

## First Aid

*Red spider mites, mealybugs, thrips, leaf miners, nematodes. (See *Pests*.)

*The buds just sit or drop, leaf tips turn brown, yellowing leaf margins, stunted, wilting, shriveling.* The problem is low humidity. This plant needs very high humidity. Spray-mist twice a day and keep the plant on a bed of wet pebbles without the bottom of the pot touching the water. A humidifier is necessary during the winter.

*No flowering while there is good growth.* The production of the runners (stolons) interferes with flower production. Pinch off new runners, and your plant will bloom more readily.

*Brown mushy leaves, discolored foliage with curled leaves, brown edges and rotting stems.* The problem is temperatures that are too cool. Cut back the plant to soil level. Move to a warm location, enclose in a plastic bag and hope new growth begins. When growth begins, remove the bag.

*Base and stems of plant turn soft and mushy.* This is a fungus called stem-rot disease and it is promoted by temperatures that are too low and overwatering. Repotting is necessary, infected areas must be removed and the plant sprayed with a fungicide. Allow the soil to dry out thoroughly before resuming normal watering.

*Yellow lower leaves, stems become soft and dark

in color, the plant wilts.* This is root-rot disease, which prevents the root system from absorbing water. Plant must be removed from the pot (see *Potting*). Remove all soil and wash the root system in warm water and repot in fresh soil. The soil must be drenched with a fungicide. Remove damaged foliage and water plants only enough to keep the plant from wilting. Once the plant has resumed normal growth, water properly.

*Black, brown or yellow damp or blistered spots, usually with yellow margins.* This is a fungus called leaf-spot disease and is caused by overwatering, chilling, low light and poor air circulation. Increase the light and temperature. Give the growing area better air circulation. Destroy all infected leaves. Let the soil dry out thoroughly before re-watering. Spray what foliage is left with a foliar fungicide.

*A mass yellowing and dropping of leaves. Rotting, wilting and bleaching of foliage, leaves can curl, tips turn brown and die back. Flowers will blight and soil is constantly wet.* The problem is overwatering. No doubt roots have been injured. Remove the plant from the pot and check the roots (see *Potting*). If they are soft and brown, the plant cannot be saved. Partial decay can be removed and the plant repotted in fresh soil, damaged foliage removed and the plant given proper growing requirements. If roots are white and healthy-looking, put it back into its pot and stir the soil gently with a fork to promote aeration of the soil. Allow the soil to dry once before giving it proper water.

The leaves of dizygotheca are narrow-fingered, jagged-edged and grow in flat palmate fans with a leathery texture. They are olive-green with a reddish brown central vein. The plant has a tendency to become woody. As the plant becomes too tall, it's necessary to cut it back. It will take a few months for the new buds to produce anything but a very small form of the leaves. When air is dry, the bottom leaves fall off, but placing small plants in strategic places will hide the aralia's baldness. It can grow to 5 feet, and older plants have large leaves and produce small, green-colored flowers.

## Location

Direct sunlight is detrimental to dizygotheca. A shaded area in a bright location is best. The plant likes normal room temperatures but not below 60 degrees.

## Soil

One part all-purpose loam, one part peat moss and one part vermiculite or perlite.

## Watering

Allow the soil to dry for no longer than one day between thorough waterings. Place on a bed of wet pebbles without the bottom of the pot touching the water and spray-mist once or twice daily.

## Fertilizer

Once a month March through September with no feeding the rest of the year.

## Propagation

Stem cuttings.

# FALSE ARALIA FINGER ARALIA— ARALIA DIZYGOTHECA

## Artificial Light

800 footcandles.

## First Aid

*Mealybugs, scales, spider mites. (See *Pests*.)

*Leaves are limp, shrivel and die. Scorch marks appear on leaves, and the plant has a general bleached-out or gray appearance. All of these symptoms indicate too much light. Move plant farther from the light source or shield the plant with other plants or a curtain. This plant prefers shade.

*Bottom leaves drop.* This is caused by air that is too dry. This is normal because the humidity necessary to retain the leaves is virtually impossible to give in the home. The plants leaves are so beautiful it's worth keeping the leaves that are left. Eventually you should cut back the plant, but new growth will soon appear. Spray-mist daily and place on a bed of wet pebbles without the bottom of the pot touching the water.

*Yellowing of foliage.* This is the result of soil that is too dry. When watering, water until you can see the water draining through the drainage holes but never allow the plant to sit in a saucer of water for more than an hour. Before watering again, let the plant dry out only enough to meet its specific requirements. Remove damaged foliage and stems.

# FERNS

There are over six thousand species of ferns, of which two thousand are suitable for growing indoors if given proper growing conditions. Ferns produce spores on the undersides of the leaves. At a certain stage, rain or soil moisture will enable the sperm to swim to the eggs, both of which are located in separate spores. Fertilized, the egg grows into the familiar fern. Tropical ferns from rain forests and jungles are the easiest and most successfully grown ferns in the house. Some are terrestrial and grow on the floors of the forest where the growing medium is spongy and full of decayed vegetable matter. Many of the terrestrials have rhizomes that grow along the surface or just below the surface of the soil. These rhizomes conserve moisture for droughts in addition to supporting the fronds. The rhizomatous type are very hardy for house culture. There are also the epiphytes which cling to tree trunks and rock crevices, deriving moisture from the rain and the high humidity of the jungle air. These are very hardy if the humidity is kept very high. These can be grown successfully in hanging baskets of sphagnum moss or attached to slabs of cork, bark and redwood. Ferns need plenty elbow room to grow; some send out long runners which never develop into foliage. These should be removed, because they take strength from the plant. Ferns like to be groomed. Remove brown fronds and dead twigs and so on.

The bird's nest fern (*Asplenium*) is an epiphyte from the South Sea Islands. Has funnel-shaped rosettes and chartreuse leaves with a leathery texture. The fronds grow to 3 feet long and 6 inches wide and have black spore groups underneath the leaves. New foliage resembles a bird's egg when it first appears deep in the black, hairlike heart of the plant before it uncurls.

Mother fern (Asplenium bulbiferum) has fragile, featherlike, scalloped fronds which grow tiny fernlets on the upper surface of their leaves and develop into miniature replicas of the larger plant. These can be potted up separately for new plants.

The maidenhair (Adiantum) has hundreds of varieties native to the tropics and subtropics. The leaflets are lacy, wedge-shaped, 1/4 to 1/2 inch across, with thin, black stems. Most species have new leaves that are pink, and as they mature they turn green. New growth emerges from a clumpy root system, and the fronds turn yellow after six to nine months. To continually have fresh new growth it is necessary to cut away all the fronds. In three or four months the plant will have new growth. The plant occasionally has a resting period and loses greenery, but soon new growth will appear. This is not a strong plant and does best in a terrarium.

The Boston fern (Nephrolepis) has sword-shaped, arching fronds that grow up to 3 feet long with 3- to 4-inch, closely set leaflets. The finely divided appearance is beautiful but the more finely divided the leaves the harder the plant is to grow. At the end of runners grow tiny plantlets which if kept in a shady place will produce many offspring by the end of summer. They can be removed and planted in fern soil to start new plants. Old, browning fronds must be constantly removed to have an attractive plant. The Boston fern seems to be the most popular and easiest of the ferns to grow indoors.

The table fern or brake fern (Pteris) has many varieties with extremely variable foliage. Some have light green leaves, frilled along the edges. There are those with silver-striped foliage. Still others have dense, dark green fronds with slender leaflets that end in crestlike clusters. The fronds usually 6 to 12 inches long.

## Location

They will benefit from a few hours of sun a day from an east or west window and will do well in bright light of a north window but must be kept away from the bright sun of a south window. They will not grow in the dark. They like temperatures between 60 and 70 degrees year round.

## Soil

Slightly acid soil. One part all-purpose loam, one part sharp sand, two parts peat moss or one part all-purpose soil, one part peat moss but adding sharp sand to improve the drainage. Repot every two years replacing all the soil. The crown of the plant must be level with the soil and don't bury rhizomes under the soil.

## Watering

The soil should be kept moist at all times and never allowed to dry out. They need high humidity and need to be kept on a bed of wet pebbles without the bottom of the pot touching the water. Spray-mist twice daily and use a humidifier during the winter. Those growing on cork or wood need to be kept sprayed sometimes as much as three or four times daily during the winter.

## Fertilizer

Use a high-nitrogen fertilizer once a month starting in late January through September. Ferns have a slight dormant period in the winter and shouldn't be fed during this period.

## Propagation

Divisions, side runners, spores.

## Artificial Light

150 footcandles.

## First Aid.

*Red spiders, mealybugs, aphids, nematodes, scale. (*See Pests.*) Chemical sprays can damage ferns; use nicotine sulfate (3/4 teaspoon per quart of warm, soapy water).

*Brown dots on the undersides of the fronds.* If the dots are arranged in lines or clustered, they are spore cases. Leave them alone—this represents a healthy plant, and new ferns can be produced from these spores. If the spots are scattered on the stems as well as fronds, these are scales. Dip plant in a soapy solution of nicotine sulfate.

*Dark tan or black dry center spots with narrow, dark margins. Tips of leaves and or leaf margins turn brown and die back.* The problem is anthracnose disease and is caused by sudden chilling. Remove infected leaves and spray or paint with a foliar fungicide. Grow plant on the dry side until the disease has cleared up.

*Dry edges curl under, lower leaves turn yellow with brown spots, drying foliage from the base upward, dropping of older leaves.* The problem is temperatures that are too warm. They need warmth but not blasts from hot radiators. Temperatures must vary only between 60 to 70 degrees.

*Yellowing leaves and yellowing leaf margins with brown leaf tips, wilting, shriveling and stunted new growth.* The problem is too little humidity. Keep the plant on a bed of wet pebbles without the bottom of the pot touching any water. Spray twice or more a day and use a humidifier during the winter.

*Yellowish green appearance, scorch marks on leaves and a general bleached-out appearance.* This is too much light. They will not tolerate the hot sun of summer and must be protected by a curtain or moved farther from the light source.

*Loss of color with ash gray spots with purple margins on the fronds.* This is tip blight. Spray with a Bordeaux mixture which can be purchased at your plant or hardware store.

*A black sooty coating on the fronds.* This is a mold that develops in very humid conditions but is not a parasite disease. It is attracted to a honeydew secreted by scales and mealybugs. Black molds can be washed off with soapy water. Give the plant good air circulation without chilling drafts. Check for pests.

*Dry, wilting, limp look. Leaves can curl under and lower leaves turn yellow with brown spots and fall.* This is underwatering or improper watering. Plant must always be moist. Water slowly over the entire soil surface until excess water runs out of the drainage hole in the bottom. Do not let the plant sit in the water-filled saucer for more than an hour. Before rewatering, allow the plant to become damp to the touch and then thoroughly water again.

The Rubber plant (*Ficus elastica*) is a very rugged plant from Eastern Asia that has many varieties. It is a vigorous, erect plant with shiny leaves. It may have dark green, broad oval leaves; broad, greenish yellow marbled leaves; narrow white yellow or multicolored leaves. Leaves can grow to 12 inches long and 6 inches wide. Dwarf varieties are also available. The young leaves appear as red points at the tips of the branches and slowly unwind into full-grown leaves. Rubber plants can grow very tall, but if you prefer a shorter plant, you can encourage branching by two methods. Either remove the growing point or cut a circular ring through the bark directly under a leaf. The sap coagulates and food collects above the cut forcing a dormant bud to develop.

# FICUS

The Fiddle-leaf Fig

The Mistletoe Fig

The Rubber Plant

§ 97

The fiddle-leaf fig *(Ficus lyrata)* is a very durable plant from West Africa that flourishes even when neglected. The 12- to 18-inch leaves are a rich green patterned with deep veins. They have a leathery texture that makes them look waxed. The edges are ruffled and irregular and resemble the body of a violin. They can grow from 2 to 10 feet tall and can be made to branch like the rubber plant.

The mistletoe fig *(Ficus diversifolia)* is tough and durable. It grows slowly to about 18 inches high. The leathery dark green or blue-green 2-inch leaves have brown marks near the base. The leaves are prominently veined and shaped like a raindrop. Inedible, yellowish red, 1/4-inch fig fruits appear near every leaf axil and often in pairs that sometimes last throughout the year and give the appearance of mistletoe.

## Location

They need bright light or filtered sunlight but must be protected from any direct sunlight. Temperatures should be between 60 and 80 degrees.

## Soil

One part all-purpose loam, one part peat moss, one part sharp sand, perlite or vermiculite. They like to be pot-bound, so don't be too hasty to repot.

## Watering

Allow the soil to thoroughly dry between waterings. Spray-mist daily and wash the leaves weekly with warm water.

## Fertilizer

Every three months.

## Propagation

Air layering, cuttings only if the stem has not become woody.

## Artificial Light

400 footcandles.

## First Aid

*Mealybugs, scales, spider mites, thrips. (See *Pests*.)

*Rustlike spots on the leaves.* This often appears to be tip scorching but in fact indicates a fungus disease. Remove severely spotted leaves. Spraying the leaves will spread the disease, so don't spray-mist the leaves for a couple of weeks. Spray with a foliar fungicide.

*Dark tan or black dry center spots with narrow, dark margins. The ends of the leaves can turn dark tan with darker bars crisscrossing the leaf. Tips of leaves and or leaf margins turn brown and die back.* This is anthracnose disease and is caused by chilling or humidity that is too high. Remove infected foliage and spray healthy leaves with a fungicide. Do not spray the foliage with water until the disease has cleared up.

*Black, brown or yellow damp or blistered spots, usually with yellow margins.* This is leaf-spot disease caused by high humidity, overwatering, chilling, too little light. Temperature, light and ventilation must be increased, and soil must dry out thoroughly between waterings. Infected areas should be removed. Spray remaining leaves with a fungicide.

*Grayish or white feltlike coatings on the leaves.*

These are mildews. They can block our light, and eventually the leaves curl and shrivel up. They are caused by too much humidity. Mildewed leaves should be removed. Lower the humidity and improve the air circulation in the growing area.

*Yellowing of leaves beginning on the outer edges spreading to the whole leaf. Older leaves will drop. Stems look weak and limp.* The problem is too little fertilizer. Fertilize more often, especially during the plant's growing season. Remove all damaged foliage.

*Occasional yellowing of one leaf.* This is usually old age. If more than one leaf turns color, then other problems are at hand.

*Lack of new growth.* This is usually from the plant being too crowded in its pot. Repot.

*Leaves droop and hang down limply, soft and discolored foliage, lower leaves turn yellow with brown spots, dry edges curl under. This is from temperatures that are too warm.* The plant likes warmth, but the growing area needs to have good air circulation. The plant cannot tolerate the heat from sunlight and must be protected from it.

*Stems look weak, limp and wilted. Leaves curl under and lower leaves turn yellow with brown spots and fall. Dark, undersized leaves with loss of older ones.* The problem is underwatering or improper watering. Water slowly over the entire soil surface until excess water runs out of the drainage hole in the bottom. Do not let the plant sit in the water-filled saucer for more than an hour. Before rewatering, allow the plant to dry thoroughly and allow to remain dry for two days before rewatering.

*A mass yellowing and dropping of leaves. Rotting, wilting, leaves can curl, tips turn brown and die back. Brown spots can also occur.* The problem is overwatering. A root check will have to take place. The plant will have to be removed from its pot (see *Potting*). At the same time, check for proper soil and proper drainage material over the drainage area. If the roots are white and healthy, repot in fresh soil, removing all damaged foliage, and water only when the soil is thoroughly dry. If the roots are partially decayed, remove them and repot in fresh soil. If all the roots are brown and mushy, the plant can not be saved and will have to be discarded, but if healthy cuttings are available, you can start a new plant.

*Plant becomes leggy.* This occurs naturally. New plants can be propagated with cuttings from the tips of the old plant that have not become woody.

# FITTONIA

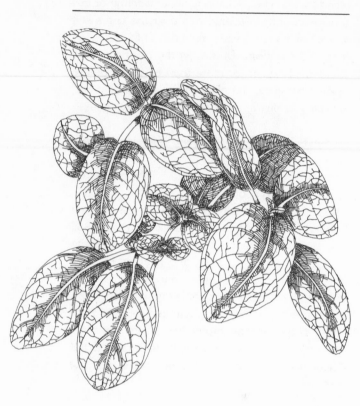

*Fittonia* is a low creeping plant from Peru. It grows 8 inches long and 4 inches high. It has 2- to 4-inch, oval, bright green leaves with rounded ends. The leaves have veined patterns that are very intricate and look like a nerve network. The veins can be white, pink or red. They can blossom with yellow flowers. Fittonias are a very good terrarium plant.

## Location

Needs bright light of an east or west window protected from any hot sun during the summer. It will thrive in a north window. *Fittonia* needs warmth, and the temperatures should never drop below 55 degrees year round.

## Soil

One part all-purpose loam, one part peat moss, one part sharp sand. Their roots grow close to the surface, and when repotting use shallow, wide pots.

## Watering

Soil should be kept moist at all times but should never be allowed to get soggy. Needs high humidity and should be kept on a bed of wet pebbles without the bottom of the pot touching the water. Spray-mist a few times a day to keep it healthy.

## Fertilizer

Once a month.

## Propagation

Stem cuttings.

## Artificial Light

150 footcandles.

## First-Aid

*Mealybugs, spider mites, leaf miners, nematodes. (See *Pests*.)

*Plant looks straggly.* As a plant gets to be over a year old it will begin to look less attractive. This is natural. Propagate new plants with the healthy stems.

*Leaves shed in winter.* This happens because the temperature is too cold. The temperature must never be below 55 degrees. It's a good idea to keep the plant in a terrarium during the winter.

*Rotting, wilting and bleaching of foliage. A mass yellowing and dropping of leaves. New growth is weak. Leaves can curl, tips turn brown and die back. Flowers will blight and soil is constantly wet.* Overwatering is the problem. The plant must be removed from its pot (see *Potting*) in order to check the roots. Also make sure the proper soil has been used and that the drainage holes have been covered sufficiently to ensure proper drainage. If roots are white and healthy, either repot in fresh soil or return to its original pot, soil and all, and aerate the surface soil by gently stirring the soil with a fork. If roots are brown, the plant may be dying, and you should remove soil, cut away injured roots and repot. Cut away damaged foliage and water carefully.

*Black, brown or yellow damp or blistered spots with yellow margins.* This is leaf-spot disease caused by high humidity, overwatering, chilling and low light. Temperature, light and ventilation need to be increased. Soil must dry out before you resume proper watering. Infected areas should be removed. Spray remaining leaves with a fungicide.

*Plant shows signs of underwatering, wilting and yellowing of leaves. Stems become soft and dark in color.* The problem is root-rot disease. Plant must be removed from its pot (see *Potting*). All soil has to be removed from the roots, which should then be washed in warm water. Remove badly injured roots and repot in fresh soil. Remove damaged foliage and water only enough to keep the plant from wilting. Drench the soil with a fungicide with its first watering. Once the plant shows signs of normal growth, resume proper watering.

*Base and stems of plant turn soft and mushy and the rest of the plant quickly follows suit.* The problem is stem-rot disease. It is promoted by too much humidity, overwatering, too high or low temperatures. Repotting is necessary. Infected areas must be removed and the wounds sprayed with a fungicide. Be very careful the soil never becomes soggy. Rewater when the soil feels barely damp.

# FLAMINGO FLOWER TAILFLOWER— ANTHURIUM

The anthurium is native to Central and South America and Hawaii. Its leaves are dark green and narrow. The small yellow flowers are clustered in a dense spike. They resemble wax and are often taken to be artificial. The clusters are surrounded by a leathery spathe of red, white or pink. The plant flowers most of the year, but needs an annual resting period of about a month. During this resting period, all food, light and water should be diminished slightly. The resting period should occur when no new flower buds appear. Both the leaf and flower stems are long and grow from the necks of the roots at the surface of the soil. If the plant sends out aerial roots, root them in sphagnum moss and keep moistened. This is a good method of getting the plant to flower more often. There are different species of anthurium, some with suedelike foliage, different shaped leaves and even some varieties of climbers.

## Location

They can tolerate winter sun of an east or west window but must be shaded completely from any sun during the summer. A north window is best in summer. The plant needs warmth and will not tolerate temperatures below 60 degrees during the winter.

## Soil

One part all-purpose loam, one part peat moss with a handful of vermiculite or perlite added. Two parts African violet prepackaged soil mix with one part peat moss and a handful of perlite or vermiculite. Repotting is only necessary every two to three years. The roots are close to the surface, so wide, flat pots with plenty of room for the roots to spread are necessary.

## Watering

Anthurium is very finicky about its water. The soil must always be moist but never soggy. The plant can be damaged by drying out one time and will rot from too much water. Spray-mist daily.

## Fertilizer

While flowering fertilize once a month. Roots are very sensitive to salts in the soil. Occasionally, three to four times a year, drench the soil in the sink twice to clean away built-up salts, but make sure to let the soil dry just barely on the top before rewatering.

## Propagation

Divisions, offsets, cuttings from climbers that have aerial roots.

## Artificial Light

150 footcandles.

## First Aid

*If the plant should be attacked by pests, nicotine sulfate is generally safe, while other insecticides will harm the plant.

*Exposed roots.* It is harmful to allow the roots to heave themselves out of the soil. Cover them with damp sphagnum moss and, if growth continues and gets out of hand, divide the plant.

*The plant doesn't bloom, flowers are small and leaf tips turn brown, leaf margins yellow, stunted or no new growth, wilting and shriveling of leaves.* The problem is low humidity. The pot needs to be put on a bed of moist pebbles without allowing the bottom of the pot to touch the water. Spray-mist the leaves once or twice daily and use a humidifier during the winter.

*Leaves curl under and lower leaves turn yellow with brown spots and fall. Brown crisp spots, scorched edges on leaves and flowers. Flower buds drop or the flowering period is short.* Anthurium resents even one underwatering. Water slowly over the entire soil surface until excess water runs out of the drainage hole in the bottom. Do not let the plant sit in the water-filled saucer for more than an hour. Allow the plant to become barely damp before rewatering.

*Spots, scorch marks on leaves turning grayish where scorched and a general bleached-out look. Plant becomes limp, shrivels and can die.* The problem is too much sun. A north window is best during the summer. During the winter it can tolerate a little sun but keep it away from the cold window.

# FLOWERING OLIVE
# SWEET OLIVE
# FALSE HOLLY—
# OSMANTHUS

An evergreen from Asia which is one of the most satisfactory flowering house plants. There are a few varieties, including plants with dark, glossy, green foliage or small, dark, spiny leaves, and green, spiny-edged leaves with creamy-white edges occasionally tinged with pink. It is easy to keep the foliage clean and shining. Heat does not dry out flower buds, and the small fragrant flowers will bloom most of the year if kept pot-bound. The plant never becomes leggy. In the spring tall growth should be pruned back.

## Location

Needs a sunny window with semishade in the hot sun of summer, but does very well in bright indirect light. Likes a cool location.

## Soil

One part all-purpose loam, one part peat moss, one part sharp sand, perlite or vermiculite. They like to be pot-bound.

## Watering

Keep the soil barely moist at all times. Allow only the surface soil to become dry between waterings.

## Fertilizer

Once in early spring and once in early summer.

## Propagation

Stem cuttings, air layering.

## Artificial Light

800 footcandles.

## First Aid

*Practically a problem-free plant. This plant will have to be abused badly before any problems occur.

A very difficult plant to raise from tropical America. There are many hybrids, all hanging plants, that have beautiful, two-toned, pendant, double or single flowers in colors that range from red, pink, magenta, violet to fuchsia and white. It blossoms continually in late winter for weeks. Stems are very brittle and will snap at the slightest pressure; thus pruning must be done carefully. If a wide plant is desired, the center of the young shoots has to be removed. The plant needs a rest, and beginning in October water less, prune back some of the top growth and either repot in a container one size larger or root-prune and keep it in the same pot. Allow to rest in a cool place until January. Then return it to its required environment.

## Location

They do best in an east or west window where protection from the sun isn't necessary in winter but they need to be protected from hot sun in summer. There are a few varieties which perform well in full sun. In order to bloom, they need cool temperatures around 65 degrees.

## Soil

One part all-purpose loam, one part peat moss, and a handful of perlite or vermiculite added. Two parts African violet prepackaged loam, one part peat moss and a handful of perlite or vermiculite. A pinch of chimney soot in the soil deepens the flower tones.

## Watering

Keep the soil moist during the growing season. When dormant water very sparingly.

## Fertilizer

Feed every other week during the growing period. Refrain from feeding during dormancy.

# FUCHSIA

## Propagation

Stem cuttings in fall, spring or winter.

## Artificial Light

800 footcandles.

## First Aid

*Aphids, whiteflies, red spider mites, mealybugs, thrips, nematodes. Older plants get attacked by cyclamen mites. (See *Pests*.)

*Leaves wilt overnight and never recover.* This is fuchsia heart attack and there's no cure. The cause of this problem has yet to be determined.

§ 105

*The plant dies back from the tips and the inner stem tissue becomes blackened.* This is a disease called verticillium wilt which attacks plants that demand a lot of water. There is no cure.

*A black coating on leaves.* This is a black sooty mold. It is not a disease parasite. It develops from humid conditions and also is attracted to honeydew left by insects. The mold can be removed with soapy water. Provide better air circulation in the growing area and be sure to check for pests.

*Black, brown or yellow damp or blistered spots, usually with yellow margins.* This is leaf-spot disease and it is caused by overwatering, chilling, low light or poor air circulation. Temperature, light and ventilation need to be improved and allow the soil to dry before resuming normal watering. Infected areas should be removed and remaining leaves sprayed with a fungicide.

*Poor flowering and dropping flowers, lower leaves turn yellow with brown spots, dry edges curl under.* The problem is from temperatures that are too warm. Plant needs to be kept cool—65 degrees year round—and kept well ventilated with fresh air.

*Poor flowering.* This problem can be caused from an improper resting period. Check the proper requirements.

*The plant produces few blooms, flowers drop and become stringy and misshapen, pale or discolored leaves. A mass of yellow foliage, tips of leaves and margins turn brown and die, older plants shed leaves from the bottom up.* The problem is too little light. Move the plant to a brighter location without direct sun or move closer to the artificial light source.

*Stunted or dying plant.* Allowing fuchsia to dry out often during its growing period will stunt or kill it, and it will never recover.

*Leaves curl under and lower leaves turn yellow with brown spots and fall. Brown crisp spots, scorched edges on leaves and flowers. Flower buds drop or the flowering period is short. Dark, undersized leaves with loss of older ones.* The problem is underwatering. Water slowly over the entire soil surface until excess water runs out of the drainage hole in the bottom. Do not let the plant sit in the water-filled saucer for more than an hour. Allow the plant to become damp before rewatering.

An evergreen shrub from eastern Asia with glossy, green, ovate or laceolate leaves. The very fragrant flowers are large, flat, waxy and white. Gardenias can flower all year round but will normally do so only from May to August. The buds are beautiful, but the art of raising gardenias is to succeed in encouraging them to flower, because the buds have a tendency to drop off. Buds should be removed in spring to encourage winter blooming. The plant grows to 3 feet and should be pruned after flowering.

## Location

Full sunlight in winter and shaded from strong sunlight in summer. Southern exposure is best. Needs warm temperature during the winter, 70 to 80 degrees, and not below 65 degrees at night. In order to flower the temperature must be 10 degrees lower at night.

## Soil

Needs acid soil. One part all-purpose loam, one part peat moss, one handful of perlite or vermiculite added. When repotting, repot in February, and plant it firmly and at the depth previously planted.

## Watering

Must be kept constantly moist and never allowed to dry out completely. Needs high humidity and must be mist sprayed once or twice a day.

## Fertilizer

Feed aluminum sulfate, which is an acid-type fertilizer containing iron. Feed weekly when there are no flower buds. No feeding when in bloom. Feeding during the winter is not recommended.

# GARDENIA— CAPE JASMINE

## Propagation

Stem cuttings, but it takes two years to produce buds.

## Artificial Light

800 footcandles.

## First Aid

*Mealybugs are the most common plague, aphids, red spiders, scales, nematodes. (See *Pests*.)

*Buds on a new plant turn black and drop.* The environmental change from greenhouse to house is traumatic due to the low light, low humidity and

§ 107

warm temperatures in the home. Proper requirements must be given, especially high humidity. Spray-mist daily and place the plant on a bed of wet pebbles without the bottom of the pot touching the water.

*Yellowing of top leaves, yellow margins, discolored leaves, retarded growth.* This is an iron or magnesium deficiency. Feed the plant with an acid fertilizer weekly when there are no flower buds. No feeding when in bloom and during the winter.

*Flowers turn brown, foliage yellows, buds drop, leaf tips turn brown.* The problem is low humidity. The pot needs to be put on a bed of moist pebbles without allowing the bottom of the pot to touch the water. Spray-mist more than once a day and use a humidifier during the winter.

*Dropping of buds or no buds at all, a pale bleached coloring, yellowing or yellow spots on leaves usually beginning on the outer edges and spreading to the whole leaf. Older leaves will drop.* This is the result of too little fertilizer. The plant needs to be fed weekly with an acid fertilizer when there are no flower buds, with no feeding at all during the winter.

*Rotting, wilting and bleaching of foliage. A mass yellowing and dropping of leaves. Leaves can curl, tips turn brown and die back. Flowers will blight and soil is constantly wet.* The problem is overwatering. The plant must be removed from the pot (see *Potting*). The roots will have to be checked, and at the same time, check to make sure the plant has been given the proper soil and that enough drainage material is covering the drainage holes. If the roots are white and healthy looking, either place back into its pot and improve watering or repot in fresh soil, removing all damaged foliage. If roots are partially brown, remove them and repot in fresh soil. If all roots are brown and mushy, the plant is beyond help and will have to be discarded.

*Plant stems look weak, limp and wilted. Lower leaves turn yellow with brown spots and fall. Flower buds drop or the flowering period is short. New growth dies back.* This is underwatering. Water slowly over the entire soil surface until excess water runs out of the drainage hole in the bottom. Do not let the plant sit in the water-filled saucer for more than an hour. Allow the soil to become barely damp before rewatering. Gardenias should never dry out completely.

*A part of the stem dies.* The problem is gardenia canker. There is no cure, and the plant will have to be destroyed.

A South African plant that comes in hundreds of varieties. Pink blooms do the best indoors: Regal or Martha Washington have the largest bloom. The fancy-leaved and scented plants very rarely bloom indoors but have beautiful foliage. There are also geranium ivies and miniature varieties. Geraniums must be kept pot-bound to produce lush blooms and will flower almost all year round if given the proper requirements. They grow from miniatures to several feet tall. To encourage flowering, dead flowers should be removed regularly. Pinching off the tips of foliage will produce a bushy plant. Only some of the geranium family goes into dormancy, but it's best to watch individual plants for any indications of dormancy. If plant goes dormant, water less and use no fertilizer.

Bring plants inside for the winter. Prune the plants and place them in a bright but cool (55 to 60 degrees) location. Keep the soil moist but let the top soil just dry out before watering. Treat as house plants. If they get leggy, just keep pruning. If the leaves yellow, increase light, lower the temperature and watch the watering. When spring comes, prune again and put them back outdoors and they'll produce many blooms.

## Location

They thrive in a south window. They will grow well in a semisunlit window or bright light but will not have many blooms. Cool temperatures are necessary to produce better flowering.

## Soil

One part all-purpose loam, one part peat moss, one part sharp sand with a handful of perlite or vermiculite. Replace the soil annually in early spring, but use a larger pot only if the plant is very root-bound. Geraniums use up a lot of nourishment by their continued flowering. After repotting cut back the plant to encourage new growth.

# GERANIUM— PELARGONIUM

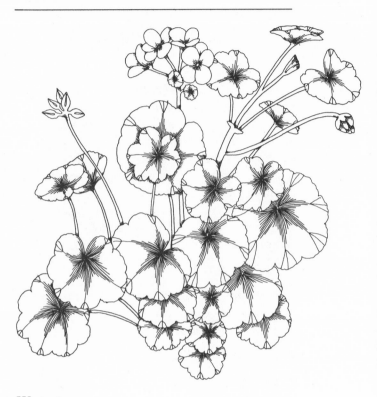

## Watering

They tolerate dry soils but flower better if the soil is allowed to dry only on the surface between waterings. If flowering should stop during the winter, water only when the soil is completely dry. Do not spray the foliage or flowers very often as they have a tendency to rot.

## Fertilizer

Feed every two weeks unless the plant is resting.

## Propagation

Cuttings that must be allowed to dry for a day before rooting, seeds.

§ 109

## Artificial Light

1,000 footcandles.

## First Aid

*Whiteflies, leaf rollers, red spiders, mealybugs. (See Pests.)

*Yellowing of foliage beginning at the outer edges, usually spreading to the whole leaf and damaging roots. Yellow spots and crisp brown spots and scorched edges on leaves, wilting and no flowering. This is the result of too much fertilizer. Soil must be literally flooded with water twice and allowed to drain well. If fertilizer salts have accumulated on the pot, remove with warm water and a stiff brush. Remove all damaged foliage. Fertilize less often or use half the amount you have been using.

*All leaf growth and no flowers. This can be too much nitrogen. Cut down on your feeding and use a fertilizer low in nitrogen and watch closely for any changes to make sure this is the problem.

*Yellowish green color on its leaves, and many plants have their leaves' undersides turning purple. This is a nitrogen deficiency. Use a fertilizer at every other feeding which is high in nitrogen.

*Brown edges. This is usually from a lack of food, especially potash. Either feed more often or use a higher-potency fertilizer.

*The leaves are abnormally dark in color and small in size. This is a phosphorus deficiency. Use a superphosphate in solution as this will improve leaf size and color.

*Yellowing of new growth and eventual rotting of the top of the plant, brown crisp spots on leaves, scorched leaf edges, new growth is thick and dwarfed, white salts accumulate on the soil and the pots' sides and rim. This is salt damage from too much fertilizing. Water heavily until water pours out of the drainage holes. Repeat. Let it drain well. Scrub off any white-salt residue from the pot with a brush and warm water. Give the plant more light, good air circulation and fertilize less often.

*Elongated, spindly growth, pale or discolored leaves. A mass of yellow foliage, tips of leaves and margins turn brown and die. Older plants shed leaves from the bottom up. The problem is too little light. Geraniums need bright light and will not grow in the shade. They need to be moved to a brighter location or closer to the artificial light source. Or add some artificial lighting to its present light source.

*No flowering. This can be due to either temperatures that are too warm or too much pinching. They must have cool temperatures of 55 to 65 degrees. Less pinching will improve flowering.

*Leaf tips turn brown, leaf margins yellow, stunted new growth, wilting and dropping of buds. The problem is low humidity. Rather than mist spraying, which can be dangerous, place the plant on a bed of wet pebbles without the bottom of the pot touching the water.

*Rotting, wilting and bleaching of foliage. A mass yellowing and dropping of leaves. Leaves can curl, tips turn brown and die back. Flowers will blight and soil is always wet. This is the result of overwatering. The plant must be removed from the pot (see Potting) and the roots checked. Check for proper soil and proper drainage material over the drainage area. If roots are white and healthy, repot plant in fresh soil and water carefully. Remove all damaged foliage. If roots are partially brown, remove them and repot in fresh soil. If all roots are brown and mushy, the plant can not be saved.

*Yellowing of leaves and rapid loss of older leaves, wilting, water stands on the soil.* The problem is improper soil. Cut off any damaged foliage and repot in proper soil.

*Leaves curl under and lower leaves turn yellow with brown spots and fall. Plant stems look weak, limp and wilted. Brown crisp spots, scorched edges on leaves and flowers.* The problem is underwatering. Water slowly over the entire soil surface until excess water runs out of the drainage hole in the bottom. Do not let the plant sit in the water-filled saucer for more than an hour.

*A gray mold that resembles bread mold on the surface of the soil or leaves.* This is Botrytis, caused by soil that is too wet, poor light, high humidity. Remove damaged foliage. Scratch mold into the soil carefully so as not to injure any roots, and with its next watering it will be washed away. Reduce watering, ventilate the growing area and keep the foliage dry. If problem continues, drench the soil with a diluted solution of a fungicide and spray the leaves with a fungicide.

*Curled and crinkled leaves with pale spots.* This is a disease called leaf curl. It cannot be cured. Don't use cuttings from this plant for new plants as they will also be infected. The disease doesn't seem to spread from plant to plant.

*Leaves wilt and die overnight even though all growing conditions have been correct.* This is probably verticillum wilt. It is usually caused from too much water and high humidity. There is no cure.

*Water-soaked corky eruptions on lower leaf surface. They appear in cool, dark, cloudy weather.* This is called edema. Just keep the foliage dry, and the eruptions will disappear when warm weather arrives.

*Base and stems of plant turn soft and mushy.* This is a disease called stem rot. It is promoted by too much humidity, overwatering and too high temperatures. Infected areas must be removed and the wounds sprayed with a fungicide. Repot in fresh soil and correct the plant's environment.

*Large yellow to brown spots which cause death of the leaf from the margins inward.* This is a bacterial stem rot and it is caused when the plant is too warm. Remove damaged foliage and move the plant to a cooler location with good air circulation.

*Black, brown or yellow damp or blistered spots, usually with yellow margins.* This is leaf-spot disease. It is caused by poor air circulation, high humidity, overwatering, chilling, low light. Temperature, light and ventilation need to be increased, and soil must dry out before rewatering. Infected areas should be removed. Spray remaining leaves with a fungicide. Once the disease has cleared up, resume proper care.

# GLOXINIA— SINNINGIA

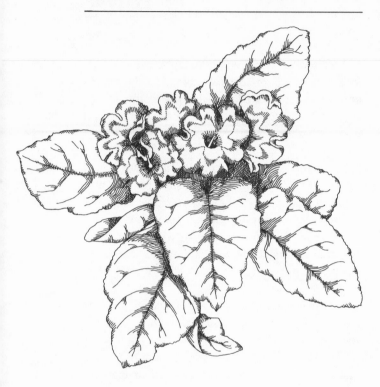

This tuberous-rooted gesneriad (a cultivated ornamental) from Brazil is a distant relative of the African violet. The trumpet-shaped flowers are 5 inches across and are in shades of pink, violet, purple and crimson or white. Blooms are ruffled, striped, frilled or variegated and have a velvety texture. The flowering period is May to October. The short stems grow to a foot tall and have very brittle leaves. The plants are sold in early summer. Buy one with many buds and few open flowers so it can be enjoyed longer. When the flowers have faded, cut off the topmost stem with one set of leaves. A new set of leaves will develop within two months and a second growth of flowers will appear before the plant goes dormant. The top stem can be propagated by rooting whole.

The resting period begins in autumn. As leaves begin to wither, reduce watering until the leaves have died. Put the plant in a cupboard or cool room not below 40 degrees and keep it dry. The tubers will rot if kept too cold. Sometimes the leaves are not lost; instead of keeping the plant in a cupboard, place it in a warm room and let the soil dry out between waterings. In February or March place the plant in a warm place (70 degrees). Place a plastic bag over the plant without securing the open end. Water carefully to prevent rotting tubers. It can be placed on a warm radiator. When new shoots are 2 inches, the tubers can be repotted in a 6-inch pot with the rounded ends of the tubers planted downward. Retain three shoots and remove the rest. When in full growth treat as an adult plant.

## Location

Sun in an east or west window during the winter, but the plant must be protected from hot summer sun. Needs warmth, 65 to 70 degrees, and never less than 60 degrees.

## Soil

One part all-purpose loam, one part peat moss, one part sharp sand, perlite or vermiculite. African violet prepackaged soil can be used with a handful of perlite or vermiculite added. Gloxinias will be happy in the same pot for two years but they can be repotted each season when they come out of dormancy.

## Watering

Allow only the surface soil to dry between thorough waterings except during dormancy, when very little water is needed. Spray-mist daily while flowering.

## Fertilizer

Use an African violet fertilizer once every two weeks but no feeding during dormancy.

## Propagation

Seeds, leaf cuttings (new plants will have a rest period so hold back watering until signs of growth), dividing tubers, cuttings from the crown which was removed to encourage a second flowering period.

## Artificial Light

500 footcandles.

## First Aid

*Cyclamen mites, thrips. (See *Pests.*)

*Shriveling, wilting of leaves, leaf tips turn brown, leaf margins yellow and buds drop.* The problem is low humidity. While the plant is flowering it must be mist sprayed daily and put on a bed of wet pebbles without the bottom of the pot touching the water.

*Elongated, misshapen growth, pale or discolored leaves, a mass of yellow foliage, tips of leaves and margins turn brown and die. New growth shrivels and dies.* This is the result of too little light. Needs bright light and will not tolerate dark places. An east or west window is best, or move closer to artificial light or add artificial light to its present light source.

*Buds turn brown, plant is limp and lifeless.* This is from general poor culture, and the plant's environment must be improved.

*A rotten tuber.* This is from too much water. It can be saved only if the crown is not affected. Cut away the bad parts carefully, dust the wounds with sulfur and let the tuber dry in the air for a week, then put in fresh soil and water carefully.

# GOLD-DUST PLANT— AUCUBA

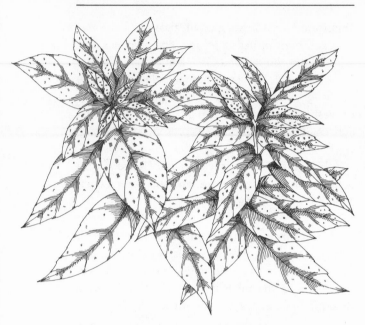

A Japanese evergreen and shrub. The most notable characteristic is the glistening effect of the 4- to 6-inch, stiff, waxy, oval leaves. All varieties have spotted leaves with different size and shape yellow markings. It may grow more than 3 feet in height. The larger plants can bear red fruits. As plants become too tall, prune to desired height in early spring as new growth develops.

## Location

Full sun during the winter, protected from hot sun during the summer. They can be successfully grown in bright light but their coloring will not be as bright. They do best with cool nights.

## Soil

One part all-purpose loam, one part peat moss, one part sharp sand, perlite or vermiculite. One-half all-purpose loam and one-half sharp sand is also suitable.

## Watering

Keep the soil moist at all times but never soggy. Spray-mist daily.

## Fertilizer

Feed every three months.

## Propagation

Tips of stem cuttings.

## Artificial Light

400 footcandles.

## First Aid

*Spider mites, scales. (See *Pests*.)

*No fruit on an older plant.*   Both male and female plants are necessary. The female plant develops the fruit but needs the male plant for pollination.

*Plant becomes leggy and spindly.*   This is natural as the plant grows tall. They can be cut successfully to desired heights in winter and early spring, and new growth will appear soon afterward.

*Scorched edges on leaves, brown crisp spots, plant stems look weak, limp and wilted. Leaves curl under and lower leaves turn yellow with brown spots and fall.*   The problem is underwatering. Water slowly over the entire soil surface until excess water runs out of the drainage hole in the bottom. Do not let the plant sit in the water-filled saucer for more than an hour. Allow the soil to become just damp before rewatering.

The genus *Cissus* used to be classified in the genus *Vitis*, for grapes, because of the tendrils which the plant uses for support. Cissus grow beautifully in hanging baskets. They grow quickly, and to keep them bushy and compact you should pinch off stem tips at any time. There are many varieties of cissus but the most popular are the grape ivy and the kangaroo vine.

Grape ivy is not a true ivy and is only called an ivy because of its tendrils and leaf formation. It must not be treated like an ivy. This plant is from the West Indies and tropical America. The leaves are diamond-shaped and grow in clumps of three. They are dark green on top with a reddish color on the undersides. New growth has a fuzzy appearance.

The kangaroo vine's large green leaves have saw edges and resemble birch leaves. Older leaves cascade downward while new top growth stretches outward. New growth has a fuzzy appearance.

## Location

Needs bright light or indirect sunlight with protection against any strong sunlight. A north or northeast location is best. Needs cool places to survive at its best but a minimum of 60 degrees in winter. Keep the plant away from hot radiators.

## Soil

One part all-purpose loam, one part sharp sand, perlite or vermiculite. Don't use any peat moss or the soil will be too acid. Yearly repotting is advisable to keep the plant healthy.

## Watering

For all species the soil should become just dry between thorough waterings. They are sensitive to too much moisture, especially in winter. Spray-mist daily.

# GRAPE IVY
# KANGAROO VINE—
# CISSUS

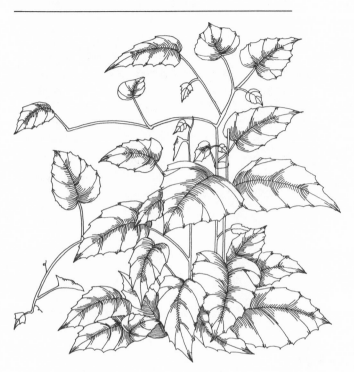

## Fertilizer

Once a month.

## Propagation

Stem cuttings any season.

## Artificial Light

400 footcandles.

## First Aid

*Their worst enemies are mealybugs and red spider mites. (See *Pests*.)

§ 115

*Spots, scorch marks on leaves turning grayish where scorched and a general bleached-out appearance. Plant becomes limp, shrivels and dies.* This is from too much light. Move plant farther from the light source or shield the plant with a thin curtain.

*A mass yellowing and dropping of leaves. Leaves can curl, tips turn brown and die back. New growth is weak. Rotting, wilting and bleaching of foliage.* The problem is overwatering. The plant must be removed from the pot (see *Potting*), and a root check must take place. At the same time, check for proper soil and proper drainage material at the base of the pot. If roots are white and healthy, either repot or return to original pot soil and allow the soil to dry between waterings. Remove all damaged foliage. If roots are partially damaged, remove them and repot. If all the roots are damaged, the plant cannot be saved, and healthy cuttings can be taken to start new plants.

*Leaves curl under and lower leaves turn yellow with brown spots and fall. Brown crisp spots, scorched edges on leaves. Dark, undersized leaves with loss of older ones. New growth dies back.* This is underwatering. Water slowly over the entire soil surface until excess water runs out of the drainage hole in the bottom. Do not let the plant sit in the water-filled saucer for more than an hour. Before rewatering, the soil should be allowed to dry.

# HOUSE IRIS
# FAN IRIS
# APOSTLE PLANT—NEOMARICA

A Brazilian plant which is a beautiful accent plant and a reliable bloomer. There are usually twelve flat, green, sword-shaped leaves that grow in the form of a fan from underground stems. In winter blue and white irislike flowers bloom and last only one day. They are 4 inches across and are touched with violet. After flowering, the leaves on which the flower was born flap over and if a leaf comes into contact with its own soil or a neighboring pot, it will give birth to a new plant from the exact place where the flower grew. The plant grows to 2 feet tall.

## Location

Can tolerate full sun during the winter but needs protection from the hot sun of summer. Will survive in a bright window. It needs temperatures of 70 degrees or less.

## Soil

One part all-purpose loam, one part peat moss, one part sharp sand, perlite or vermiculite. Likes to be pot-bound, so don't repot unless absolutely necessary.

## Watering

Keep the soil moist but never soggy. The soil must never be allowed to dry out. Spray-mist daily.

## Fertilizer

Feed once a month.

## Propagation

Plantlets from the flowering stems treated like stem cuttings. Division of rhizomes.

## Artificial Light

500 footcandles.

## First Aid

*Apparently impervious to insects.

*Leaf tips turn brown, yellowing leaf margins, stunted new growth, wilting, shriveling, dropping buds.* The problem is too little humidity. Place the pot on a bed of moist pebbles without allowing the bottom of the pot to touch the water. Spray-mist the leaves daily and use a humidifier during the winter.

---

A Mascarene Islands evergreen bush relatively new as a plant for the home. A good north-window plant. It has branching, cinnamon-brown stems and 1- to 2-inch, indented, succulent leaves. The leaves resemble oak leaves in shape and have a metallic-blue cast. The species is naturally bushy, and pinching new growth makes it more so. The plant grows to 18 inches tall.

## Location

The plant prefers sun but will grow in a bright north window. They like a cool location but must be kept out of drafts during the winter.

## Soil

One part all-purpose loam, one part peat moss, one part sharp sand, perlite or vermiculite.

## Watering

Keep the soil moist at all times. The soil should never dry out completely. Spray-mist daily.

# INDOOR OAK—NICODEMIA

§ 117

## Fertilizer

Feed once a month from spring to midsummer but do not fertilize the rest of the year.

## Propagation

Stem cuttings in spring or summer.

## Artificial Light

800 footcandles.

## First Aid

*Red spider mites. (See *Pests*.)

*Plant stems look weak, limp and wilted. Leaves curl under and lower leaves turn yellow with brown spots and fall. Brown crisp spots, scorched edges on leaves. Dark, undersized leaves with loss of older ones.   This is the result of underwatering. Water slowly over the entire soil surface until excess water runs out of the drainage hole in the bottom. Do not let the plant sit in the water-filled saucer for more than an hour. Allow the plant to become just damp and then rewater.

# IVY—HEDERA

There are hundreds of varieties of ivy, but only five species: *Hedera helix* (English ivy), *Hedera canariensis* (Canary Island ivy), *Hedera colchica* (Persian ivy), *Hedera nepalensis* (Nepalese ivy), *Hedera rhombea* (Japanese ivy). There are many shapes, sizes, veins and different colors of the leaves. Even older leaves on the same plant can look different from younger ones. If you have two plants of the same variety, put into different environments, they each can take on a different appearance, or even suddenly produce a new kind of leaf or shoot. These new shoots can be propagated and you will have a totally different plant from the mother plant. No true ivy will grow from seeds. In the juvenile stage they have climbing stems that cling to upright surfaces with aerial roots that sprout from the stems and work their way into any available crevice. The young never form flowers. Given a support, they can be trained to grow upward or they can cover fanciful shapes formed by wires stuffed with sphagnum moss or they can cascade over the sides of pots or hanging containers. The adult stage of the plant produces a bushy plant with no aerial roots. The tendency to climb disappears and the adults will eventually flower. To induce bushiness pinch off stem tips at any season.

## Location

Ivies are shade lovers. They will also thrive in sunlight but must be protected from hot sun. They need a cool environment.

## Soil

One part all-purpose loam, one part peat moss, one part sharp sand, perlite or vermiculite.

## Watering

Allow the surface soil to dry between waterings. They need to be sprayed with water daily and washed under a faucet weekly to keep spider mites under control, which are the worst enemy.

## Fertilizer

Feed once a month with a balanced fertilizer such as 10-10-10, 15-15-15. Feed variegated plants less often or the leaves will turn solid green.

## Propagation

Stem cuttings, layering, runners.

## Artificial Light

800 footcandles.

## First Aid

*Red spider mites, cyclamen mites (the most destructive pest to ivies), aphids, mealybugs, scales, thrips. (See Pests.)

*Dark tan or black dry center spots with narrow, dark margins. The ends of the leaves can turn dark tan with darker bars crisscrossing the leaf. Tips of leaves and or leaf margins turn brown and die back.* This is a fungal disease called anthracnose and is caused by high humidity or sudden chilling. Remove infected foliage. Keep plant fairly dry and avoid water on the foliage until the problem clears up. The growing area should be well ventilated. Spray remaining leaves with a foliar fungicide.

*Black, brown or yellow damp or blistered spots, usually with yellow margins.* This is leaf-spot disease and it is caused by poor air circulation, high humidity, overwatering, chilling, low light. Temperature, light and ventilation need to be increased, and soil must dry out thoroughly before watering. Infected leaves should be removed and remaining leaves sprayed with a fungicide. When disease clears up, resume proper watering.

*Leaf tips turn brown, leaf margins yellow, stunted growth, wilting, shriveling.* The problem is too little humidity. The plant needs to be sprayed daily if hanging. If the plant is grounded, place the pot on a bed of wet pebbles without the bottom of the pot touching any water. Humidifiers are necessary during the winter.

*Dry edges curl under, drying foliage from the base upward, dropping older leaves, and a leggy and elongated plant.* This is from temperatures that are too warm. Ivies need a cool location to remain healthy. Keep near a window without drafts and keep the air circulating well in the growing area.

*Plants stems look weak, limp and wilted. Leaves curl under and lower leaves turn yellow with brown spots and fall. Dark, undersized leaves with loss of older ones.* The problem is underwatering. Water slowly over the entire soil surface until excess water runs out of the drainage hole in the bottom. Do not let the plant sit in the water-filled saucer for more than an hour. Before rewatering allow the surface soil to dry.

*Rotting, wilting and bleaching of foliage. A mass yellowing and dropping of leaves. New growth is weak.* The problem is overwatering. The plant must be removed from the pot (see Potting) and the roots checked. At the same time, make sure it has the proper soil and enough drainage material over the drainage holes. If the roots are white and healthy looking, repot in fresh soil, remove all damaged foliage and water more carefully. If roots are partially browned, remove them and repot in fresh soil. If all the roots are brown and mushy, the plant can not be saved. Take healthy cuttings and start new plants.

# JADE—CRASSULA

Crassula

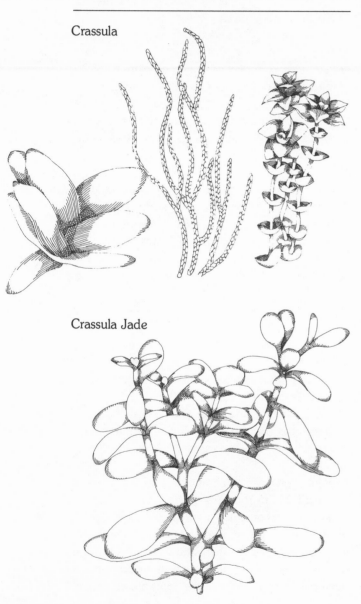

Crassula Jade

There are hundreds of crassulas but the most popular is the jade plant, a small, sturdy treelike succulent from South Africa. The plant has a thick trunk with numerous branches covered with fleshy round or oval leaves often edged with red. The plant has lacy, white, fragrant flowers in early spring, but in order to flower the plant needs to be six to eight years old and 2 feet or more tall. The plant can grow up to 3 feet tall with leaves 1 to 2 inches long. There are many varieties of jade which have leaves marked with combinations of white, yellow, pink, red and purple. There is also a dwarf jade with small leaves. They are very sturdy house plants and can withstand lack of moisture in both air and soil. It needs to be pruned and pinched to keep the plant bushy. When pinching out new growth, the parts removed must be very tiny. If they are too large, the subsequent growth will be misshapen.

## Location

Need sun but must be protected against hot noon sun during the summer. They will grow well in bright light. Dark green crassulas will survive without sunlight but the gray or blue crassulas need sun to keep their light colors. The red-edged leaves on some jade plants will only remain red if given some sun daily. They can tolerate a temperature range from 40 to 100 degrees. The best temperature is the lower seventies.

## Soil

One part all-purpose loam, one part peat moss, one part sharp sand. The plants like to be root-bound and generally live for years in the same pot. The surface soil, however, should be replaced annually.

## Watering

Crassulas should remain dry for several days between thorough waterings. Water much less in the winter.

## Fertilizer

Feed every three months with a cactus fertilizer. This fertilizer has less nitrogen, and crassulas thrive with low nitrogen.

## Propagation

Stem cuttings, leaf cuttings.

## Artificial Light

1,000 footcandles.

## First Aid

*Nematodes, mealybugs. (See Pests.) Crassulas can not tolerate Malathion, which is effective in fighting mealybugs, and using hard sprays of water, to combat pests, will break off foliage. The safest method to fight mealybugs is with swabs of alcohol.

*No flowering. This is usually a matter of age. The plant must be six to eight years old. Some never bloom indoors. Some young plants have surprised their owners by flowering, but this is unusual.

*Flowering crassula dies soon after blooming. You probably purchased one of the few annual varieties.

*Leaf drop, leggy growth, elongated, misshapen with underdeveloped leaves and inadequate branching. The problem is too little light. The plant needs to have additional light added to its present source, or move it closer to artificial lights, if they are its only light source.

*Rotting, wilting and bleaching of foliage. A mass yellowing and dropping of leaves. This is overwatering. It can usually be cured by simply watering less frequently. If the symptoms get worse, the plant will have to be removed from its pot (see Potting) and the roots checked. Also check for proper soil and proper drainage material over the drainage holes. If roots are white and healthy, repot in fresh soil and water carefully. If partial rotting of the roots has taken place, remove the damaged roots and repot in fresh soil. If all the roots are brown and mushy, the plant cannot be saved and cuttings or leaf cuttings should be taken to start new plants.

*Leaves turn yellow and shrivel, plant's stems look weak, limp and wilted. This is the result of underwatering. Water slowly over the entire soil surface until excess water runs out of the drainage hole in the bottom. Do not let the plant sit in the water-filled saucer for more than an hour. Allow the soil to remain dry for several days before rewatering. During the winter allow the soil to remain dry much longer.

*Growth soft and discolored. This is from too much humidity. Humidity must be lowered, ventilate the growing area well and move the plant away from plants that demand high humidity.

*Plants become leggy and elongated, lower leaves turn yellow with brown spots, drying foliage from the base upward, dropping older leaves. The problem is temperatures that are too warm. The growing area must be well ventilated. This rarely happens unless you have the plant close to a hot radiator during the winter.

*Base and stems of plant turn soft and mushy.* This is stem-rot disease. It is promoted by too much humidity and overwatering. Repotting is necessary. Infected areas must be removed and the wounds needs to be sprayed with a fungicide. If the infection doesn't look too severe, first try dipping the plant in a hot bath for twenty to forty minutes. Allow the plant to dry for several days before re-watering.

*Yellow lower leaves, stems become soft and dark in color and show signs of underwatering.* This is root-rot disease which prevents the root system from absorbing water. Plant must be removed from its pot (see *Potting*). All soil has to be removed and the roots washed in warm water. Remove any badly damaged roots. Repot in fresh soil. Remove damaged foliage and water only when the soil has been dried for several days. At the first wa-

tering, the soil should be drenched with a fungicide.

*A black coating on leaves.* This is a black mold from too much humidity. It is not a disease. Good ventilation is necessary. Wipe the mold off the leaves with soapy water. Lower the humidity and give the plant more sun. Check for pests as black mold is sometimes attracted to the honeydew substance that insects leave on the foliage.

*Gray or white covering on soil surface or foliage.* This is mold and it is from too much fertilizer or overwatering. This mold impairs drying out of the soil and can cause other problems. Soil molds can be scratched gently into the soil. Watering and fertilizing should be reduced. Wash the mold off the foliage gently with warm water. If the problem persists, drench the soil with a diluted solution of a fungicide.

A very durable plant that survives lack of attention and adverse conditions. A plant will last many years without getting too large for the house. The large, shiny, light green leaves grow up to 16 inches wide and have from five to nine lobes. The plant grows more than 4 feet tall. Removing the insignificant flower buds will promote even larger leaves. New leaves are covered with thick gray felt, which generally appears in winter and vanishes as the leaves grow older. Mature plants need to have the leaves dusted frequently or sponged with warm water. The japonica variegata has green and silver blotched leaves.

## Location

Fatsias prefer some sun but not the hot noon sun of summer. They do very well in bright light. They survive very cold temperatures if the soil is allowed to remain on the dry side.

## Soil

One part all-purpose loam, one part peat moss and one part vermiculite or perlite.

## Watering

Let the soil just barely dry between thorough waterings. Spray-mist daily.

## Fertilizer

Once a month March through September, with no feeding the rest of the year.

## Propagation

Stem cuttings.

## Artificial Light

800 footcandles.

# JAPANESE ARALIA—
# FATSIA JAPONICA
# ARALIA

## First Aid

*Aphids, red spider mites, scales. (See *Pests*.)

*Leaves shrivel.* This is the result of air that is too dry or too much hot summer sun. Mist-spray plant frequently and protect from hot noon sun in summer by using curtains or moving it farther away from its light source.

*Yellow leaves with brown spots that curl under and fall. Stems that look weak, limp and wilted. Brown, scorched edges on leaves.* All of these are signs of underwatering. The soil should be kept damp but never soggy. When watering, make sure you water slowly over the entire soil surface until

§ 123

excess water runs out of the drainage hole in the bottom but don't allow the plant to sit in a saucer of water for more than an hour. Before rewatering, allow the plant to dry out slightly.

*A mass yellowing of leaves and dropping. Leaves curl, tips turn brown and die. Rotting, wilting and bleaching of foliage.*   This is the result of overwatering, and if allowed to continue, a fungal disease will take precedence and it will be almost impossible to save the plant. The plant must be removed from the pot (see *Potting*), and a root check must take place. While checking the roots, make sure the plant has proper soil and the drainage holes are covered with enough material and also that the holes are not clogged with soil. If the roots are white and healthy looking, put the plant back in its pot and stir the surface soil to promote aeration and allow the soil to dry out slightly or repot in fresh soil. Remove all damaged foliage and keep the plant in a warm, well-ventilated location until new growth appears when it can be moved back to its proper location. If a few roots are damaged, remove them and repot in fresh soil. If all the roots are soft and mushy, the plant cannot be saved. Perhaps some healthy cuttings can be taken and new plants propagated.

*The leaves will turn yellow and drop, dry edges curl under, foliage becomes dry, brittle and shrivels from the base upward.*   This is the result of too warm temperatures. Keep away from hot radiators in winter and improve the air circulation around the growing area without causing any cold drafts.

# JAPANESE PITTOSPORUM— PITTOSPORUM

A beautiful foliage plant with shiny, thick, leathery leaves 2 to 4 inches long. The clusters of white flowers have a fragrance resembling orange blossoms or jasmine. There is a variegated variety with grayish green and creamy-margined leaves. They grow to 3 feet and are as wide as they are high. If they become too large, prune them in early spring just before new growth appears.

### Location

It needs sun to flower but will thrive with handsome foliage in bright light. The plant is durable in both warm and cool conditions.

### Soil

One part all-purpose loam, one part peat moss, one part sharp sand, perlite or vermiculite; likes to be pot-bound.

### Watering

Allow the soil to dry between thorough waterings. Spray-mist daily.

### Fertilizer

Feed once in early spring and once in early summer.

### Propagation

Seeds, stem cuttings, air layering.

### Artificial Light

800 footcandles.

### First Aid

*Aphids, scales, mealybugs. (See *Pests*.)

*Leaf tips turn brown, yellowing leaf margins, wilting, shriveling and buds drop.* The problem is too little humidity. Spray-mist daily and place the plant on a bed of wet pebbles without the bottom of the pot touching any water.

*Leaves curl under and lower leaves turn yellow with brown spots and fall. Brown crisp spots, scorched edges on leaves and flowers. Flower buds drop and plants stems look weak, limp and wilted.* The problem is underwatering. Water slowly over the entire soil surface until excess water runs out of the drainage hole in the bottom. Do not let the plant sit in the water-filled saucer for more than an hour. Before rewatering, allow the soil to dry, but not for more than one or two days.

An undemanding, bulbous, perennial plant with fleshy roots from South Africa. There are varieties with wide and narrow dark green leaves. They branch out alternately on both sides, and four to six new leaves can be produced yearly with proper care. The plant can grow 18 to 24 inches tall. The blooms are trumpet-shaped and grow in clusters of ten to twenty scarlet, salmon or orange flowers. They grow atop 20-inch, flat stems. The plant usually blooms in January but sometimes also in the early autumn. Only plants that are several years old will flower. When the flowers die, the stems should be cut as close to the soil surface as possible and when the remaining stem dries, it should be removed. Strong foliage growth begins after flowering, and the dead flowers can take strength away from the growth. The flower stems can be left intact if you want to use the ripe seeds for propagating. Once the plant is placed in the proper location, it must not be moved, and the pot must not be turned or the flowers will drop. *Clivia* must rest during the winter. After mid-October the water supply must be slowly reduced and the plant should remain completely dry from November to January. During this

# KAFFIR LILY— CLIVIA

period it should be kept in a bright, cool (but not below 50 degrees) location. When flower buds appear, move it to a warmer location (60 to 65 degrees) but let the soil remain dry until flower stalks are 6 inches tall and then resume proper watering.

## Location

Can tolerate a small amount of filtered sunlight, but beginning in the late spring it must be moved away from any sun. It does very well in bright light alone.

## Soil

One part all-purpose loam, one part peat moss, one part sharp sand, perlite or vermiculite. It needs to be repotted only every three to five years. When roots start growing over the surface soil, repot after flowering has ceased. Careful watering is necessary after repotting.

## Watering

While flowering, keep the soil moist but never soggy. After flowering, when foliage growth begins, let the plant dry out between thorough waterings. No watering during the resting period. Spray-mist plant daily.

## Fertilizer

Feed every other week between May and August. Do not get fertilizer on the leaves as it can cause rot in the center of the plant.

## Propagation

Offsets, division.

## Artificial Light

500 footcandles.

## First Aid

*Mealybugs. (See *Pests*.)

*No flowers, flower buds drop, brown crisp spots, scorched edges on leaves and flowers, plants stems look weak, limp and wilted.* The problem is underwatering. Soil must be kept moist while flowering and allowed to dry between waterings at other times.

*No flowering.* This can be from neglecting the resting period, or from lack of light. They don't like direct sun but they will not grow in the dark. Keep it in bright light near a sunny window without ever being placed directly in the sun.

*Short flower stems with flowers blooming down between the leaves and soft, discolored foliage with curled leaves, brown edges.* This is the result of too cool temperatures during the development of flowers. Needs 70-degree temperatures and never below 60 to 65 degrees. Move into a warmer location out of any cold drafts.

*The plant wilts, lower leaves yellow, stems become soft and dark in color.* This is a fungus called root-rot disease which prevents the root system from absorbing water. Plant must be removed from its pot (see *Potting*). All soil has to be removed and the roots washed in warm water. Remove badly damaged roots and repot in fresh soil. The soil must be drenched with a fungicide and all damaged foliage removed. Take special care to water properly.

There are many varieties of these extremely easy-to-grow succulents from tropical Africa and Madagascar. They are popular for their unusual colored foliage. Plants will bloom in December if the length of the day is shortened during September by giving them complete darkness from 6 P.M. to 6 A.M. Here are three of the most popular varieties:

Blossfeldiana (brilliant star, Tom Thumb) has red, stiff, waxy blossoms appearing in flat-headed clusters that bloom all winter. They can grow to 15 inches. When flowers fade in the spring, the tops must be severely pruned and the plant placed in a shady window and given very little water. Resume required watering and move back into the sun in September.

Daigremontiana (mother-of-thousands) has 1- to 3-inch blue-green leaves with a reddish purple cast. The leaf edges have shallow teeth and tiny replicas of the whole plant are continuously produced between each pair of teeth. The leaves grow on slender, single stems which grow up to 18 inches tall.

Tormentosa (panda plant) has leaves 2 to 3 inches long and a light gray-green in color. They are thick and inflexible. The leaves are covered with silvery-white hairs resembling fur with brown hair markings along the edges and tips. They can grow to 2 feet tall but are usually found as a 6- to 8-inch plant.

## Location

Needs plenty of sunlight and cool temperatures.

## Soil

Two parts all-purpose soil, two parts sharp sand, one part peat moss or cactus prepackaged mixture with peat moss added.

# KALANCHOE

## Watering

Soil must be allowed to dry between thorough waterings.

## Fertilizer

Feed every six months with a cactus fertilizer which is low in nitrogen.

## Propagation

Plantlets, leaf cuttings, stem cuttings.

## Artificial Light

1,000 footcandles.

§ 127

## First Aid

*Mealybugs. (See Pests.) Do not use Malathion, for it will kill kalanchoes. Use nicotine sulfate.

*Dropping leaves.* This problem can be from too little or too much water. Treat it for too much watering first by cutting down on how often you water. If the problem continues water more often.

*Dropping leaves with a mass yellowing of foliage, rotting, wilting and bleaching of foliage. Flowers will blight and soil is constantly wet.* The problem is overwatering. The plant must be removed from the pot (see Potting) and the roots checked. Also check for proper soil and make sure that enough drainage material was used over the drainage holes. If the roots are white and healthy looking, repot in fresh soil or return to its original pot and allow the soil to dry thoroughly between waterings. If a few roots are damaged, remove them and repot in fresh soil. If all the roots are brown and mushy, the plant can not be saved, but healthy cuttings can be taken to start new plants.

*Blackened stems, rotting flower stalks, base and stems turn soft and mushy.* This is stem-rot disease and is promoted by too much humidity, overwatering and temperatures that are too high or low. First try dipping the plant in a hot bath for twenty to forty minutes. If this, along with improving its environment, doesn't help, the plant should be repotted (see Potting) in more porous soil and not planted too deep. Remove all infected parts and allow the soil to dry thoroughly between waterings. The cut wounds must be treated with a spray of a fungicide.

*Growth is soft and discolored.* The problem is too much humidity. Humidity must be cut down by moving the plant into brighter light and ventilating the growing area. Move the plant away from plants that are high-humidity lovers.

*Plant gets elongated, straggly, misshapen with underdeveloped leaves and no blooms.* This is the result of too little light. Move to full sun, add artificial light to its present light source or move closer to its artificial light source.

*Yellowing leaves that fall suddenly, with glossy, translucent plant tissue. Plant does not bloom. Rotting look.* This is due to sudden changes in temperature. The plant does best near a window where the changes in temperature are minimal. Keep the growing area well ventilated.

*No blooming during the winter.* This is probably due to improper lighting in the fall. They need to be in darkness from 6 P.M. to 6 A.M. during the month of September in order to bloom in December.

*Dark tan or black dry center spots with narrow, dark margins. The ends of the leaves can turn dark tan with darker bars crisscrossing the leaf. Tips of leaves and or leaf margins turn brown and die back.* This is a fungal disease called anthracnose. This disease is caused by high humidity. Infected leaves must be destroyed. The growing area must be well ventilated, and be sure to move the plant away from plants that love humidity. The soil must be thoroughly dry between waterings. Spray healthy leaves with a foliar fungicide.

*A gray or white feltlike coating on the foliage.* This is mildew which blocks out the light and forces the leaves to curl and shrivel. It is a parasitic organism caused by high humidity. If leaves have not been damaged, rinse them off in warm water. The damaged leaves must be removed. Increase ventilation in the growing area. Keep the plant away from high-humidity plants and give the plant more sun.

A plant from the Dutch East Indies with green foliage that has a texture like rough sandpaper. The lavender blossoms are very pungent and the fragrance can be smelled several feet away. It trails and spreads in a hanging basket very quickly until the appearance is like a cascading sheet of color. The longer stems should be pruned regularly to keep blossoming all winter. After flowering, cut back the entire plant to encourage new growth.

## Location

Needs a sunny window and adapts well to heat. Temperatures should not go below 65 degrees.

## Soil

One part all-purpose loam, one part peat moss, one part sharp sand, vermiculite or perlite. Small plants need to be repotted yearly and should be pruned severely once or twice a year.

## Watering

The soil must be kept just moist at all times but never let it remain soggy.

## Fertilizer

Feed once a month.

## Propagation

Stem cuttings.

## Artificial Light

1,000 footcandles.

## First Aid

*Mealybugs, whiteflies (See *Pests.*)

# LANTANA

*No blooms, pale or discolored leaves, a mass of yellow foliage, tips of leaves and margins turn brown and die. No new growth.* The problem is too little light. Lantanas need no less than full sun. If you can't provide this, add artificial light to their present light source or move them closer to the artificial light source.

*No blooms, yellowing leaves that fall suddenly.* This problem is usually due to improper temperatures. Temperatures must be warm, which is usually easy to manage if the plant is kept in full sun. It must be kept out of drafty areas, especially during the winter.

*No blooming, flower buds drop or the flowering period is short. Plant stems look weak, limp and wilted, brown crisp spots, scorched edges on leaves*

§ 129

*and flowers.* The problem is underwatering. Water slowly over the entire soil surface until excess water runs out of the drainage hole in the bottom.

Do not let the plant sit in the water-filled saucer for more than an hour. Before rewatering, allow the surface of the soil to feel just damp.

# LAUREL
# SWEET BAY—
# LAURUS

This is the popular bay leaf used in cooking. When young it is single-stemmed with leathery leaves. The leaves grow 3 to 4 inches long and 1 inch wide. As it matures, it usually develops multiple stems and thick foliage. It needs to be pruned to keep at a desirable height of 2 to 4 feet.

## Location

Prefers direct sunlight but will survive in bright light. It needs to be kept cool and will survive drafty places.

## Soil

One part all-purpose loam, one part peat moss, one part sharp sand, perlite or vermiculite. It can go a few years without being repotted.

## Watering

The soil must remain moist at all times without being soggy.

## Fertilizer

Every two months from spring to the middle of summer with no feeding the rest of the year.

## Propagation

Stem cuttings, air layering.

## Artificial Light

800 footcandles.

## First Aid

*Mealybugs, scales. (See *Pests*.)

*Yellowing and shedding of leaves in winter.* This is from too much water. Keep the soil barely moist. If you feel you have been watering properly, water less even if it means the soil drys out slightly between watering.

A beautiful herbaceous plant from Japan. The long-stemmed, glistening leaves are rounded, with their edges slightly scalloped. The patterns and spots on the leaves are a shimmering gold color. The plant has flowers, of the same color as the leaves, which bloom in midsummer.

## Location

Prefers filtered sunlight and needs protection from hot direct sun but can tolerate full sun in winter. Will grow well in a north window and adapts well to cool places.

## Soil

One part all-purpose soil, one part peat moss, one part perlite or vermiculite.

## Watering

Soil should be kept moist. Water slightly less in winter, if the plant is kept in a shady north window, where in cool damp weather the soil doesn't dry out quickly enough.

## Fertilizer

Feed once a month.

## Propagation

Divisions.

# LEOPARD PLANT— LIGULARIA

## Artificial Light

500 footcandles.

## First Aid

*A very easy-to-grow, problemless plant. Overwatering and underwatering don't seem to be a problem because of the durability of the plant. It can deal with a temporary change without any damage to the plant.

§ 131

# LIPSTICK VINE— AESCHYNANTHUS

A gesneriad, member of the Gesneriaceae family, a cultivated ornamental, from the Asiatic tropics. Young growth is soft and a grayish lavender color. The mature leaves are dark green and stiff-pointed. They grow opposite each other on vines. Tubular flowers grow at the tips of branches in clusters of four or more and are red or orange. The flowers bloom at all seasons. The flowers should be allowed to fall off the plant naturally as new stems grow from the places where the flowers have died.

## Location

Can tolerate morning or late-afternoon sun, but it must be protected from hot noon sun of summer. It needs a bright window for good bud formation. Can tolerate extremes in temperature.

## Soil

One part all-purpose loam, one part peat moss, one part sharp sand, perlite or vermiculite or use two parts African violet prepackaged soil with one part perlite or vermiculite.

## Watering

The surface soil should become dry between waterings and be kept completely dry during May, to allow the development of flower buds. Spray-mist daily.

## Fertilizer

Feed once a month.

## Propagation

Cuttings.

## Artificial Light

500 footcandles.

## First Aid

*Pests don't seem to bother this plant.

*An occasional dead stem.* This seems to be part of the plant's natural growth pattern. Cut it off, and new growth soon appears.

*No new growth for a while in winter.* This is due to temperatures that drop too low. Reduce watering, don't fertilize and resume proper growing requirements only when new foliage appears.

*Spindly growth.* This is natural as stems grow

older. Pinch the tips of the branches to produce new growth to make the plant look bushier.

*No blooms, buds drop, leaf tips can turn brown, yellowing leaf margins, wilting, shriveling.* These symptoms indicate low humidity. Since the plant is usually hanging, it will have to be spray misted more often and a humidifier used during the winter in the growing area.

*No blooms, pale or discolored leaves. A mass of yellow foliage, older plants shed leaves from the bottom up. New growth, if any, shrivels and dies.* These problems are caused by too little light. The plant needs a bright exposure, and artificial light can be added to its present light source. Or move the plant closer to its artificial light source.

*White salts accumulate on the soil and the pot's sides and rim. Brown crisp spots appear on leaves. Leaf edges become scorched. New growth is thick and dwarfed.* This is salt damage from fertilizer-salt buildup. Flush out excess salts by watering heavily and repeatedly until water pours out of drainage holes. Scrape any salt off the pot's rim and sides with warm water and a brush. Give the plant more light. Fertilize less frequently or cut down to half the amount you have been administering.

A twining plant that grows easily and vigorously. The shoots grow to 3 feet long. The leaves are dark green and oval in shape with a leathery texture. The fragrant, tubular, waxy white flowers grow in clusters of eight to ten in the leaf axils. The flowering period is May to October; however, they do not flower well for the first few years. The first few years, the plant does not need to be tied to stakes, but after a few years the new shoots should be tied up regularly, so the leaves and flowers can unfold freely. The flowers usually bloom at the tips of new shoots, so distribute the growth evenly over your trellising. They don't flower as well if they are allowed to grow without being stacked. They need a rest in the winter, so water less and keep the temperature cool (60 degrees).

## Location

Needs sun in winter in an east or west window but must be protected from the hot sun in summer. It likes normal room temperatures but a cool room in winter.

# MADAGASCAR JASMINE— STEPHANOTIS

§133

## Soil

One part all-purpose loam, one part peat moss, one part perlite or vermiculite.

## Watering

The soil must be moist at all times from May to October but should never be allowed to become soggy. During the winter let the soil dry between waterings. Spray-mist daily.

## Fertilizer

Feed monthly from February through October. The rest of the year refrain from feeding.

## Propagation

Stem cuttings in early spring.

## Artificial Light

500 footcandles.

## First Aid

*Scales, mealybugs, red spider mites. (See *Pests.*)

*Yellowing foliage, water stands on the soil after watering, general deterioration of the plant.* This indicates poor drainage. Remove any damaged foliage and repot (see *Potting*) in proper soil and make sure the drainage holes are covered with enough drainage material.

*Yellow spots on leaves, scorch marks on leaves that turn grayish where scorched and a general bleached-out appearance.* These symptoms indicate too much light. Either move it farther away from its light source or filter the light with a curtain.

*Failure to bloom, poor blooming, pale or discolored leaves, new growth shrivels and dies, plant becomes elongated, misshapen.* This is from too little light. Needs a very bright location but should not be subjected to the hot sun of summer.

*Poor growth and flowering.* This can be from not giving the plant a winter rest period. Water less and keep it cool.

*Poor blooming, flower buds drop or the flowering period is short. Plant stems look weak, limp and wilted. Leaves can curl under and lower leaves turn yellow with brown spots and fall.* The problem is underwatering. Water slowly over the entire soil surface until excess water runs out of the drainage hole in the bottom. Do not let the plant sit in the water-filled saucer for more than an hour. Before rewatering, allow the soil to become damp and during the winter let the soil dry between waterings.

A rhizomatous gesneriad (a member of the Gesneriaceae family that includes cultivated ornamentals) from Central America which is very easy to grow. Has cone-shaped stem tubers. Leaves are oval and serrated with a velvety texture. Both leaves and stems are purplish and covered with hairs. Flowers are bell-shaped and tubular with single or double flowers that are pink, red, violet, blue or purple and resemble the petunia. The flowering period is June through October. Achimenes are usually available as flowering plants in July and August. Some varieties make good hanging baskets.

Achimenes goes dormant in the fall, usually in September or when the foliage dries up. At that time, the plant should be kept completely dry in its own pot and kept in a cool dark place at temperatures not below 45 degrees. The tuberous roots should be repotted in February in fresh soil. Repot three to seven tubers in the same clay pot, which should be wider than it is high, and place the tubers an inch deep into the soil. Water and cover with a plastic bag, secured to the pot with a rubber band, and don't remove the cover until new growth is visible, usually three weeks to a month. When new growth appears, remove the cover a little each day to gradually accustom the plant to the air in the room. Place the plant in a sunny room but out of any direct sun and mist-spray the soil. When buds form, water properly. Sometimes the new growth is weak and needs to be tied to a support.

## Location

They need a sunny room but should be protected from direct sunlight. The temperatures should never fall below 65 degrees.

## Soil

One part peat moss, one part sharp sand or one part all-purpose loam, one part peat moss, one part sharp sand, perlite or vermiculite.

# MAGIC FLOWER— ACHIMENES

## Watering

Keep soil moist but never soggy. During dormancy keep completely dry. Needs high humidity but resents water dripping on the leaves and flowers. Put the plant on a bed of wet pebbles without the bottom of the pot touching any water.

## Fertilizer

Once a month from March through August.

## Propagation

Dividing the conelike rhizomatous roots.

## Artificial Light

500 footcandles.

## First Aid

*Aphids. (See Pests.)

*Scorch marks on leaves that turn grayish where scorched. A general bleached-out appearance. The problem is too much light. The plant needs a very sunny room but must be protected from any direct sunlight or moved farther away from its artificial light source.

*Flowers drop before they are dead. This is due to a location that is too sunny, too dark or too dry.

All growing requirements must be improved. Dropping flowers indicates neglect of the plant.

*Leaf tips turn brown, leaf margins yellow, wilting, shriveling, and buds drop. The problem is low humidity, but the plant resents being mist sprayed. Place on a bed of wet pebbles without the bottom of the pot touching the water.

*The base and stems of plant turns soft and mushy. This is stem-rot disease and is promoted by too much humidity, overwatering and changes in temperature. Repotting in fresh soil is necessary. Infected areas must be removed and the wounds sprayed with a fungicide. Give the plant better growing conditions.

# MINIATURE ROSES

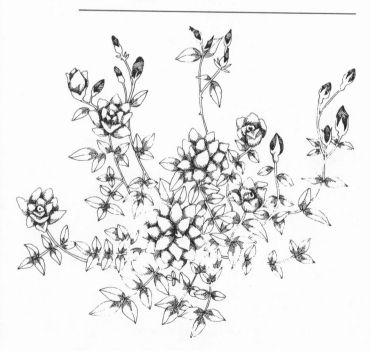

This is the only rose that can be successfully grown indoors, and its success depends on sunshine, humidity and moderate temperature. The tiny buds that develop are 3/4 inch in diameter. There are many varieties in a wide range of colors. The plant grows from 3 to 6 inches tall, although there are varieties that grow as tall as 15 inches. When purchased they should be transplanted into fresh soil (the soil they are bought in is usually the incorrect kind of soil for the plant), and blooms will appear in about six weeks. Buds do not open all at once, but slowly one after another. When flowers fade, pinch them off to promote more blooming. They bloom as long as the conditions are perfect. They grow well in terrariums.

## Location

They need the sun of a south window with good air circulation and cool temperatures (65 to 70 degrees).

## Soil

Two parts all-purpose loam, two parts peat moss, one part sharp sand. Needs ample root room. A 5-inch clay pot is the best size.

## Watering

Soil should be kept moist. Water less, prune less and give less sun in November and December. Return to proper conditions in January. Needs high humidity. Spray-mist daily and place the plant on a bed of wet pebbles without the bottom of the pot touching any water.

## Fertilizer

Feed monthly while flowering but do not overfeed.

## Propagation

Cuttings.

## Artificial Light

1,000 footcandles.

## First Aid

*Miniature roses are commonly afflicted with pests. Spider mites, thrips, leaf rollers. (See *Pests*.) They should be sprayed with a diluted insecticide weekly to keep them under control.

*Curling of leaves and a gray or white feltlike coating on foliage.* This is mildew, a parasitic organism. It is the result of high humidity and cold drafts. Lower the humidity and have good air circulation without cold drafts. Remove damaged leaves. Rinsing foliage in warm water may prevent the necessity to remove any foliage unless the leaves have already been damaged.

*Black, brown or yellow damp or blistered spots, usually with yellow margins.* The problem is leaf-spot disease and it is caused by poor air circulation, high humidity, overwatering, chilling, low light. Temperature, light and ventilation need to be increased, and soil must dry out before rewatering. Infected areas should be removed and remaining foliage sprayed with a fungicide. Resume proper care.

*Water stands on the soil, wilting, slow growth, yellowing of leaves with rapid loss of older leaves.* This is improper drainage. Repot in proper soil and make sure enough drainage material is covering the drainage holes. Remove damaged foliage and resume proper care.

*Leaves curl under and lower leaves shrivel and turn yellow with brown spots. Brown crisp spots, scorched edges on leaves and flowers. Flower buds drop or the flowering period is short.* The problem is underwatering. Plant must always be kept moist except during November and December when the soil should dry between thorough waterings.

*Rotting, wilting and bleaching foliage. A mass yellowing and dropping of leaves. Leaves can curl, tips turn brown and die back. New growth is weak. Flowers will blight and soil is constantly wet.* The problem is overwatering. The plant must be removed from the pot (see *Potting*) and the roots checked. Also check the drainage to make sure there is enough drainage material. If the roots are white and healthy looking, put the plant back in its pot, stir the surface soil gently with a fork to promote aeration and allow to dry according to proper watering requirements. Or you can repot in fresh soil. Remove all damaged foliage. If roots are partially brown, cut them away and repot in fresh soil. If all roots are brown and mushy, the plant can not be saved, but cuttings can be taken to start new plants.

# MOSES-IN-A-BOAT
# MOSES-IN-A-CRADLE
# MAN-IN-A-BOAT—RHOEO

An easy-to-grow plant from Mexico and Florida. The 8- to 15-inch, glossy, deep green and purple, stiff, swordlike leaves have bright purple undersides. The plant grows in rosettes with the leaves growing from the center of the short stem. It quickly grows many offshoots and soon becomes a very bushy plant. The tuberlike white flowers are half-hidden between two, purple, boat-shaped bracts, which look like flowers but are the leaflike part of the flower with the actual flower growing in the center of these bracts. *Rhoeo* grows to a foot tall.

## Location

Needs full sun in winter but protection from hot sun from March to September. Not dependent on full

sun to grow, will also grow in bright light. Likes average room temperatures but keep away from cold windows in winter.

## Soil

One part all-purpose loam, one part peat moss, one part sharp sand, perlite or vermiculite.

## Watering

Keep the soil moist at all times, but water less in winter. Spray-mist daily.

## Fertilizer

Feed every two weeks during the summer, once a month during the winter.

## Propagation

Offsets, division, seeds, cuttings.

## Artificial Light

400 footcandles.

## First Aid

*Pests don't seem to bother this plant.

*Plant becomes straggly as it grows older.  Older plants seem to naturally deteriorate. Propagate new plants.

*Leaf tips turn brown, yellowing leaf margins, stunted or no new growth, wilting, shriveling and dropping of buds.  The problem is low humidity. Spray-mist daily and place the plant on a bed of wet pebbles without the bottom of the pot touching any water and use a humidifier during the winter.

*Leaves curl under and lower leaves turn yellow

with brown spots and fall. *Brown crisp spots, scorched edges on leaves and flowers. Dark, undersized leaves with loss of older ones.* This is the result of underwatering. Water slowly over the entire soil surface until excess water runs out of the drainage hole in the bottom. Do not let the plant sit in the water-filled saucer for more than an hour. Before rewatering, allow the soil to be just damp. During the winter, allow the soil to dry out completely before rewatering.

A miniature evergreen from South Africa related to the silver fir, which grows to 200 feet in its natural habitat. The branches are arranged on symmetrical tiers and grow up a central stalk at regular intervals. A year's growth includes a new tier, usually of six branches, and the distance between each tier is approximately 6 inches. Branches are thickly covered with bright green, furry, ½-inch needles. The needles are soft and pliable when touched. To keep the plant from growing too tall, keep it very pot-bound.

## Location

In winter they can tolerate full sun but need to be protected from any sun during the summer. Northeast, northwest or north window. They do not like high temperatures—60 to 70 degrees in summer, 40 to 50 degrees during the winter. Don't buy araucarias if your room is always warm.

## Soil

They grow well in many soils. One part all-purpose loam, one part peat moss, one part sharp sand, perlite or vermiculite, or use African violet soil prepackaged with a large handful of sharp sand, perlite or vermiculite to improve drainage. Use one part peat moss, one part sharp sand. Repot at three- to four-year intervals and only when very overcrowded. Be careful not to plant too deep.

## Watering

Allow the soil to remain dry one day between thorough waterings. Needs high humidity. Place on

# NORFOLK ISLAND PINE— ARAUCARIA

a bed of wet pebbles without bottom of the pot touching any water and spray-mist twice a day.

## Fertilizer

Feed every three months.

## Propagation

Cuttings of branches will take root, but new growth will grow sideways rather than upward. Cuttings in

August or November from the top, but original plant's shape will be ruined. The top can be removed with two rings of branches but not immediately under a ring of branches in order to avoid wounds. The cuttings should be coated with a rooting medium and allowed to dry out for one day. Place the cuttings in a rooting medium and cover with plastic. Treat like cuttings.

## Artificial Light

400 footcandles.

## First Aid

*Mealybugs. (See Pests.)

*Green tiers will drop one by one, browning needles falling and leaving behind bald branches. These problems are caused from dry soil, dry air, lack of good air circulation or too warm temperatures. Allow the soil to remain dry only one day between waterings, place on a bed of wet pebbles without the bottom of the pot touching any water. Spray twice daily and use a humidifier during the winter. Improve the air circulation and keep the plant cool.

# OLIVE—OLEA

A very durable indoor plant. The leathery leaves grow 1 to 3 inches long and the plant occasionally has tiny, fragrant white flowers. The blossoms are so hard to pollinate that fruit is rarely produced indoors. They grow very tall, but you can pinch off the tips of long stems to keep it bushy. It's desirable to prune drastically in early spring to promote strong new growth. Their growth is very slow in winter while resting.

In order to grow olive pits, two or three black-olive pits can be planted in loose soil in a 5-inch pot. Water and cover with plastic. Keep the medium moist. It takes up to three months to germinate. When they start to grow, repot using proper soil for olive plants. Spray-mist and give it lots of light and a warm room and let the soil dry one day between waterings.

## Location

They like direct sun but will thrive in a bright location. They tolerate temperatures as low as 15 degrees in winter and as high as 100 degrees during their active growing period.

### Soil

One part all-purpose loam, one part peat moss, one part sharp sand, perlite or vermiculite. *Olea* should remain very pot-bound before transplanting into a larger pot.

### Watering

Allow the soil to remain dry for one day between thorough waterings, but allow to remain dry a little longer during the winter depending on how cloudy and damp the weather is.

### Fertilizer

Feed once in early spring and once in early summer.

### Propagation

Stem cuttings.

### Artificial Light

800 footcandles.

### First Aid

*A problemless plant. Because it tolerates so many diverse conditions, it is not prone to attack by any pests or susceptible to any problems. If a problem should occur, check general problems in Part Three of this book.

---

The orange tree is from tropical regions. When purchased they usually have fruit on the tree and are very expensive, but it can last a lifetime if not longer. It's an evergreen with shiny, leathery leaves. The flowers are pink-tinged and smell like orange blossoms. They remain open for weeks on the plant. The golden-orange fruits follow after artificial cross-pollination is performed. Hand-pollinate using a small brush and spread the powdery pollen from one flower onto the stigma of another. Pollinate only when the stigma is moist and sticky. Flowers and fruit can appear at the same time, and pollination should be constant. The fruit remains bright orange for weeks, but their taste is so tart that they are not edible. A second flowering can occur in Autumn, but if pollinated, these fruits will take nearly a year to mature. The spring flowering will take less time to have full-grown fruits. A light pruning for symmetry, cutting out only any extra-long shoots, should be performed in early spring. The plant can grow 1 to 3 feet tall.

# ORANGE TREE—CITRUS

§ 141

## Location

Needs full sun. In summer it must be placed by an open window to get the necessary ventilation. It cannot tolerate heat and needs a cool location year round. During the winter it likes 40 to 50 degrees at night.

## Soil

Acid soil. One part all-purpose loam, one part peat moss, one part sharp sand. It likes to be pot-bound and at three years old it will probably need a 11-inch pot. The plant needs to be potted firmly; ram the pot soil around the sides hard.

## Watering

Keep the soil moist while flowering; at other times let it dry between thorough waterings. Never spray-mist the plant while flowering, but at other times it will benefit the plant.

## Fertilizer

While flowering and while fruit is developing, use an acid fertilizer every three weeks. Nitrogen content of fertilizer should not be too high. Don't feed at other times.

## Propagation

Cuttings taken from half-ripened wood of plants that have already had fruit. They need some kind of bottom heat to root, either a hot radiator or special equipment from a nursery can be purchased to provide this kind of heat. Seeds from store-bought oranges. Some seed won't germinate if oranges have been treated in any way.

## Artificial Light

1,000 footcandles.

## First Aid

*Aphids, mealybugs, spider mites, scales, nematodes, thrips, whiteflies. (See *Pests*.)

*Dark tan or black dry center spots with narrow, dark margins. The ends of the leaves can turn dark tan with darker bars crisscrossing the leaf. Tips of leaves and or leaf margins turn brown and die back.* This is anthracnose disease and is caused by high humidity or sudden chilling. Infected leaves must be destroyed. Keep the plant fairly dry. Avoid cold drafts while keeping the area well ventilated. The healthy leaves need to be sprayed with a foliar fungicide. When the disease has cleared up, resume proper watering.

*A black coating on leaves.* This is sooty mold but is not a disease parasite. It is attracted to honeydew secretions of insects or develops from very humid conditions. The leaves should be washed with soapy water. Increase air circulation in the growing area. Check for insects.

*Failure to flower, dropping of buds, flowers and small fruit. Pale or discolored leaves. A mass of yellow foliage, tips of leaves and margins turn brown and die. Older plants shed leaves from the bottom up, underdeveloped leaves.* All these problems are due to lack of light. The citrus needs full sun, no less.

*Failure to flower, dropping of buds, flowers and small fruit. Soft and discolored foliage, lower leaves turn yellow with brown spots, dry edges curl under, drying foliage from the base upward, dropping older leaves.* The problem is temperatures that are too warm. Needs to be kept cool near an open window during the summer and kept in a cool location without cold drafts, but good air circulation during the winter.

*Yellowing of top leaves or yellow margins, discolored leaves, retarded growth.* This is an iron or magnesium deficiency. The citrus needs to be fed an acid fertilizer every three weeks. If the symptoms persist, perhaps feeding every two weeks will be necessary.

*Dropping of buds, flowers and small fruit, plant stems look weak, limp and wilted. Leaves curl under and lower leaves turn yellow with brown spots and fall.* The problem is underwatering. Water slowly over the entire soil surface until excess water runs out of the drainage hole in the bottom. Do not let the plant sit in the water-filled saucer for more than an hour. Before rewatering, allow the soil to become damp while flowering; at other times let it dry out.

---

There are over thirty thousand species, and each species has many varieties. They are found in open fields, under waterfalls, next to streams, in the tops of trees and high in the mountains. Some are epiphytes that receive nourishment and moisture from the air and debris on tree limbs, and grow clinging to trees by their roots. Others grow in soil where their roots are always damp but never wet and they are called terrestrial. It is necessary to find out the exact requirements for the orchid you have purchased, because there are no set conditions which suit them all. Begin growing the easy types such as the cattleya (lavender and white florist orchid) or the cypripedium, which is long lasting. Actually they aren't any more difficult to grow than the philodendron, a companion of orchids in their native habitat.

## Location

In order to manufacture plant food, orchids need sunlight, direct sunlight in winter, a south or west window. Must be protected from hot sun from April to October, given a north or east window. During winter days the temperature should range from 68 to 80 degrees. They need night winter temperatures of 60 degrees. Most orchids will grow where a

# ORCHID—ORCHIDACEAE

day and night temperature averages 70 degrees. If proper light is given, leaves will grow upright and will be a dark green color. Too much sun produces leaves of a light green color and injures the leaf tissue. Too little sun produces horizontal growth to the leaves. They need good air circulation.

## Soil

Most orchids are grown successfully in chopped or shredded bark, fir, pine, cedar or birch bark or osmundine, which is the roots of the osmund fern. Potting material must be coarse. Fast drainage and good ventilation are necessary to allow the roots to dry out between waterings. Repotting is usually necessary only every two or three years. When roots extend over the pot from the base of the new growth, it is then necessary to repot. Remove the plant from its pot and take out all the potting medium. With a sharp knife cut away all brown, dead roots. Fill the new pot one-third full of crocking. Place small pieces of the new medium on top of the crocking to fill the pot half way. Place the plant in position and slowly insert the medium until the plant is held tightly in place. Use a wooden stick for packing in the medium. There are clay pots especially designed for orchids since they need exceptionally fast drainage.

## Watering

You must always remember that not all orchids require the same watering. The following are generalities. The plant will survive under these, but it's best to find out the exact requirements when purchased. Too much or too little water is detrimental, but overwatering is deadly. The medium must be thoroughly dry between waterings. They prefer to be quickly dipped into water rather than soaked. Plants growing in osmundine need less watering than the ones grown in bark. They need a humidity of 70 percent. Spray-mist daily and put them on a bed of wet pebbles without the bottom of the pot touching the water.

## Fertilizer

They are not heavy feeders. Once a month if using osmundine, every three weeks when bark is used. Use 30-10-10 or 23-19-17 plant food. There are fertilizers made especially for orchids.

## Propagation

Division.

## Artificial Light

650 footcandles.

## First Aid

*Spider mites, scales, thrips, sow bugs, centipedes. (See Pests.) Kelthane is advisable to use on orchids instead of Malathion.

*Orchid's leaves turn yellow-green and appear very thin.* This is probably from too much fertilizer. Repot in fresh medium but give the roots a good rinse in warm water first. Hereafter, feed only once a month with an orchid fertilizer.

*Large brownish black spots form suddenly on the leaves.* If the spots are hard, too much sun is the villain. Protect the plant with a curtain or move it to a less bright location. If the spots are soft, a fungus is to blame. The spots must be carefully cut out with a knife going well behind the affected area. Treat the wound with a fungicide.

*A fungus develops at the points where the orchid flower has been cut off.* This is from leaving too much of the flower sheath when a flower is cut. The plant can be killed if the disease is not cut out and treated with a fungicide. When cutting flowers, remove as much of the sheath as possible.

Palms come from all over the world. There are more than one thousand tropical and subtropical varieties. The leaves are usually in the shape of feathers or fans and divided into many leaflets. They grow outward from a single long, flexible stem. They do not branch, and the stem will die if the terminal of the stem is injured or removed. They have no real rest period, but growth slows down during the winter. Culture requirements are the same all year except for fertilizing.

## Location

Filtered sun or bright light, but should never be exposed to direct sunlight. They need warm temperatures and must be kept away from cold drafts during the winter.

## Soil

One part all-purpose loam, one part peat moss, one part sharp sand. They need to be pot-bound. When repotting use deep narrow pots, so the aerial roots are not too high. Planting must be firm. Ram the soil in carefully around the edges.

## Watering

Palms need to be kept moist at all times. Water slightly less during the short days of winter. Mist-spray daily.

## Fertilizer

Once every two months, April to October. No feeding during the winter. Feed with an acid fertilizer at every other feeding.

## Propagation

Seeds, but it can take years to grow suitable plants.

# PALM—PALMACEAE

## Artificial Light

400 footcandles.

## First Aid

*Mealybugs, scales, spider mites. (See *Pests*.)

*Tips of leaves or whole leaves turn brown and dry up, rotting, wilting and bleaching of foliage.* The problem is overwatering. The plant must be removed from the pot (see *Potting*) and the roots checked. Also check for proper soil and enough drainage material over the drainage holes. If the roots are white and healthy, either put back into its pot or repot in fresh soil. Remove all damaged leaves, increase humidity and water slightly less. If the roots are partially brown, cut them off and repot in fresh soil. If all the roots are brown and mushy, discard the plant.

*The palm takes on a yellow appearance.* This is

§ 145

usually from underwatering or lack of light. Water slowly over the entire soil surface until excess water runs out of the drainage hole in the bottom. Never allow the plant to sit in the water-filled saucer for more than an hour. The plant should always be kept moist except during the winter when it should dry out slightly. Move the plant closer to its light source without exposing it to direct sunlight.

*Only the tips of the leaves turn brown.* This is from dry air and underwatering. If the plant dries out only once, the brown spots appear and they never disappear. Plant must be kept moist, drying out slightly in winter. Mist-spray daily.

*Dried tips.* This can be caused also by fertilizer damage. This occurs because palms are usually kept in plastic pots, which are best for palms, but they accumulate salts which cannot be seen. Water heavily twice to flush out salts. Fertilize less frequently or half the regular amount and give the plant more light without sunlight.

*Dried tips.* This can also be caused by constant touching and brushing against the foliage. In this case give the plant more space in which to grow.

*The roots lift the plant above the soil level.* This indicates a need for more root space. This is characteristic, but as long as two or three new leaves develop yearly and they are as healthy as the earlier ones, do not shift to a new pot.

*Yellowing of top leaves or yellow margins, discolored leaves, retarded growth.* This is an iron or magnesium deficiency. Palms need slightly acid soil. Use a fertilizer for acid-loving plants every other feeding.

*Dark tan or black dry center spots with narrow, dark margins. Tips of leaves and or leaf margins turn brown and die back.* This is anthracnose disease and is caused from high humidity or sudden chilling. Infected leaves must be destroyed. To cure this disease, grow plant on the damp side, almost dry, and avoid mist spraying until the disease is cleared up. The growing area should be well ventilated without any cold drafts. The healthy leaves need to be sprayed with a foliar fungicide.

*Black, brown or yellow damp or blistered spots with yellow margins.* This is leaf-spot disease and is caused by poor air circulation, high humidity, overwatering, chilling, low light. All growing requirements must be improved. Infected areas should be removed and the remaining leaves sprayed with a fungicide. Allow the soil to become almost dry before rewatering.

*Top growth wilts, new growth dies back, yellow lower leaves, stems can become soft and dark in color.* This is root-rot disease which prevents the roots from absorbing water. Plant must be removed from the pot (see *Potting*). Remove all soil and wash the roots in warm water and repot in fresh soil. Remove damaged foliage and water plant only enough to keep the plant from wilting. Drench the soil with a fungicide. Once the plant has resumed normal growth, water regularly but only enough to keep the soil moist.

A South African succulent that looks like small stones and pebbles and adopts the coloring of stones and pebbles. Their leaves grow in pairs split by a central fissure from which large anemonelike flowers emerge annually, often in August. Lithops usually grow in thick clumps, and the growing period is mainly in summer and autumn. At the top of the thick, flat, nearly spherical leaves is an area through which the plant absorbs light into the photosynthetic tissue that nourishes each leaf, even when nearly covered with sand. They grow from 1 inch to 3 inches tall, and most species are easy to care for.

## Location

They can tolerate full sun, but slightly broken sunlight gives the best results. They can tolerate extremes in temperature.

## Soil

One part all-purpose soil, one part sharp sand with a handful of peat moss added or use three parts all-purpose loam, one part sharp sand with a handful of peat moss added. Prepackaged cactus soil with a handful of peat moss added can also be used. They live for many years in the same pot and should never be repotted unless absolutely necessary. When you do repot, always put a few of them, even of different species, in one larger pot rather than each one in a tiny pot.

## Watering

Never totally saturate the soil or allow water to stand on any part of the plant. During the winter, water once a month unless the plant shrivels, in which case give it a few drops of water. Never water on cloudy or wet days.

# PEBBLE PLANT—LITHOPS

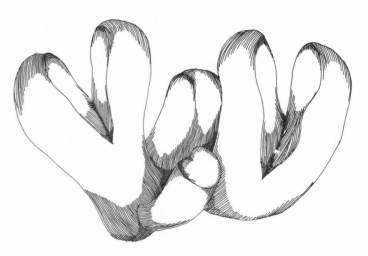

## Fertilizer

Once every spring.

## Propagation

Seeds purchased from a nursery.

## Artificial Light

800 footcandles.

## First Aid

*Very rarely attacked by pests.

*Plant turns soft and mushy.* The greatest and only problem that seems to affect lithops. This is stem-rot disease, a fungus. It spreads quickly and is promoted by overwatering, high humidity, too high or too low temperatures. Repot in dry soil and remove infected leaves. Dust wounds with a fungicide. The plant likes to be dry, and you should only give it dribbles of water at each watering. Lithops need to have a layer of pebbles between the base of the plant and the surface of soil to prevent wet soil from touching the foliage. They can't tolerate being wet or even being near water but of course they need some moisture to keep alive. Avoid humidity and never grow them near foliaged plants that like humidity. Grow them with other cacti.

# PEPEROMIA

A small plant with many species. Some are succulent while others are semisucculent. All are from tropical South America and are of the pepper family. Some species trail, some grow erect or form clusters. They range from small-leafed vines to large-leafed bushes. Some have woody trunks and branches while others send out leaves from a main central core. Foliage ranges from solid shiny green to variegated and fleshy. The blunt-leaved plants are easy to grow. They have roundish leaves with a smooth texture and are irregularly edged with creamy white. All peperomias have tiny bisexual flowers growing atop a spike and they look like mouse tails. When a flower matures it will bend over and snap at the axil, for easy picking off. They grow up to 12 inches tall, which makes them perfect for windowsill culture.

## Location

They do best in bright indirect or curtain-filtered sunlight but they will adapt to a north exposure easily. They need a warm room in winter and must never be near cold drafts.

## Soil

One part all-purpose loam, one part peat moss, one part sharp sand, perlite or vermiculite. They rarely outgrow their pot.

## Watering

They are semisucculent naturally, and the soil should become dry between thorough waterings. Water less in winter. They rest but don't lose foliage while doing so. Spray-mist daily.

## Fertilizer

Feed monthly while strong growth.

## Propagation

Full-grown leaf complete with stem, stem cuttings, dividing crown of old plants. Rooting can be very slow, so be patient.

## Artificial Light

400 footcandles.

## First Aid

*Aphids, spider mites. (See *Pests*.)

*Loss of leaves.*   This will happen if the temperature is too cool. They need temperatures 60 to 65 degrees year round.

*Older, lower leaves will yellow.*   This is natural aging. To remove, pinch off the leaf, leaving the stem to die back on its own. This occurs in a few day. Then you can lift the stem off without injury to the rest of the plant.

*Weak new growth, old leaves turn yellow, wilting and darkening of leaves and a rotting look. Flowers blight and soil is always wet. Scablike swelling on the undersurface of leaves.*   These problems indicate overwatering. The plant must be removed from the pot (see *Potting*), and a root check must take place. Also make sure the plant has the proper soil and the proper drainage material covering the drainage holes. If the roots are white and healthy, repot in fresh soil, removing all damaged foliage and allowing the soil to dry between waterings. If partial browning of the roots, remove them and repot in fresh soil. If all the roots are brown and mushy, the plant can not be saved.

*Dark tan or black dry center spots with narrow, dark margins. The ends of the leaves can turn dark tan with darker bars crisscrossing the leaf. Tips of leaves and or leaf margins turn brown and die back.*   This is anthracnose disease and is caused from sudden chilling. Infected leaves must be destroyed. The growing area should be well ventilated to prevent recurrence of disease, but keep the plant out of cold drafts. The healthy leaves need to be sprayed with a foliar fungicide.

*Black, brown, or yellow damp or blistered spots, usually with yellow margins.*   This is leaf-spot disease and is caused by poor air circulation, high humidity, overwatering, chilling, low light. All conditions must be improved. Infected areas should be removed. Spray remaining leaves with a fungicide.

# PEPPER
# CHRISTMAS PEPPER—
# CAPSICUM

A plant with many varieties from Brazil which is sold around Christmastime. It's an evergreen shrub covered with cone-shaped, 1-inch fruit in colors of yellow, purple or red. The peppers are hot but edible and with little care will remain on the plant for months. Plant can grow up to 15 inches tall. The tall branches should be cut back to give the plant a nice shape. After the fruiting period is over, the plant should be cut back to half its previous size and repotted in fresh soil. The roots should not be allowed to extend over the edge of the pot while it is in full growth or there will be a strong leaf growth and the flowers will not set fruit. Turning the plant regularly will prevent this from happening. To help the plant set fruit, be careful not to overwater during August and September, while it is in its flowering period. At the end of September the tips of the

branches should be pinched to prevent fuller growth and thereby produce better fruit.

## Location

Likes full sun or a bright window. Needs a cool place except when it fruits. A warm room will help hold fruit longer.

## Soil

One part all-purpose loam, one part peat moss, one part sharp sand.

## Watering

When in fruit, keep the soil constantly moist. Other times of the year let it barely dry on the surface between thorough waterings. Spray-mist daily.

## Propagation

Seeds.

## Artificial Light

800 footcandles.

## First Aid

*Aphids, spider mites and its worst enemy—whiteflies. (See *Pests*.)

*No peppers form.* This is due to a lack of light. Needs very strong light or full sun to flower and subsequently form fruit.

*Pale or discolored leaves. A mass of yellow foliage, tips of leaves and margins turn brown and die. Older plants shed leaves from the bottom up. No new growth, or new growth that shrivels and* dies. Soft and discolored growth, no blooming, dropping of buds. The problem is lack of light. The plant needs very bright light or full sun. Move closer to artificial lights or add artificial light to its present window light.

*Fruit shrivels and buds can drop, leaf tips turn brown, yellowing leaf margins, stunted or no new growth, wilting, shriveling. The problem is low humidity. Place the pot on a bed of wet pebbles without the bottom of the pot touching any water and spray-mist daily. Use a humidifier during the winter.

*Soft, discolored foliage with curled leaves, brown edges. This is the result of cold drafts. This plant can tolerate cold but must be moved away from any drafty window during the winter.

*Plant stems look weak, limp and wilted. Dropping of buds, with scorched edges on both leaves and flowers. Leaves curl under and lower leaves turn yellow with brown spots and fall. This is under-watering. Water slowly over the entire soil surface until excess water runs out of the drainage hole in the bottom. Do not let the plant sit in the water-filled saucer for more than an hour. When in fruit, allow the soil to become just barely damp before rewatering. At other times of the year allow the soil to become dry on the surface.

---

# PHILODENDRON

There are hundreds of species of philodendron from tropical America. They come in all shapes and sizes. Some are vines that climb with their aerial roots. Others have their leaves on long stems growing directly from the soil with large aerial roots that grow out of the soil and can lift the plant right out of its pot. These aerial roots should never be removed. They do not hurt the plant, and even if the plant is lifted out of the soil, it is not injurious unless it goes to extremes. The most common philodendrons are the heart-shaped vines. They do flower but are shy bloomers in the living room.

### Location

They like sun during the winter but can not tolerate sun during the warm months and must be protected or moved away from direct sunlight in the summer. They do, however, need bright light.

### Soil

One part all-purpose loam, one part peat moss, one part sharp sand with added wood shavings, char-

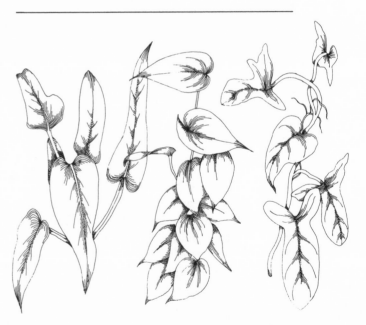

coal, vermiculite or perlite. They seldom need re-potting, but every year the top 2 inches of soil should be replaced with fresh soil.

§ 151

## Watering

If the soil is on the dense side, it should be allowed to dry between thorough waterings. If you have repotted your plant into loose soil, it can tolerate a lot of water and can be kept moist at all times. If your plant is climbing on bark, the bark should be sprayed daily to ensure the roots clinging to the bark can draw water to keep the leaves healthy. Spray-mist daily.

## Fertilizer

Once every two months.

## Propagation

Stem cuttings, leaf cuttings with long stems, air layering, layering.

## Artificial Light

400 footcandles.

## First Aid

*Mealybugs, red spider mites, aphids. (See *Pests*.)

*A mass yellowing and dropping of leaves. Rotting, wilting and bleaching of foliage. Leaves can curl, tips turn brown and die back. New growth is weak.* The problem is overwatering. The plant must be removed from the pot (see *Potting*) and the roots checked. Also, check for proper soil and proper drainage material over the drainage holes. If the roots are white and healthy, repot in fresh soil, remove damaged foliage and water as required. If partial root decay has taken place, remove the damaged roots and repot in fresh soil. If all the roots are brown and mushy, the plant can not be saved.

*Plant stems look weak, limp and wilted. Leaves curl under and lower leaves turn yellow with brown spots and fall. Dark, undersized leaves with loss of older ones.* The problem is underwatering. Water slowly over the entire soil surface until excess water runs out of the drainage hole in the bottom. Do not let the plant sit in the water-filled saucer for more than an hour. Before rewatering, allow the soil to dry out enough to meet its proper requirements.

*Browning at tips and edges of leaves.* This can be due to the plant being pot-bound. Repot.

*The plant shows all the signs of overwatering, but you have been watering properly.* The problem is probably improper soil. The plant should be repotted in more porous soil.

*Leaves get smaller and smaller and farther apart on the stems. Leaves become pale or discolored. Older plants shed leaves from the bottom up. No new growth.* This indicates too little light. The plant can not tolerate sun but does need bright light. Add artificial light to its present light source or move closer to its artificial light source.

*Limp, weak yellowish color, scorch marks.* The problem is too much light. Move the plant out of the sun or farther away from its artificial light source.

*Leaf tips turn brown, leaf margins yellow, stunted or no new growth, wilting, shriveling, and new leaves are very small.* The problem is low humidity. Spray-mist daily and use a humidifier during the winter.

*Soft and discolored foliage, lower leaves turn yellow with brown spots, dry edges curl under, drying foliage from the base upward, leaves get smaller and smaller and grow farther apart. These symptoms indicate too much warmth. The air must circulate freely around the growing area and the plant must be kept away from hot radiators during the winter.

*A pale, bleached coloring. Yellowing or yellow spots on leaves, usually beginning on the outer edges and spreading to the whole leaf. Older leaves will drop, there is a reduction in leaf size. The problem is too little fertilizer. Feed every other month. If you have been feeding every other month, try feeding monthly.

*Small leaf growth. This can also be due to improper soil. Repot in fresh, loose soil.

*Base and stems of plant turn soft and mushy. This is stem-rot disease and is promoted by too much humidity, overwatering and changes in temperatures. Repotting is necessary. Infected areas must be removed and the wounds need to be sprayed with a fungicide. Give the plant a better growing environment.

From western North America the piggyback plant has broad, attractive, heart-shaped leaves. They are many pointed and are nearly stemless. The leaves are covered with a delicate, downy fuzz. Tiny light green plantlets are carried piggyback on the surface of the darker green older leaves. They have green flowers but rarely bloom indoors. *Tolmiea* grows to 8 inches tall and 15 inches wide and develops into a bushy beauty.

## Location

It will tolerate partial sun but does very well in the bright light of a north window. It does not like to be hot, so a shaded location is best.

## Soil

One part all-purpose loam, one part peat moss, one part sharp sand, perlite or vermiculite.

## Watering

Keep the soil moist at all times without allowing it to become soggy.

# PIGGYBACK PLANT— TOLMIEA

## Fertilizer

Feed once a month.

## Propagation

Plant the stem of the parent leaf bearing the tiny plantlets up to its base in ordinary soil. Treat like a leaf cutting, and soon the plantlet will take root.

## Artificial Light

400 footcandles.

## First Aid

*Mealybugs, whiteflies. (See *Pests*.)

*Scorch marks on leaves turning grayish where scorched, looks generally bleached-out in appearance. Becomes limp, shrivels, and dies.* The problem is too much light. Can not tolerate hot sun and needs a shady location with bright light.

*Pale or discolored leaves. A mass of yellow foliage, tips of leaves and margins turn brown and die. Older plants shed leaves from the bottom up. No new growth.* The problem is too little light. Needs a shady spot but should not be in the dark. It needs bright light away from any direct sun.

*Plant stems look weak, limp and wilted, leaves curl under and lower leaves turn yellow with brown spots and fall.* The problem is underwatering and watering improperly. Water slowly over the entire soil surface until excess water runs out of the drainage hole in the bottom. Do not let the plant sit in the water-filled saucer for more than an hour. Before rewatering, allow the soil to become damp but never dry. If this plant is allowed to wilt too many times, it will die.

# PINK POLKA-DOT PLANT— HYPOESTIS

A very attractive plant from Madagascar that has a few varieties. The plant has dark green, oval, pointed leaves with tiny, pink-colored spots. They grow rapidly up to 20 inches tall and need to be pruned frequently. The stems of the plant are very wiry. Sometimes after a strong growing period it may die back, but pruning drastically will promote strong new growth. There are species with white markings and fiery red veins on dark green leaves.

## Location

Needs filtered sunlight or very bright light to bring out the colorful spots. It will grow in a shaded area but the leaves will be solid green.

## Soil

One part all-purpose loam, one part peat moss, one part sharp sand with a small amount of perlite or vermiculite added. Repot annually in new soil, but not necessarily a new pot.

## Watering

Keep plant moist at all times except after the plant dies back. During this period withhold watering except when the soil becomes very dry. Spray-mist daily.

## Fertilizer

Once a month while growing, do not feed the rest of the year.

## Propagation

Stem cuttings.

---

An extremely durable plant with many dark green or yellowish green leaves with the underneath a bluish green. The leaves are slender, about 1/4 inch wide and up to 3 inches long, with a leathery appearance. The leaves grow on woody stems. A podocarpus will develop into a beautiful bush if pruned regularly.

## Location

It prefers bright light or indirect sunlight. Cool temperatures make it happy but it is almost immune to heat or cold.

## Soil

One part all-purpose loam, one part peat moss, one part perlite or vermiculite. Prefers acid soil.

## Watering

Soil should be kept moist but never wet.

## Artificial Light

800 footcandles.

## First Aid

*A virtually problemless plant that doesn't seem to be attacked by pests unless other plants are badly infected and they spread.

*Plant dies back and loses its leaves.* This is natural. Prune back drastically, and new growth will soon appear.

*Plant becomes leggy and bare at its base.* This is a natural growth pattern. Constant pruning will prevent this from being too noticeable, because the plant will develop into a bushy plant.

---

# PODOCARPUS

## Fertilize

Once a month. Every other month use a plant food for acid-loving plants.

## Propagation

Stem cuttings.

## Artificial Light

400 footcandles.

## First Aid

*Mealybugs, spider mites, nematodes, scales. (See Pests.)

*Discolored leaves, yellowing of top leaves or yellow margins, retarded growth.* This is an iron or magnesium deficiency. The peat moss in the soil is an acid substance, but it also acts as a buffer to absorb both excess acid and alkaline elements. Therefore it is necessary to feed the plant an acid fertilizer every other month.

*Soft and discolored foliage, lower leaves turn yellow with brown spots, dry edges curl under, drying foliage from the base upward.* This is the result of temperatures that are too warm. Podocarpuses are almost immune to heat or cold, but if the plant has a hot radiator blowing on it, these symptoms will appear. Move to a better location.

# POINSETTIA—EUPHORBIA

Poinsettia is a succulent. When buying the plant around the December holidays, pick a plant which has abundant dark green foliage. The red leaves are bracts, not flowers. They surround the tiny flowers in the center which are green or red button-shaped. The flowers should be a good size with little or no pollen showing. When brought home, care must be taken not to shift the plant around. Injury to the stems will cause the milky white poisonous sap to run out. Most plants are discarded after the holidays, but it is possible to keep them over for another year. Stop watering when the bracts fall. All leaves will now be lost, and the plant should be cut back to 3 or 4 inches, treating all wounds with powdered charcoal. The plant must be kept in a warm, shaded place and kept constantly dry. In April repot carefully in its required soil. Place it back in a sunny window or bright light and water sparingly at first. As new growth appears, water according to its requirements and feed weekly. In order to set buds and produce flowers in December, they must be on a long night schedule with short days beginning in September and ending late November or the beginning of December.

The poinsettia should be in total darkness (even car lights, lamplight, night light, streetlights will affect it) from 5 P.M. to 8 A.M. the next morning. The temperature should be maintained around 60 degrees after the beginning of September with a leeway of a few degrees below or above. Higher temperatures will prevent setting of buds, and the plant will not flower until January or later. Fertilizing weekly will help the plant to flower.

## Location

Indirect sunlight, filtered sunlight, but it must have six hours of bright light daily to survive. Day temperatures should be 70 degrees and not less than 60 degrees at night. Temperatures below 50 degrees cause problems.

## Soil

Two parts all-purpose loam, two parts sharp sand, one part peat moss.

## Watering

The surface of the soil should be barely dry between thorough waterings. Spray-mist daily.

## Fertilizer

Feed weekly when flowering at half the recommended dosage on the label.

## Propagation

Stem cuttings can be taken through August and still make fine Christmas flowers.

## Artificial Light

800 footcandles.

## First Aid

*Mealybugs, root aphids. (See *Pests*.)

*Yellowing leaves that fall suddenly with glossy, translucent plant tissue, no flowering.* The problem is sudden changes in temperature. Day temperatures must be at a minimum of 70 degrees and not less than 60 degrees at night. Fifty-degree temperatures or below will cause these problems. Keep out of drafts from air conditioners and hot radiator blasts.

*Pale or discolored leaves. A mass of yellow foliage, tips of leaves and margins turn brown and die. Older plants shed leaves from the bottom up, no blooming, poor blooming.* The problem is the result of too little light. The plant needs very bright light or filtered sun for a minimum of six hours daily. Move to a brighter location or add artificial light to its present light source or move closer to its artificial light source.

*Leaf tips turn brown, yellowing leaf margins, stunted or no new growth, wilting, shriveling and dropping of buds and leaves with yellowing of foliage.* The problem is too little humidity. Place the plant on a bed of wet pebbles without the bottom of the pot touching any water and spray-mist daily.

*Failure to flower.* This may be from excess artificial light at night (streetlamps, indoor lamps, night lights, etc.). Place in complete darkness at 5 P.M. and bring it back into light at 8 A.M. the next morning.

*Plant stems look weak, limp and wilted, leaves curl under and lower leaves turn yellow with brown spots and fall, flower buds drop or flowering period*

§ 157

is short.  The problem is underwatering. Water slowly over the entire soil surface until excess water runs out of the drainage hole in the bottom. Do not let the plant sit in the water-filled saucer for more than an hour. Before rewatering, allow the surface soil to just dry.

*The plant wilts, new growth dies back, lower leaves yellow, stems become soft and dark in color.*  This is root-rot disease which prevents the root system from absorbing water. Plant must be removed from the pot (see *Potting*) and all soil removed. Wash the roots in warm water and repot in fresh soil. Remove damaged foliage and water plant only enough to keep the plant from wilting. The soil must be drenched with a fungicide. Once the plant has resumed normal growth, water properly.

*Rotting, wilting and bleaching of foliage. A mass yellowing and dropping of leaves, new growth is weak, flowers will blight and soil is constantly wet.*  The problem is overwatering. The plant must be removed from the pot (see *Potting*) and the roots checked. Also check for proper soil and proper drainage material covering the drainage holes. If the roots are white and healthy looking, repot in fresh soil, remove all damaged foliage and water more carefully. If only a few roots are brown, cut them away and repot in fresh soil. If all the roots are brown and mushy, the plant will have to be discarded.

# PRAYER PLANT—MARANTA

There are two varieties from Africa and Brazil. One has velvety, grayish green leaves with reddish brown markings that look like rabbit tracks. These markings change to dark green as the leaf ages. The other variety is velvety green, and the color progression toward the center turns to dark green with a very light green stripe in the center. The veins are red and the undersides are purple. It is noted for the fishbone pattern of its veins. The leaves fold upward at night like prayer hands. New growth is tightly rolled and protrudes at the end of stems. In the fall it has a dormancy period, and old leaves should be cut away to stimulate new growth. It grows 6 to 8 inches tall, and a large plant can be used for a hanging basket.

## Location

They like an east or west window shaded from any hot sunlight. They will grow in a north window but they will probably need brighter light during the winter.

## Soil

One part all-purpose loam, one part peat moss, one part sharp sand. Plant should be repotted annually in early spring, if not in a new pot then at least fresh soil. Do not pack the soil too firmly or it will not be porous enough to allow the plant to grow well. Use shallow pots, as the roots grow close to the soil surface.

## Watering

The soil must be kept moist at all times while growing. During the fall dormancy period, the soil should be allowed to dry between thorough waterings. Newly potted plants should be allowed to dry between waterings until new growth begins. Spray-mist daily.

## Fertilizer

Feed once a month with no feeding during the winter.

## Propagation

Dividing in early spring when repotting.

## Artificial Light

400 footcandles.

## First Aid

*Spider mites. (See Pests.)

*Brown crisp spots, scorched edges on leaves, leaves curl under and lower leaves turn yellow with brown spots and fall. The problem is underwatering. Marantas can not stand drought. Water slowly over the entire soil surface until excess water runs out of the drainage hole in the bottom. Do not let the plant sit in the water-filled saucer for more than an hour. Before rewatering, allow the soil to become damp except during the winter when the soil should become just dry.

*Leaf tips turn brown, yellowing leaf margins, stunted or no new growth, wilting, shriveling. The problem is low humidity. Spray-mist daily and place the plant on a bed of wet pebbles without the bottom of the pot touching any water and use a humidifier during the winter.

*Soft, discolored foliage with curled leaves, brown edges. Stems can rot. This is from temperatures that are too cool. They must be kept away from windows during the winter. I put mine under a lamp where it gets extra light when the lamp is used.

# PRIMROSE—PRIMULA

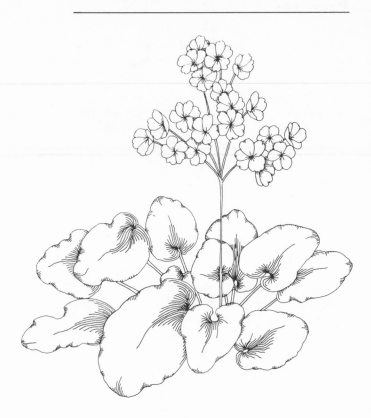

A gesneriad, a member of the Gesneriaceae family, and a cultivated ornamental, with leaves of many shapes and sizes. Primroses have glandular hairs on their stems that give a skin rash to people allergic to it. Rose, red, magenta, purple, sky blue or white flat clusters of flowers bloom atop 6-inch stems that grow from the heart of the plant. It blooms all season, often for a whole year. Remove old blooms to encourage new growth. They grow to 12 inches tall.

Primrose is usually considered an annual. Because of its constant bloom, the vitality and strength is usually depleted in one season, and its strength never seems to be established again. However, it is really a perennial and needs to be rested during the summer to force strong new growth and blooms to appear again. In May repot and put in a cool, damp, semishaded location. Water less and fertilize once a month. In August, stop feeding until October and then resume all proper growing requirements. When repotting, be careful not to plant too deep or the soft center may rot.

## Location

Needs the brightest light possible without direct sun. Needs cool temperatures as low as 45 degrees at night.

## Soil

One part all-purpose loam, one part peat moss, one part sharp sand. When repotting keep the crown slightly above the soil surface so water does not settle in the center and cause rot.

## Watering

Must never be allowed to dry. Keep the soil moist except during the summer when watering should be slightly lessened.

## Fertilizer

Once a month except in August and September when feeding is stopped.

## Propagation

Easily from seeds in spring.

## Artificial Light

800 footcandles.

## First Aid

*Whiteflies. (See *Pests*.)

*Rash on hands.* The hairs on the plant sometimes causes a rash which requires first aid for people.

*Base and stems turn soft and mushy.* This is from planting the crown of the plant too deep into the soil. Water settles here and rots the plant. Once the plant has rotted, it is probably too late to save it. You can try to repot making sure the crown is slightly above the soil level. Arrange the soil to slope away from the crown so the water will drain quickly.

*Gray or white mold on leaves, flowers and soil.* This is usually caused by soil that is too wet or by overusing fertilizer. It happens more often when plastic pots are used. Wash the foliage in warm water. Remove any damaged leaves and keep foliage dry. If mold is on soil, it can be scratched gently into the soil. Reduce watering.

Ventilate the growing area. If the problem continues, drench the soil with a diluted solution of a fungicide. When fertilizing, use half the amount listed on the label.

*Yellowing of foliage beginning at the outer edges and usually spreading to the whole leaf and damaging roots. Yellow spots and crisp brown spots and scorched edges on leaves, wilting and no flowers.* This problem is too much fertilizer. Soil must be literally flodded with water twice and allowed to drain well. If fertilizing properly, feed less often or use half the amount of fertilizer.

*Leaves curl under and lower leaves turn yellow with brown spots and fall. Brown crisp spots, scorched edges on leaves and flowers, flower buds drop.* This problem is underwatering. Water slowly over the entire soil surface until excess water runs out of the drainage hole in the bottom. Do not let the plant sit in the water-filled saucer for more than an hour. Before rewatering, the soil should be allowed to become just damp but never be allowed to dry.

§ 161

# ROSARY VINE
# HEART VINE—
# CEROPEGIA

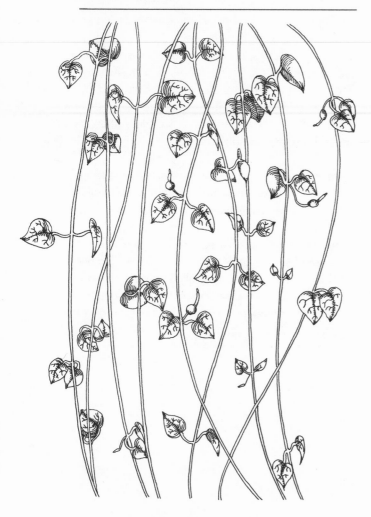

A succulent plant from Rhodesia. A very easy plant to grow but it needs sufficient room to hang free. The flexible, pendant stems grow several feet long from bulblike storage tissue called a tuber. These small tubers also develop along the stem itself. Ceropegias' tiny leaves are shaped like hearts.

They are dark green with gray markings, marbled white on green or white on copper and have purplish undersides. During the summer, pink flowers appear along the stems at the leaf joints. Some will grow year round without a resting period but others indicate a desire to rest by appearing to wilt. Water should be withheld completely for one month during the resting period no matter how much they wrinkle.

## Location

It can tolerate full sun even in a south window. It can survive without sun but is healthiest with it. Tolerates dry air and likes average room temperatures.

## Soil

One part all-purpose loam, one part peat moss, one part sharp sand. One part all-purpose loam, one part sharp sand. Cactus soil prepackaged mix with a small amount of peat moss added. After repotting, keep the plant out of direct sun and water sparingly for one month.

## Watering

Allow soil to dry between thorough waterings from spring to fall. Water only enough to keep the plant from shriveling during winter. No water for one month during the resting period which usually occurs during the winter.

## Fertilizer

From spring to fall feed monthly. If it grows too quickly, feed less. No feeding during the winter.

## Propagation

Stem cutting with a tuber attached, seeds.

## Artificial Light

A minimum of 400 footcandles.

## First Aid

*Pests don't seem to attack this plant.*

*The plant has been growing well and all of a sudden it seems to wilt.* The plant is dormant. This is a natural occurence. Let it remain dry for a complete month, no matter how much it wilts, until new growth appears. It will revive and be healthy as ever.

*Rotting, wilting and bleaching of foliage. A mass yellowing and dropping of leaves. Leaves can curl, tips turn brown and die back. Flowers will blight and soil is constantly wet.* The problem is overwatering. The plant must be removed from the pot (*see Potting*) and the roots checked. Also check for proper soil and proper drainage material over the drainage holes. If the roots are white and healthy looking, repot in fresh soil, remove damaged foliage and allow the soil to dry between waterings. If the roots are partially brown, cut them away and repot in fresh soil. If all the roots are brown and mushy, the plant can not be saved. If there are healthy cuttings, use them to start new plants.

*Elongated, misshapen, underdeveloped leaves, soft and discolored foliage, no blooming or poor blooming.* This is the result of too little light. They need full sun to perform well. Artificial light can be added to its present location or move the plant closer to its artificial light source.

---

A very handsome plant from China, with many varieties. Hibiscus is a slow-growing plant with oblong, pointed leaves with coarsely toothed edges. The leaves can be colored with pink or white and some have white edges. The spectacular blooms can be pink, yellow or white with single or double blooms that grow atop long stems. They appear in June through early autumn, and though a bloom lasts for only four hours, new flowers appear continuously. With careful attention it can bloom all year round. They grow 2 to 4 feet tall. After blooming they should be pruned to prevent the plant from looking straggly, and as stems get long, pinch the tips back and use them for cuttings. When purchased they are usually in bloom. Once placed in its home location it should not be moved or the buds will drop. It is difficult to keep through the winter because it cannot tolerate cool rooms. Hibiscus needs to rest for the winter in a temperature not below 50 degrees. Give it a small amount of water and cease feeding until spring. In March repot, prune back

# ROSE OF CHINA—
# HIBISCUS

half the foliage, begin watering and feeding and move it into proper light.

## Location

Needs full sun but must be protected from the hot noon sun during the summer. The temperatures can never be below 50 degrees.

## Soil

One part all-purpose loam, one part peat moss, one part sharp sand with a small amount of perlite or vermiculite added. When repotting after its resting period, put it in a pot two sizes larger. It needs plenty of root space to grow.

## Watering

Soil must be kept moist at all times except during the resting period when the soil should dry thoroughly between thorough waterings. Spray-mist daily.

## Fertilizer

Feed monthly except during the resting period when no food should be given.

## Propagation

Stem cuttings.

## Artificial Light

800 footcandles.

## First Aid

*Aphids, mealybugs, spider mites, scales, white-flies. (See *Pests*.)

*Leaf tips turn brown, yellowing leaf margins, stunted or no new growth, wilting, leaves roll up and buds drop.* The problem is low humidity. Place the plant on a bed of wet pebbles without the bottom of the pot touching any water. Spray-mist daily.

*No blooming in winter.* This is natural. The plant usually rests during the winter. Blooms best in summer and fall but has beautiful foliage all year round.

*Buds drop, soft and discolored foliage with curled leaves, brown edges and stems can rot.* This is from temperatures that are too cool. The temperature can never go below 50 degrees without causing problems. Also, if plants are moved to different locations, or the pot turned in different directions, buds will drop. Buds always face the light and, if the position is changed, the buds twist off their axils by turning to face the light.

A trailing plant from tropical America that's a good choice for hanging baskets. Browallia needs plenty of space to grow because it spreads and reaches up to 15 inches tall. An undemanding plant, it has bright, attractive, blue or white bell-shaped flowers, and it is possible to keep them in bloom constantly from late summer to spring, although only a few appear simultaneously. The blooms can reach 2 inches across. The leaves are broad and pointed. To enable the plant to continue flowering, cut back and pinch back the plant after each main flowering period. This plant usually only lasts one year and by spring it will probably look a shambles. Take cuttings, at least five cuttings to a pot, and start a new plant. Discard the old plant.

## Location

Likes partial sun in a west or east window and needs protection from hot noon sun in the summer. Will survive in bright light. Likes normal room temperatures unless it gets too hot. The west or east window is cooler than other windows.

## Soil

One part all-purpose loam, one part peat moss, one part sharp sand, perlite or vermiculite.

## Watering

The soil must remain moist at all times without being soggy. Needs high humidity and should be mist sprayed once or twice daily.

## Fertilizer

Every two months.

## Propagation

Stem cuttings, using at least five cuttings to a pot. Seeds.

# SAPPHIRE FLOWER— BROWALLIA

## Artificial Light

800 footcandles.

## First Aid

*Leaf miners, aphids, spider mites, whiteflies. (See *Pests*.)

*A *straggly and leggy plant.*   To prevent this you must prune and pinch back regularly.

*Darkening and dropping of leaves.*   This is from too little humidity and soil that is too dry. Water slowly over the entire soil surface until excess water drains out of the drainage hole in the bottom. Do not let the plant sit in the water-filled saucer for more than an hour. Before rewatering, allow the plant to dry only slightly. Set the plant on a bed of wet pebbles without the bottom of the pot touching the water and spray-mist twice daily.

# SCREW PINE—
# PANDANUS

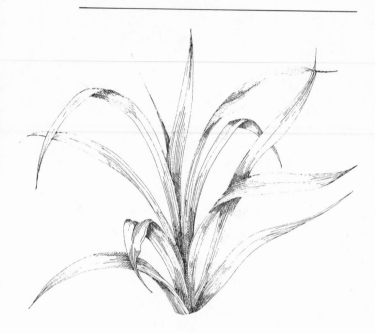

A very durable plant from Malaysia. It is not a true pine but acquired the name because of the pine-cone fruit which occurs when the plant is grown outside. Screw pine can have both variegated and plain green leaves. The swordlike leaves grow 2 feet long and 3 inches wide, with serrated, sharp edges. The plant grows in spiral arrangement rising from a rosette. The leaves are not strong for their length and will sometimes collapse. The plant grows very slowly but can grow up to 5 feet tall. Usually the rosette develops into a stem as the plant grows taller. As it grows taller, the base of the stem sends out large aerial roots. They can remain hanging over the sides of the pot or can be pushed into the soil. These roots support the plant and should never be removed. Sometimes the plant will be lifted out of the soil by these roots. If this happens, the plant should be repotted.

## Location

Does best near an east or west window but must always be protected from the sun. Needs a warm location all year round.

## Soil

One part all-purpose loam, one part peat moss, one part sharp sand, perlite or vermiculite. Can go several years without being repotted. When the plant heaves itself out of the pot by its aerial roots, it's time to transplant. Use gloves to protect your hands from the sharp edges.

## Watering

Allow the soil to barely dry between thorough waterings. Spray-mist daily.

## Fertilizer

Feed every three months.

## Propagation

Suckers at the base which should be 6 inches before removing.

## Artificial Light

400 footcandles.

## First Aid

*Insects don't seem to attack this plant.

*Bottom leaves will sometimes collapse. They are pulled down by their own weight. This is natural. Remove the leaves only if they appear to be badly damaged.

*Lifts itself out of its pot by its large aerial roots. This is natural and does not injure the plant, but transplanting into a larger pot is a good idea.

A very attractive plant from Peru and Brazil which is both easy to grow and a fast grower. The smooth-edged, leathery, 2- to 3-inch leaves are heart-shaped. They have rich purple undersides and an olive-green surface that is striped silver-gray with a metallic sheen and a puckered texture that resembles the fabric seersucker. They grow in clumps up to a foot tall. Blue flowers appear annually in dense clusters.

## Location

Needs sun but needs protection from the hot sunlight of summer. Needs warm temperatures of around 72 degrees year round. Will grow in dimmer light but will not remain compact.

## Soil

One part all-purpose loam, one part peat moss, one part sharp sand, perlite or vermiculite.

## Watering

The surface of the soil should become dry between waterings. Never allow the soil to become soggy. Spray-mist daily.

## Fertilizer

Feed monthly during the growing period and every two months during the winter.

## Propagation

Offshoots, stem cuttings. Propagate often, because younger plants are the most handsome.

## Artificial Light

400 footcandles.

# SEERSUCKER PLANT— GEOGENANTHUS

## First Aid

*Mealybugs, spider mites. (See *Pests*.)

*Scorch marks on leaves turning grayish where scorched, general look, bleached-out small new growth. The problem is too much sun. Move the plant farther away from its light source or filter it with a curtain. It can not tolerate hot sun of summer.

*Rotting, wilting and bleaching of foliage. A mass yellowing and dropping of leaves. Leaves can curl, tips turn brown and die back. New growth is weak. This problem is overwatering. The plant must be removed from the pot (see *Potting*) and

§ 167

the roots checked. Also check for proper soil and proper drainage material over the drainage holes. If the roots are white and healthy, repot in fresh soil, remove damaged foliage and allow the soil to become almost dry before rewatering. If the roots are partially brown, cut them away and repot in fresh soil. If all the roots are brown and mushy, the plant cannot be saved, and healthy cuttings can be taken to start new plants.

*Plant stems look weak, limp and wilted. Leaves curl under and lower leaves turn yellow with brown spots and fall. Brown crisp spots, scorched edges on leaves, flowers drop.* The problem is underwatering. Water slowly over the entire soil surface until excess water runs out of the drainage hole in the bottom. Do not allow the plant to sit in the water-filled saucer for more than an hour. Before rewatering, allow the soil to become almost dry.

# SHRIMP PLANT—BELOPERONE

A handsome plant from Mexico. Its main attractions are the beautiful white flowers emerging from the terminals of the delicate hanging clusters of shrimp-pink bracts. The bracts are leaves and not flowers. There are also rare varieties with lime-green to yellow bracts and those with golden-yellow bracts. They all have shiny green leaves. These flowers soon die along with the bracts, but the plant is in constant bloom from November through April. It becomes a small shrub and grows to 20 inches tall and begins flowering at 10 inches. It needs to have its woody branches constantly pruned to be kept shapely, especially after flowering in the spring. The early flowers should also be pinched in order to have more vigorous leaf growth and a more bushy plant.

## Location

Does well with east or west sunlight, especially during its blooming period. Grow in the warmest area of the room.

## Soil

One part all-purpose loam, one part peat moss, one part perlite. Likes acid soil. Should be repotted every spring if not in a larger pot at least in fresh soil.

## Watering

Allow the soil to become just dry between thorough waterings. Keep the plant on a bed of wet pebbles without the bottom of the pot touching the water. A humidifier should be used during the winter. Never spray water on leaves or flowers.

## Fertilizer

Feed once a month with an acid fertilizer.

## Propagation

Nonflowering cuttings. Put three to four cuttings together and root in the sun.

## Artificial Light

800 footcandles.

## First Aid

*Mealybugs, red spider mites. (See *Pests*.)

*Leggy Plant.* Shrimp plants have a tendency to become leggy and lose lower leaves. Start new plants from cuttings. Constantly pinch and prune plants when young to promote bushiness so that the legginess won't be as noticeable.

*Leaves curl under and lower leaves turn yellow with brown spots and fall. Brown crisp spots, scorched edges on leaves and flowers. Flower buds drop and plants stems look weak, limp and wilted.* The problem is underwatering. Water slowly over the entire soil surface until excess water runs out of the drainage hole in the bottom. Do not let the plant sit in the water-filled saucer for more than an hour. Before rewatering, allow the soil to become dry but not for more than one day.

*Discolored leaves, yellowing of top leaves or yellow margins.* This problem is an iron or magnesium deficiency. Plant must be fed monthly with a fertilizer for acid-loving plants. It needs fresh soil yearly to keep the soil acid.

# SILKY OAK
# AUSTRALIAN SILKY OAK—
# GREVILIEA

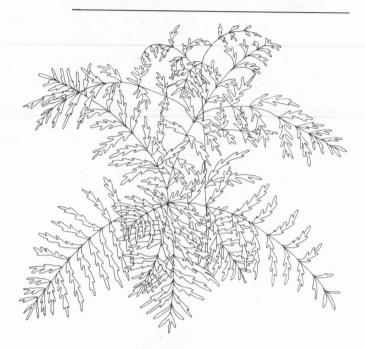

A fast-growing evergreen from Australia which grows up to a foot a year. The curving branches grow up to 18 inches long and develop clusters of lacy, fernlike foliage with silky undersides. The leaves are dark green, soft and very delicate. Red flowers can appear but rarely do indoors. It can grow to 10 feet.

## Location

Will tolerate full sun during the winter but must be protected from the hot sun of summer. Prefers a cool room but will adapt to almost any temperature, but temperature should never reach below 45 degrees during the winter.

## Soil

One part all-purpose loam, one part peat moss, one part sharp sand. When purchased they are usually in small pots and should be repotted as soon as possible. Never repot when light-colored new growth appears or it may be damaged.

## Watering

Keep the soil moist but never soggy. This is one plant that prefers a little water every day rather than too much at one time. During the winter allow the soil to dry thoroughly between thorough waterings. Mist-spray around the plant, but it resents water on the leaves.

## Fertilizer

Feed once a month except during the winter when feeding is withheld.

## Propagation

Seeds grown in full sun. Stem cuttings.

## Artificial Light

800 footcandles.

## First Aid

*Pests never seem to attack.

*No flowers.  This is due to the fact that they rarely bloom indoors.

*Roots growing out of the pot, but the plant isn't root-bound.  This is natural, but to keep roots under control the pot should be lifted and turned weekly.

*Plant loses its shape after a few years.* This is natural, and the plant will need to be propagated and replaced by new plants. While still young, as much as half the length of the branches can be pruned every spring and new growth will appear quickly and the plant will keep its shape longer.

*Scorch marks on leaves turning grayish where scorched, a general bleached-out appearance.* The problem is too much sun. Either filter the sun with a curtain or move the plant farther away from its light source or move it to a new location.

*Rotting, wilting and bleaching of foliage. A mass yellowing and dropping of leaves, new growth is weak, flowers will blight and soil is constantly wet.* The problem is overwatering. The plant must be removed from the pot (see *Potting*) and the roots checked. Also check for proper soil and proper drainage material covering the drainage holes. If the roots are white and healthy looking, repot in fresh soil, remove all damaged foliage and water more carefully. If only a few roots are brown, cut them away and repot in fresh soil. If all the roots are brown and mushy, the plant will have to be discarded.

A plant from Africa with thick, almost succulentlike leaves that is among the most durable house plants. The leaves are stiff and slim and they grow up to 30 inches tall and 2 to 3 inches wide. They are green with thick yellow trim or all green with grayish white or pale green horizontal stripes. They rise from thick stems or rhizomes that grow underground and form rosettes. Each rhizome has up to ten leaves. If given proper care, fragrant green-white or pale yellow flowers, dripping with honey, grow on tall thin stalks rising from the heart of each rosette. There is also a low-growing rosette variety. Remove flower stems after flowering.

## SNAKE PLANT— SANSEVIERIA

### Location

Will tolerate any exposure but needs a small amount of protection from hot southern sun during the summer. It needs sun in order to flower. It likes average room temperatures and 60-degree temperatures during the winter.

### Soil

One part all-purpose loam, one part peat moss, one part sharp sand. The snake plant can go without repotting from three to five years without affecting growth.

## Watering

Water when thoroughly dry during the summer and spring. Water as little as every two weeks during the winter. Wash leaves with warm water occasionally.

## Fertilizer

Once a month without feeding during the winter.

## Propagation

Leaf cuttings, 3-inch pieces of leaves set upright in a growing medium and treated like a leaf cutting. Leaf cuttings produce only plants without stripes. Division or suckers are the only methods that produce striped plants.

## Artificial Light

From 150 footcandles to 800 footcandles.

## First Aid

*Pests rarely attack.

*Plant dies during the winter, neck of the roots rot and or brown spots appear on the leaves, rotting, wilting and bleaching of foliage. A mass yellowing of leaves and dropping. Leaves can curl, tips turn brown and die back. The problem is overwatering or root-rot disease. In either case the plant will have to be removed from its pot (see Potting) and the roots checked. Also check for proper soil and proper drainage material over the drainage holes. If the roots are white and healthy looking, remove all soil and wash the roots in warm water and repot in fresh soil removing all damaged foliage. If partial decay of roots has taken place, cut them away, wash the remaining roots in warm water and repot in fresh soil. Spray all wounds with a fungicide. If all the roots are brown and mushy, the plant can not be saved. Take healthy cuttings and propagate new plants.

*Stems rot and plant dies during the winter. This is from cold drafts. The plant will have to be discarded, but take healthy cuttings and start new plants.

*No flowers, pale or discolored leaves. The problem is too little light. They can tolerate almost any location except the dark. In order to flower it needs sun but not direct hot noon sun during the summer.

*Scorch marks on leaves turning grayish where scorched, a general bleached-out appearance. This is the result of too much sun. Either filter the plant from the sun with a curtain or move it farther away from its light source or move it to a new location.

*Reddish brown, black or yellow damp or blistered spots, usually with yellow margins. This is a fungal or bacterial invasion called leaf-spot disease and it is caused by high humidity, overwatering, chilling, low light. Temperature, light, ventilation need to be increased, and soil must dry out before rewatering. Infected areas must be removed and the remaining leaves sprayed with a fungicide.

The narrow, leathery leaves, with cream-yellow margins, grow in clusters with leaves 6 to 10 inches long and closely set around slender, supple stems. As they grow larger, their weight will bend them into a horizontal position. They can grow to 4 feet or more but grow very slowly.

## Location

Bright light or shaded from direct sun.

## Soil

One part all-purpose loam, one part peat moss, one part sharp sand, perlite or vermiculite.

## Watering

Keep the soil moist at all times and spray-mist daily.

## Fertilizer

Once every three months or every month very diluted.

## Propagation

Stem cuttings.

## Artificial Light

400 footcandles.

# SONG OF INDIA— PLEOMELE

## First Aid

*A problemless plant.

*Loss of lower leaves.  This is natural for this plant, but the beauty of the remaining leaves is worth a denuded base.

# SPATHE FLOWER— SPATHIPHYLLUM

A Central American plant with many species that are all easy to grow. Here are descriptions of a few varieties: large, oval, dark green leaves; lance-shaped leaves with deep center ribs that twist and bend and are a light green color; long, thin, shiny, dark green leaves that grow very large or a variety that remains small. All varieties have lilylike flowers called spathes that are snowy white with a touch of lilac. As they open, they reveal very small white blossoms within. The spathes appear on the ends of long stems growing out from the heart of the plant. The size of the flower is determined by the size of the plant. The flowering period is usually from early spring through summer and sometimes even through late fall.

## Location

Can tolerate winter sun in an east or west window but must have filtered sun the rest of the year. Does very well in bright light. Likes average room temperatures but must be kept out of cold drafts during the winter.

## Soil

One part all-purpose loam, one part peat moss, one part sharp sand. Should be repotted each fall, not necessarily in a larger pot but with fresh soil.

## Watering

The soil must be kept moist at all times. Water slightly less in winter, but plant has no resting period. Must be kept on a bed of wet pebbles without water touching the bottom of the pot. Mist-spray daily.

## Fertilizer

Once a month.

## Propagation

Dividing into several sections. Seeds formed in the spathes.

## Artificial Light

400 footcandles.

## First Aid

*Pests don't seem to attack this plant.

*Most problems with the spathe are due to spent

soil. It needs fresh soil every year, so be sure to repot regularly.

*Plant stems look weak, limp and wilted. Leaves curl under and lower leaves turn yellow with brown spots and fall. Brown crisp spots, scorched edges on leaves and flowers.* The problem is underwatering. Water slowly over the entire soil surface until excess water runs out of the drainage hole in the bottom. Do not let the plant sit in the water-filled saucer for more than an hour. Before rewatering, allow the soil to become just damp.

*Leaf tips turn brown, leaf margins yellow, stunted or no new growth, wilting, shriveling and dropping of buds.* The cause is too little humidity. The plant must be put on a bed of wet pebbles without the bottom of the pot touching any water. Spray-mist daily and use a humidifier during the winter.

*Scorch marks on leaves turning grayish where scorched. General bleached-out appearance.* The problem is too much light. It can tolerate direct sun during the winter but sometimes the southern exposure during the winter can be too much. Filter the light or move the plant to a new location.

# SPIDER PLANT— CHLOROPHYTUM

An easy-to-grow hanging plant from South Africa, the spider plant has streamers of leaves 4 to 16 inches long and up to 1 inch wide. Leaves are green with white or yellow stripes down the middle or pale green leaves with white edges, or all green. They arch from the center of the plant's fleshy roots. Older plants develop long wiry stems up to 2 feet long that cascade over the sides of the pot at the end of which small plants develop. Small, white flowers develop on the runners just before the new plantlets are formed. The plantlets can live on the plant for many years, increasing in size.

## Location

It can tolerate full winter sun but must be protected from hot noon sun in summer. Does best in bright light or curtain-filtered sunlight. Needs average room temperatures.

## Soil

One part all-purpose loam, one part peat moss, one part sharp sand, perlite or vermiculite. Repotting is

necessary if any white roots appear on the surface soil. They can push themselves out of the soil. When repotting, use large, wide pots as the roots need plenty of space to grow.

## Watering

Keep the soil moist at all times; drying out can injure the plant. They can tolerate dry atmospheres, but it's wise to spray-mist daily.

## Fertilizer

Feed once a month.

## Propagation

Division, small plantlets with six or seven leaves treated like cuttings.

## Artificial Light

400 footcandles.

## First Aid

*Pest-free.

*Yellowing mottled leaves, a mass of yellow foliage, tips of leaves and margins turn brown and die. Older plants shed leaves. During winter the growth is soft and discolored. The problem is too little light. Needs bright light, and curtain-filtered sunlight is best.

*Tips of leaves and or leaf margins turn brown and die back. This is from bruising. Cut off damaged sections of foliage, keeping as much of each leaf or stem intact as possible. Move the plant to a location where people are less likely to brush against it.

*Leaf tips turn brown, leaf margins yellow, stunted or no new growth, wilting, shriveling. This is the result of too little humidity. Spray-mist daily and use a humidifier during the winter.

*Leaves curl under and lower leaves turn yellow with brown spots and fall. Brown crisp spots, scorched edges on leaves, new growth dies back. The problem is the spider plant's worst enemy—underwatering. Water slowly over the entire soil surface until excess water runs out of the drainage hole in the bottom. Do not let the plant sit in the water-filled saucer for more than an hour. Before rewatering, allow the plant to become just damp. Never allow the plant to dry out.

A hard plant to find but a very easy one to grow. The most popular is a 3- to 4-inch, oval, bluish-green leaved variety accented with silvery central ribs. The undersides and leaf stems have a reddish color. There is also a variety with green oval leaves that grow to 12 inches long and have light green undersides and hairy leaves. Leaves spiral around the stems rather than growing opposite or alternating from each other. In the spring they occasionally have 3-inch flowers of red, yellow or a brilliant orange. The plant grows to 3 feet tall.

## SPIRAL FLAG— COSTUS

### Location

Filtered sun in an east or west window. Costus likes a warm room year round.

### Soil

One part all-purpose loam, one part peat moss, one part sharp sand, perlite or vermiculite.

### Watering

Allow the surface soil become just barely dry between thorough waterings. Spray-mist daily.

### Fertilizer

Feed every three months.

### Propagation

Division, stem cuttings.

### Artificial Light

400 footcandles.

### First Aid

*A problemless plant.

# STONECROP
# BURRO'S TAIL—SEDUM

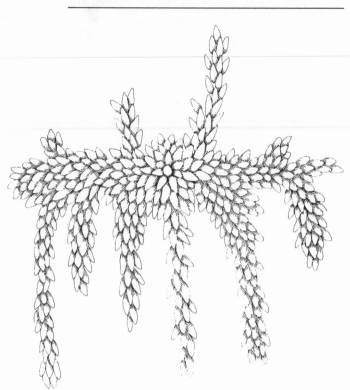

A succulent. There are many kinds but the most popular has blue-green, 1-inch, tear-shaped leaves with a silvery cast and they are densely settled on pendant stems, a foot or more in length, that trail over the pot or basket. The succulent leaves are covered with "bloom," which is a powdery blue dust. Bloom is also found on blue berries and plums. Brilliant scarlet flowers appear at the stem tips annually.

## Location

To remain compact and flower, they need as much sun as possible and grow best in cool or cold locations. They can survive in bright light.

## Soil

One part all-purpose loam, one part sharp sand or one part all-purpose loam, one part peat moss, one part sharp sand. They should not be repotted unless absolutely necessary. Their leaves are so brittle that transplanting would damage most of them. Feed and water older plants more often to keep from repotting. Try every two years to replace some surface soil in order to provide the plant with good nutrition.

## Watering

Allow the soil to dry between thorough waterings. During winter only water enough to keep leaves from shriveling.

## Fertilizer

Feed once in early spring, late spring and late summer. Do not feed any other time of year.

## Propagation

Stem cuttings. Leaf cuttings, inserting the bottom of the entire leaf into rooting medium. Water carefully so as not to rot the cuttings.

## Artificial Light

1,000 footcandles.

## First Aid

*Mealybugs, sow bugs, slugs, and snails. (See *Pests*.)

*Falling leaves.* The leaves will fall at the slightest touch, so the plant must be hung where it will not be brushed against.

*Rotting, wilting and bleaching of foliage, leaves turn yellow, new growth is weak, blackening of foliage.* The problem is overwatering. Because the plant is so fragile, a root check is risky, so first try removing damaged foliage and aerating the surface soil with a fork to promote oxygen to the roots. Soil must dry out thoroughly between waterings. If the problems continue, the plant will have to be removed from the pot (see *Potting*) and the roots checked. Break the pot away from the soil so as not to injure too much foliage. If roots are white and healthy, repot in fresh soil and remove damaged foliage. If partial root decay is evident, cut the damaged roots away and repot in fresh soil. If all roots are brown and soft, the plant can not be saved, and cuttings should be taken to start new plants.

*Base and stems of plant turn soft and mushy.* This is stem-rot disease and it is promoted by too much humidity, overwatering, and changes in temperatures. Try dipping the plant in a hot bath for twenty to forty minutes. If the problem persists, repot in fresh soil, removing infected areas, and spray the wounds with a fungicide. Give the plant proper growing requirements.

*Top growth shrivels, lower leaves yellow, stems become soft and dark in color.* This is root-rot disease which prevents the root system from absorbing water. Plant must be removed from its pot by breaking the pot to save as much foliage as possible. Remove all soil and wash roots in warm water. Repot in fresh soil and drench the soil with a fungicide. Remove damaged foliage and water only when the soil becomes thoroughly dry.

*Black, brown or yellow damp or blistered spots on the leaves, with yellow margins.* This is leaf-spot disease which is caused by high humidity, overwatering, chilling, low light. Temperature, light and ventilation need to be increased and the soil must dry out thoroughly before rewatering. Infected areas should be removed. Spray plant with a fungicide.

*Soft and discolored growth.* This is from too much humidity. Humidity must be cut down. Move it into brighter light and away from humidity-loving plants and ventilate the growing area well.

*Underdeveloped, elongated, misshapen growth.* The problem is too little light. Move into a sunny location, add artificial light to its present light source or move closer to its artificial light source.

*Shriveling, yellow foliage.* This is the result of underwatering. Water slowly over the entire soil surface until excess water runs out of the drainage hole in the bottom. Do not let the plant sit in the water-filled saucer for more than an hour. Before rewatering, allow the soil to dry thoroughly.

# SWISS CHEESE PLANT— MONSTERA

become deep green as they mature. As they grow older they can be grown against bark-covered slabs of wood. The stems send out roots, some hang in midair and others will penetrate the support or soil. The aerial roots are a sign of a very healthy plant and should never be removed. Long stems can be cut back both to encourage side shoots to grow and to reduce its height. Mature plants have cream-colored flowers that resemble lilies.

## Location

The plant can not tolerate sunlight from March to October, and sunlight during these months must be filtered. Bright indirect filtered sunlight is best. It likes average room temperatures, with 55- to 70-degree temperatures during the winter.

## Soil

One part all-purpose loam, one part peat moss, one part sharp sand. Monstera likes to be root-bound and should be repotted only when roots stream over the surface and through the drainage holes.

## Watering

The soil should become dry between thorough waterings. Spray-mist daily and wash the leaves with warm water weekly.

## Fertilizer

Feed once a month except during winter, when no feeding is necessary.

## Propagation

Air layering, seeds, leaf cuttings, stem cuttings. If the cutting is removed below an aerial root, it will develop into a new plant quickly.

A tropical evergreen from Mexico and Guatemala. Most people mistake this plant for a philodendron. As a young plant it is a normal pot plant but with age develops into an impressive climber. The leaves grow up to 12 inches and are roughly circular. Young leaves have deep incisions and older plants are irregularly perforated with holes or slashed. The leaves are leathery and shiny. As the young leaves unfold they are light green but they

## Artificial Light

400 footcandles.

## First Aid

*Red spider mites. (See *Pests*.)

*Straggly and leggy.* If the plant is not pruned and pinched constantly, it has a tendency to become leggy. New plants will have to be propagated and the old plant discarded.

*Soft, discolored foliage with curled leaves, brown edges. Stems can rot.* This is from temperatures that are too cool. The plant needs warmth and cannot tolerate any cold during the winter. Must be kept in a warm location all year.

*Rotting, wilting and bleaching of foliage. A mass yellowing and dropping of leaves. Leaves can curl, tips turn brown and die back. New growth is weak.* This problem is overwatering. The plant must be removed from the pot (see *Potting*) and the roots checked. Also check for proper soil and proper drainage material over the drainage holes. If the roots are white and healthy, repot in fresh soil. Remove all damaged foliage and allow the soil to thoroughly dry between waterings. If roots are partially brown, remove them and repot in fresh soil. If all roots are brown and mushy, the plant cannot be saved. Propagate new plants from healthy cuttings.

*Stems of plant turns soft and mushy.* This is stem-rot disease and is promoted by too much humidity, overwatering and too cold temperatures. Repotting in fresh soil is necessary. Infected areas must be removed and the wounds sprayed with a fungicide. Water only when the soil is dry and keep the plant in a warm location. Keep the plant's foliage dry until the problem has cleared up.

# TEMPLE BELLS—
# SMITHIANTHA

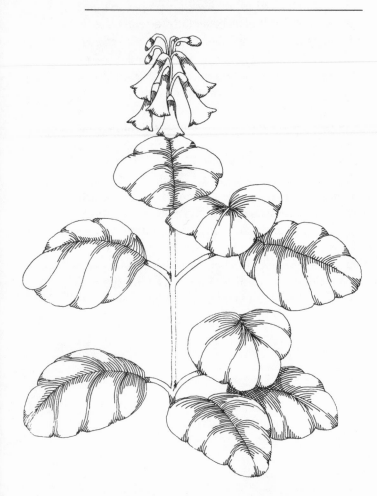

A rhizomatous gesneriad, a member of the Gesneriaceae family, which are cultivated ornamentals, from Guatemala and Mexico. The leaves are velvety green and heart-shaped with purple veins and are densely covered with fuzz. The stems and leaves are very brittle and must be handled carefully. Clusters of bell-like flowers appear on top of the central stalk. The flowers are scarlet with yellow undersides, and the throats are yellow with crimson

spots. New buds bloom continuously from June to October. The plant grows from 6 to 15 inches tall. It has a dormant period in winter. As the plant stops producing foliage, water less until all foliage is lost. Then remove the rhizomes from the soil, place them in plastic bags and put in a warm place. If they look like they're drying out, sprinkle water on them occasionally to keep them from shriveling. The dormant period lasts about three months. After that time, place them in fresh soil in a sunny place and water sparingly until new growth appears. They sometimes are slow to start new growth, but if they're kept in a sunny place they will usually come back to life. Once new growth appears, resume proper watering.

## Location

Needs a sunny exposure filtered from hot noon sun during the summer.

## Soil

One part all-purpose loam, one part peat moss, one part sharp sand. This plant can also grow in the new soilless potting mediums.

## Watering

Keep soil moist at all times until dormant. Needs high humidity. Keep the plant on a bed of wet pebbles without the bottom of the pot touching any water. Spray-mist around the plant; it does not like to have its foliage wet.

## Fertilizer

Feed monthly except while resting.

## Propagation

Seeds, dividing rhizomes.

## Artificial Light

800 footcandles.

## First Aid

*Red spider mites, thrips. (See *Pests*.)

*Round brown spots on the leaves.* These are water spots from spraying. Do not spray water directly on foliage and flowers, especially cold water. Warm water can be used occasionally to clean plants.

*Pale or discolored leaves. A mass of yellow foliage, tips of leaves and margins turn brown and die. Older plants shed leaves from the bottom up, no blooming, poor blooming.* The problem is the result of too little light. The plant needs a sunny exposure but must be protected from the hot noon sun of summer. Move the plant to a brighter location or add artificial light to its present light source or move closer to its artificial light source.

*Leaf tips turn brown, yellowing leaf margins, stunted or no new growth, wilting, shriveling and dropping of buds and leaves with yellowing of foliage.* The problem is too little humidity. This plant cannot be sprayed with water. Place the plant on a bed of wet pebbles without the bottom of the pot touching any water.

*Plant stems look weak, limp and wilted, leaves curl under and lower leaves turn yellow with brown spots and fall, flower buds drop or flowering period is short.* The problem is underwatering. Water slowly over the entire soil surface until excess water runs out of the drainage hole in the bottom. Do not let the plant sit in the water-filled saucer for more than an hour. Before rewatering, allow the soil to become damp.

# TI PLANT—CORDYLINE

A beautiful plant from the South Pacific islands. The wide, lancet-shaped, deep green leaves are irregularly colored with red, maroon, deep green or pink or are variegated with two or more of these colors. The leaves spiral up the plant's woody stem in a rosette form rather than growing opposite each other or alternating up a central stem. The leaves grow 12 to 18 inches long. Most plants grow up to 3 feet tall although some may reach to 6 feet. Some of the taller varieties tend to lose bottom leaves. Oversized plants can be pruned at any season to a desired height and to force new growth at the base of the plant. The white, blue or violet flowers appear in the leaf axils sometimes producing red berries. The Ti plant sends out runners which can be propagated.

## Location

They like full sun during the winter to keep their brightly colored foliage but should be shaded from the noon sun during the summer. They will grow in bright light but will have less colorful foliage. Summer temperatures should be 70 to 77 degrees. In winter 65 to 70 during the day and not below 60 degrees at night.

## Soil

One part all-purpose loam, one part peat moss, one part sharp sand, perlite or vermiculite. They like to be pot-bound, not needing to be repotted very often.

## Watering

Keep soil constantly moist but never soggy. Allow the soil to dry slightly between waterings during the winter. They can grow in water alone but, grown this way, they may dry up and die sooner than those grown in soil. Need high humidity and must be placed on a bed of wet pebbles without bottom of pot touching any water. Spray-mist daily and wash leaves weekly with warm water.

## Fertilizer

Feed monthly, less in winter.

## Propagation

Air layering. Inch-long sections of the stem as leaf cuttings, either place them horizontally on the soil or in the soil. Division. Seeds, but plants are not reproduced true from seed. Cuttings from leafy tops which are usually only taken when the plant becomes leggy with age. The wounded ends should dry for a day or two before propagating.

## Artificial Light

800 footcandles.

## First Aid

*Red spider mites, aphids. (See *Pests*.)

*Leggy and straggly growth.* With age the ti plant tends to become leggy. Cuttings should be taken and the old plant discarded.

*Leaf tips turn brown, leaf margins yellow, bottom leaves fall off, wilting, shriveling.* The problem is low humidity. The pot has to be put on a bed of wet pebbles without the bottom of the pot touching the water. Spray-mist once or twice daily and use a humidifier during the winter.

*Rotting, wilting and bleaching of foliage. A mass yellowing and dropping of leaves. Leaves can curl, tips turn brown and die back. New growth is weak, blackening of foliage.* The problem is overwatering. The plant must be removed from the pot (see *Potting*) and the roots checked. Also check for proper soil and proper drainage material over the drainage hole. If the roots are white and healthy, either put it back into its pot with the same soil or repot in fresh soil. Remove damaged foliage and water properly. If roots are partially brown, cut them away and repot in fresh soil. If all the roots are brown and mushy, the plant can not be saved. If there is any healthy foliage left, propagate new plants.

# UMBRELLA SLEDGE
# UMBRELLA PLANT—
# CYPERUS

A plant from Madagascar related to the Egyptian papyrus with many species. A beautifully graceful plant with twenty or more 4- to 8-inch long, slender leaflets atop a bare, slender stalk 1 to 2½ feet tall. They appear as ribs of an umbrella. They can grow from small species of 12 inches tall to the larger variety that can grow to 4 feet tall. Above the crown of leaves, clusters of small brownish green flowers

appear in the spring. Dying leaf shoots should always be removed. Older plants can be pruned back completely, and soon new growth will appear.

### Location

Can withstand full sun year round in a east or west window but needs protection from sun in a south window. Will thrive, however, in the bright light of a north window. Prefers temperatures of 50 to 55 degrees but the plant is adaptable to almost any conditions.

### Soil

One part all-purpose loam, one part peat moss, one part sharp sand.

### Watering

A swamp plant. *Cyperus* needs to have constant wet feet. Place the pot in a pebble tray of water with the bottom of the pot *in* the water. It will die if allowed to become dry. Always keep its saucer filled with water. Spray-mist daily.

### Fertilizer

Needs to be fed weekly from early spring to late summer to ensure firm stems and healthy leaves. Do not feed during the winter.

### Propagation

Division. Seeds. Cuttings root easily. Cut off a leaf rosette with about a 2-inch stem, cut the leaves leaving a third of their length. Root in a medium or water. Buds will appear in the axils of leaves and develop roots quickly.

### Artificial Light

800 footcandles.

## First Aid

*Pest-free.

*Withered leaf shoots.* This is natural and the shoots should be removed from the base. Older plants can be pruned back completely.

*Leaf tips turn brown, leaf margins yellow, stunted or no new growth, wilting, shriveling.* The problem is low humidity. The plant must always be kept in water and spray misted often. The dark ends of the foliage can be cut off, but unless a small amount of the dead section is left, the wound will develop new dead parts.

*Plant stems look weak, limp and wilted, leaves curl under and lower leaves turn yellow with brown spots and fall. The plant can die if this happens once.* The problem is underwatering. The plant must constantly be wet. Place the pot in a tray of water with the bottom of the pot in the water, or keep water in the saucer at all times.

---

# VELVET PLANT— GYNURA

A beautiful trailing plant from Java. The iridescent leaves are rich, velvety purple. The stems and foliage are covered with tiny hairs giving the plant a soft, plush appearance. The purple coloring is very bright on the young leaves. The older leaves are dark green with purple hairs and grow to 3½ inches long. Has inconspicuous clusters of yellow or orange flowers which bloom during the summer and should be removed. They take away strength from the foliage and sometimes cause the leaves to lose the violet hairs. It's a very fragile plant and must be pruned and pinched frequently to keep it from becoming straggly. Goes into a semidormant period during the winter.

## Location

Likes full sunlight, and even the hot summer sun will do no damage. It will grow well in bright light, but the color will not be as vivid. Temperatures must never go below 55 degrees.

## Soil

One part all-purpose loam, one part peat moss, one part sharp sand, perlite or vermiculite. Plant may need to be repotted yearly. The roots like a lot of

room to grow. An overcrowded plant should be transplanted into a pot two sizes larger.

## Watering

The soil should be kept moist except November to March when the soil should dry between waterings.

## Fertilizer

Feed monthly while growing strongly and every other month when growth slows down.

## Propagation

Stem cuttings. Put three or four cuttings together to have a bushier plant.

## Artificial Light

800 footcandles.

## First Aid

*Aphids are its deadly enemy. (See *Pests*.)

*Straggly and leggy.*   This is natural. Older plants become leggy and straggly, and new plants should be started from cuttings. Younger plants must be pinched and pruned frequently to keep them bushy. If it's a young plant, sometimes too much fertilizer will cause this growth. Cut down on the amount of fertilizer given and the frequency of feeding.

*No flowers.*   The flowers appear only on plants that are a few years old. Many plants become leggy and are discarded before flowering.

*Pale or discolored leaves. A mass of yellow foliage, tips of leaves and margins turn brown and die. Older plants shed leaves from the bottom up. No new growth, if any growth at all. Young plants get elongated and misshapen with inadequate branching.*   The problem is too little light. This plant likes full sun. Add artificial lights to its present light source, move to a brighter location or move it closer to its artificial light source.

*Soft, discolored foliage with curled leaves, brown edges. Stems can rot from cold drafts.*   The problem is temperatures that are too cool. The temperature can never be below 55 degrees. Move to a location where the plant has bright light but no drafts from the window.

*Only new growth is small.*   This is probably due to being overly pot-bound. Repot in a larger pot with fresh soil.

*Rotting, wilting and bleaching of foliage. A mass yellowing and dropping of leaves, new growth is weak, flowers will blight and soil is constantly wet.*   This is the result of overwatering. The plant must be removed from the pot (see *Potting*) and the roots checked. Also check for proper soil and proper drainage material covering the drainage holes. If the roots are white and healthy-looking, repot in fresh soil, remove all damaged foliage and water more carefully. If only a few roots are brown, cut them away and repot in fresh soil. If all the roots are brown and mushy, the plant will have to be discarded.

A carnivorous plant natural to the savannas of South Carolina, the Venus flytrap is quickly becoming extinct. There are about forty different species. The plant produces low-growing, hugging rosettes, 4 to 6 inches across at maturity, that rise from a rhizome underground. The jawlike traps at the ends of its leaves have rows of teeth and within each leaf half it has three trigger hairs. A sweet, sticky substance is secreted within the jaws to lure its prey. Also, depending on the sunlight given, the lining of the trap is red to lure prey. If an insect touches any of these trigger hairs twice or touches two different hairs, it triggers the jaws to snap shut. Within the plant are enzymes to digest the trapped creature. A few days later the trap opens and a dried skeleton falls out. With no insects to dine upon, the flytrap derives its nourishment from the soil, or you can feed it raw hamburger. A caught fly can be fed to the plant a couple times a year. A finger can cause the trap to shut, but one trap will only close a few times before becoming exhausted. When they die they turn black, but new growth soon appears. In May or June flowers appear, rising up to 12 inches above the plant. They have a dormant period during the winter. When the growth stops, probably as soon as it starts to become cold, put the plant in a cool, but not freezing, place. Keep the soil barely damp and do not try to force growth with too much light. When strong new growth appears, move it back to its proper environment. They do very well in terrariums.

## Location

Full sun or as much light as possible. Prefers a temperature of 60 degrees. If grown in a terrarium, shade from hot sun so the plant does not get overheated.

# VENUS FLYTRAP— DIONAEA MUSCIPULA

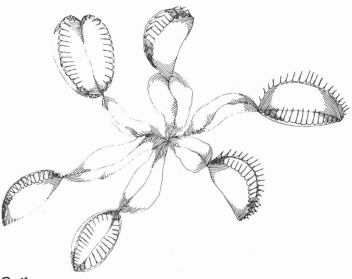

## Soil

One part sphagnum moss, nine parts of sharp sand or living green sphagnum moss of a small, slow-growing variety. Never needs transplanting.

## Watering

Keep moist at all times and spray-mist tops frequently. The slightest drying of air or soil will kill the plant.

## Fertilizer

None.

## Propagation

Kits sold at plant stores or specialists.

### Artificial Light

800 footcandles.

### First Aid

*Pests don't attack.

*While flowering, traps stop forming.* This is natural because flowering takes all the strength from the plant. If you want traps to continue to develop, flowers should be removed.

*After flowering, the plant weakens.* This is natural as flowering weakens this hard-to-grow plant. The next flowers to appear should be removed as they develop.

*Flattened-out leaves.* This is due to full sun and is natural.

*The leaf stem or petiole appears 1/4 inch across, but in the shade the stem widens and becomes more like a leaf.* This is natural. The stem widens to have more photosynthetic surface.

*The leaves and stems turn black.* This is from being exhausted by closing more than a few times. New growth will soon appear.

*Plant looks weak, limp and wilted and dry. New growth dies back.* The problem is underwatering. Venus flytraps cannot tolerate drying out even once, and you may have lost it. If you can't keep it moist, put it in a terrarium. Spray-mist frequently and water only slightly less in winter.

# WANDERING JEW—ZEBRINA INCH PLANT— TRADESCANTIA

The wandering Jew and its many varieties are all members of the Tradescantia family. All need the same care. They are all climbers and trailers and are very easy to grow. They will flower with correct environmental conditions. Leaves grow from 1 to 3 inches long. Some color varieties are: Four-color, irregularly striped leaves of green, purple, pink and white, with edges and undersides a deep red; bronze-green center stripe with a purplish cast; broad central strip in silver with narrow green stripes; green with yellow or white stripes with purple undersides; green with silvery edges; all green with purple undersides; some are almost completely white or cream; dark green with white fluff and purple undersides; there is a variety with purple hairs and also a variety that's all purple.

## Location

Sunlight brings out their coloring best, but they should be protected from hot noon sun during the summer. They survive in bright light. Can tolerate almost any room temperature but prefer warmth.

## Soil

One part all-purpose loam, one part peat moss, one part sharp sand, perlite or vermiculite. They hardly ever need repotting but when they become leggy, which is natural, they should be propagated and the old plant discarded.

## Watering

Allow the soil to just dry between thorough waterings. Spray-mist daily.

## Fertilizer

Feed every two months. Don't overfeed or their growth will be uncontrollable.

## Propagation

Stem cuttings—start them in 5-inch pots and place a few cuttings in the one pot. In a month or two a good plant will establish itself.

## Artificial Light

400 footcandles.

## First Aid

*Red spider mites. (See *Pests*.)

*Leggy and straggly.* This is natural. Plants grow very fast and, despite pinching and pruning, they eventually will have to be discarded. Propagate new plants from healthy stems. When the plant is still young, branches can be bent back and pinned down in the center of the pot with hairpins. New growth will be produced and help the plant to age more slowly.

*Leaves that overhang the pot wither.* This is natural for older plants. Cut off tips and start new plants.

*Plant stems look weak, limp and wilted. Leaves curl under and lower leaves turn yellow with brown spots and fall. Brown crisp spots, scorched edges on leaves.* The problem is underwatering. Water slowly over the entire soil surface until excess water runs out of the drainage hole in the bottom. Do not let the plant sit in the water-filled saucer for more than an hour. Before rewatering, allow the surface soil to dry.

*Leaf tips turn brown, leaf margins yellow, stunted or no new growth, wilting, shriveling.* The problem is low humidity. Since this is a hanging plant, spray misting once or twice daily and using a humidifier during the winter is the only way to increase the humidity.

*Leaves lose their variegated coloring, pale or discolored leaves, a mass of yellow foliage, tips of leaves and margins turn brown and die. Older plants shed leaves from the bottom up, no new growth, or new growth that shrivels and dies. Young plants get elongated, misshapen.* The problem is too little light. They can survive in very bright light, never shade, but to have bright colors they need sun and protection only from hot noon sun during the summer.

# WAX PLANT—HOYA

A trailing succulent from Indonesia. The wax plant has fleshy stems and thick, green, leathery leaves. There are also variegated forms with rims of white maturing to pink and also pink-tinged leaves with white borders. The hoya has a distinct front and back, with the upper surface of the leaves always turning to one side. The trailing stems must never be removed or your plant will never flower. The environment must be perfect to get them to flower, and a young plant will not bloom for three to four years. The flowers are very fragrant pinkish white and star-shaped with red or brown centers. Their texture is waxy, and they form in clusters in the leaf axils. They secrete a honeylike fluid that drips from the flowers. Blooming period is usually March to September. As buds appear, feeding must be withheld. Dead flowers should be left to fall off the plant naturally as the new flower buds will develop in the same place sometimes twice a year or the following year. Hoya has a winter dormancy period, and watering should be very light until new growth appears. Aerial roots sometimes develop and should not be removed.

## Location

Needs sun to bloom but needs to be protected from hot sun of a southern exposure during the summer. In an east or west window no protection is necessary. Warm temperatures, no lower than 50 degrees during the winter.

## Soil

One part all-purpose loam, one part peat moss, one part sharp sand. To flower it must be pot-bound. Repotting is rarely necessary.

## Watering

Allow the soil to just dry between thorough waterings. During the winter water only enough to keep plant from shriveling. Spray-mist daily during growing period.

## Fertilizer

Do not feed while buds are forming or during dormancy. Feed monthly at other times.

## Propagation

Use one-year-old stem cuttings; do not root them in the sun. If it has an aerial root on the cutting, the new plant will develop more quickly.

## Artificial Light

800 footcandles.

## First Aid

*Mealybugs, red spider mites, nematodes, scales, thrips. (See Pests.)

*No flowers.   They are naturally slow to flower. They seldom flower until three to four years old and must be grown in the sun and be pot-bound.

*Flowering poorly.   If full sun is given and the plant is sufficiently pot-bound, the plant probably needs to be older before it flowers strongly. Also, the stems should never be removed or flowering will stop.

*Flower buds drop.   This is from moving the plant or feeding while buds are forming. Buds will twist off by turning to face the sun if moved. If you suspect overfeeding, drench the soil twice to wash out as much fertilizer as possible and only feed when no flowering is occurring.

*Shriveling, wrinkled yellow appearance.   This is the result of underwatering. Water slowly over the entire soil surface until excess water runs out of the drainage hole in the bottom. Do not allow the plant to sit in the water-filled saucer for more than an hour. Before rewatering, allow the surface soil to dry and only water enough during the winter to keep this problem from happening.

*Rotting, wilting and bleaching of foliage. A mass yellowing and dropping of leaves. Foliage has a blackening appearance.   This problem is overwatering. The plant must be removed from the pot (see Potting) and the roots checked. Also check for proper soil and proper drainage material over the drainage hole. If the roots are white and healthy looking, repot in fresh soil, remove damaged foliage and allow the soil to dry between waterings. If partially decayed roots appear, cut them away and repot in fresh soil. If all the roots are brown and mushy, the plant can not be saved. Take healthy cuttings and start new plants.

# WOOD SORREL—OXALIS

A tuberous, compact little plant from warm or tropical regions. The wood sorrel needs a minimum of attention. There are over three hundred species. They have four-bladed, edible, cloverlike leaves. During the winter and spring five-petaled flowers appear in colors of red, pink, yellow or white. Both flowers and leaves close up at night, on cloudy dark days, in hot sun or if the soil becomes too dry. Some have a resting period during the summer, after flowering. After the foliage withers, during the summer, store the plant in a plastic bag. Place it in a shady location without any water. In the fall repot and resume proper growing conditions, and new growth will soon appear.

## Location

Full sunlight, even a southern exposure, is necessary to produce lasting blooms and vigorous

growth. Likes a cool room. During the dormancy period in the summer, it rests in a shady location.

## Soil

One part all-purpose loam, one part peat moss, one part sharp sand, perlite or vermiculite.

## Watering

Allow the soil to barely dry between waterings while in bloom, gradually water less after flowering as dormancy approaches, at which time watering is ceased.

## Fertilizer

Feed monthly during the flowering period. No feeding while dormant.

## Propagation

When repotted each fall, rhizomes can be divided with a sharp knife and treated like divisions.

## Artificial Light

800 footcandles.

## First Aid

*Spider mites. (See *Pests*.)

*Leaves folding up at night and dark cloudy days. This is natural. They reopen when bright light shines on them.

*A mass yellowing and dropping of leaves. Rotting, wilting and bleaching of foliage. Leaves can curl, tips turn brown and die back. New growth is weak, flowers will blight, and soil is constantly wet.   The problem is overwatering. The plant must be removed from the pot (see *Potting*) and the roots checked. Also check if the proper soil has been given and that enough drainage material is covering the drainage hole. If the roots are white and healthy looking, repot in fresh soil, remove damaged foliage and water only when the soil is dry. If all roots are brown and mushy, the plant can not be saved, but if they are partially browned, cut the brown roots away and repot the plant in fresh soil.

*Yellowing of leaves, rapid loss of older leaves and general deterioration of the plant, with water standing on the soil after watering, and wilting and slow growth.* The problem is compacted soil. Repot (see *Potting*) in fresh soil, remove all damaged foliage and water properly. This is likely if just purchased, since they are usually in improper soil and need to be transplanted.

*Yellowish green color, and some plants have their undersides turn purple.* This is due to a nitrogen shortage. Use a fertilizer every other feeding which is high in nitrogen.

*Yellowing lower leaves with brown spots, falling leaves. Plant's stems look weak, limp and wilted. Brown crisp spots, scorched edges on leaves and flowers. Flower buds drop. Dark, undersized leaves, with loss of older ones.* The problem is underwatering. Water slowly over the entire soil surface until excess water runs out of the drainage hole in the bottom. Do not let the plant sit in the water-filled saucer for more than an hour. Allow the soil to dry between waterings while in bloom, water less while going into dormancy and no watering during dormancy.

*Older foliage will turn yellow.* When this happens occasionally, it is natural. The yellow foliage can be removed by pulling the stem from the soil. If too many leaves yellow, then one of the above problems is to blame.

# ZEBRA PLANT— APHELANDRA

A very attractive plant from Brazil. The zebra plant has shiny, dark green, leathery leaves with white mid-rib and veins. There is also a variety with gray-green, leathery leaves. Spikes appear in the fall with bright, yellow-orange, waxy flowers or orange flowers that turn red as they open. The plant tends to become leggy and needs pruning. The plant must have a four- to six-week resting period after flowering. The flower stems must be cut away. Place the plant in a cool place with no feeding and very little water. Try to keep the foliage from drying up by spraying or covering with a plastic bag. In early spring repot in fresh soil and prune back, leaving only three pairs of leaves.

## Location

The plant can not tolerate hot sun. It needs complete protection from sun in a southern window.

Curtain-filtered sun in an east or west window is best. The temperature for best results is 65 to 75 degrees.

## Soil

Two parts peat moss, one part all-purpose loam, one part sharp sand, perlite or vermiculite. They like to be pot-bound. After the resting period, when repotting, using larger pots is not always necessary as long as they have fresh soil.

## Watering

Keep the soil moist, especially while flowering. The plant needs high humidity. Place on a bed of wet pebbles without the bottom of the pot touching the water. Spray-mist daily and wipe leaves with warm water weekly.

## Fertilizer

Feed twice monthly while flowering if you want the flowers to last longer. Feed monthly at other times except while resting.

## Propagation

After the resting period, cuttings taken from the plant. They need to be kept very warm, even over a hot radiator or stove. It's difficult to do in the house, because they usually aren't kept warm enough and die before they root.

## Artificial Light

800 footcandles.

## First Aid

*Spider mites. (See *Pests*.)

*Legginess.* This is hard to control since it is a

natural tendency. New plants can be started every year from cuttings, but this is difficult. Pruning after resting period may promote new growth from the base, but it usually requires some leaves to be left on the plant. You can simply purchase new plants. But since it is a natural tendency, why not let it get tall and leggy as sometimes the stems curve in interesting and unusual patterns.

*Shedding leaves.* Leaves are naturally shed sometimes after flowering. Plant needs to be rested after flowering.

*Plant stems look weak, limp and wilted. Leaves curl under and lower leaves turn yellow with brown spots and fall. Brown crisp spots, scorched edges on leaves and flowers, flower buds drop, or the flowering period is short.* The problem is underwatering. Water slowly over the entire soil surface until excess water runs out of the drainage hole in the bottom. Do not allow the plant to sit in the water-filled saucer for more than an hour. Before rewatering, the surface of the soil should become just damp.

*Leaf tips turn brown, leaf margins yellow, stunted or no new growth, wilting, shriveling, and buds drop.* The problem is low humidity. The plant must be put on a bed of wet pebbles without the bottom of the pot touching any water. Spray-mist daily and use a humidifier during the winter.

# Part Three:
# Quick-Reference First Aid Charts

This section serves as a general overview of all plant problems, their causes and their cures.

In some cases, your sick plant will not be one of those listed in the Plant Dictionary section. In other cases, the plant will be listed in the Dictionary but its problem will not be entered under the particular plant. In both the above cases, the answers will be found in this section.

Symptoms are listed alphabetically with the cause or causes listed next to them. Once you have determined the proper cause or causes, check the cure chart which immediately follows the symptom/cause chart. If you suspect insects or bugs, check the *Pest* section (page 20).

Take great care in determining the cause of the problem with your plant and then enjoy the positive results of the cure.

# Symptom/Cause Chart

| SYMPTOM | CAUSE |
| --- | --- |
| Black coating on leaves | Mildew, molds (disease) |
| Blisters/moist spots on leaves | Leaf-spot disease |
| Brown hard disks on leaf and stems | Scale insects |
| Brown or black flying insects | Fungus gnats |
| Brown crisp spots on leaves | Underwatering, overfertilizing, air pollution |
| Cactus: | |
| Mushy, soil stays soggy, green scum forms on clay pots | Too much water |
| Become yellow | Too little water, too much water |
| Weak new growth | Too little light |
| Chewed leaves | Animals, caterpillars, cockroaches, earwigs, millipedes |
| Cottony white fluff | Mealybugs |
| Curled leaves, dropping of leaves | Drafts, temperature too cool, overwatering, thrips (insects) |
| Dark, undersized leaves and stunted growth | Lack of moisture, lack of phosphorus |
| Dwarfism with yellow leaves | Root insects: nematodes, millipedes, centipedes, slugs |
| Dropping all leaves | Underwatering, air pollution, inadequate light |
| Dropping leaves in new plants | Physiological adjustment to new environment. Shock causes plant to drop a few, usually older, leaves as it adjust to a new environment. |
| Dropping older leaves | Underwatering, inadequate light, compacted soil, needs repotting, too high temperature |

| SYMPTOM | CAUSE |
| --- | --- |
| Drying foliage from base upward | Inadequate light, dry soil, too high temperature, leaking gas. (if single leaves dry up now and then, could be dying from old age) |
| Edges of leaves scorched | Insufficient water, excess fertilizer, sunburn, lack of enough humidity (ferns and begonias suffer most) |
| Edges of leaves brown | Root insects, accumulation of fertilizer salts on edges of pot, cold drafts |
| Edges brown | Plant has been allowed to dry out frequently, soil then being flooded with cold water, damaging roots |
| Edges of leaves dry and curl under, lower leaves turn yellow with brown spots and fall off | Insufficient water, too much heat |
| Flowers, none | Too little or too much fertilizer, insufficient light, improper day-length, thrips |
| Flower buds drop | Low humidity, insufficient water or light, insects (mites, whiteflies, thrips), moving plant from one location to another |
| Flowers deformed, discolored | Thrips |
| Flowers have short life | Insufficient water, excess heat |
| Gall on roots | Nematodes |
| Grayish cast with pale, bleached coloring | Mites, excessive light, insufficient fertilizer, underwatering, air pollution |
| Growth, soft, discolored | During winter, a combination of too much heat and insufficient light. Otherwise: air pollution, overwatering, extreme temperatures, excess humidity, crow- or stem-rot disease |
| Growth, new, thick and dwarfed | Salt damage |
| Growth, lack of new | Usually caused by insufficient light. Compacted soil, needs repotting, improper acidity of soil |
| Holes, cuts in leaves | Physical damage, caterpillars, cockroaches, springtails, slugs |
| Jumping insects in soil | Springtails |

| SYMPTOM | CAUSE |
| --- | --- |
| Leggy plants | Lack of light, excessive heat |
| Papery scars on leaves | Thrips |
| Rolled leaves inward at tips | Leaf rollers (insects) |
| Root deterioration | Root-rot disease, overwatering, overfertilizing, salt damage, pH factor, underwatering, poor repotting, insects: nematodes, fungus gnats, centipedes |
| Rotting at base and crown | Fungi, bacteria, aggravated by overwatering |
| Rusty spots on leaves or stems | Rust |
| Tan sesame-seed-like specks on underside of leaves | Whiteflies |
| Seedlings: | |
| Young plants rot at base and fall over | Damping-off disease, insufficient light |
| Chewed or cut off at soil level | Slugs, cockroaches, ants |
| New growth stunted, weak, distorted | Insufficient fertilizing, lack of enough light, insufficient humidity, needs repotting |
| Small leaves | Usually due to poor light; can be also caused by too much light (African violets). If leaves are also pale green and lower leaves turn yellow, means too little fertilizer |
| Soft black or brown areas on leaves | Overwatering, excess humidity |
| Soil, dry, hard packed | Underwatering, or compacted from improper soil |
| Specks of excrement | Caterpillars, cutworms, leaf miners, thrips |
| Spider webs | Mites |
| Spots on leaves | Too much sun, too hot or cold water |
| Stems long and stretch toward light | Too little light |
| Stems, weak and limp | Underwatering, underfertilizing |
| Sticky substance on leaves | Aphids, mealybugs, scales, whiteflies. They leave residue on foliage |
| Succulents: | |
| Mushy, soggy soil, green scum on clay pots | Too much water |

| SYMPTOM | CAUSE |
| --- | --- |
| Become yellow | Too much water, too little water, too much heat |
| New growth looks weak | Too little light |
| Tips of leaves and/or leaf margins turn brown and die back | Bruising (especially ferns, palms, spider plants), overwatering, too low light, too warm, air pollution, too low humidity, salt damage, anthracnose disease |
| Trails, smooth and shiny on leaves, pots, saucers | Slugs |
| White crust on rims of pot, top soil | Salt damage from too much fertilizer |
| White flying insects | Whiteflies |
| White fuzzy or feltlike spots on leaves | Powdery mildew disease, molds, mealybugs |
| Wilt | Overwatering, poor drainage, underwatering, too much light, too high temperatures, overfertilizing, air pollution, low humidity, compacted soil, repotting |
| Winding trails on leaves | Leaf miners |
| Yellowish green color | If roots healthy, it is sign of lack of nitrogen. Many plants' underside of leaves will turn purple |
| Yellow lower leaves, stems soft and dark in color | Root-rot disease from overwatering |
| Yellowing of top leaves, or yellow veins | Too much fertilizer, lack of iron, too alkaline soil |
| Yellowing of leaves followed by shedding, and poor growth | Poor drainage, lack of moisture, most likely improper soil |
| Yellowing of leaves, beginning at outer edges, spreading to whole leaf | Lack of nutrients, or damage to roots caused by too many nutrients |
| Yellowing of leaves | Soil too alkaline, natural process of leaf aging. If mass defoliation, can be overwatering or underfeeding |
| Yellowing or brown patches with leaves turning yellow on one side of plant | Too much light, sunburn |
| Yellow leaves that fall suddenly, plant tissue looks glossy and translucent | Sudden changes of temperature |
| Yellow spots | Incorrect fertilizing, air pollution, leaf-spot disease, mites, scales |
| Yellow or white rings on leaves | Watering with cold water |

§ 203

# Problem/Cause/Cure Chart

| PROBLEM | CAUSE | CURE |
| --- | --- | --- |
| *ANTHRACNOSE:* A fungal disease causing dark tan or black spots on plant, with narrow dark margins. Ends of leaves may turn dark tan and be crisscrossed with dark tan bars. Tips of leaves and leaf edges turn dark and die back. | High humidity or sudden chilling. | Destroy infested leaves. Spray healthy leaves with a foliar fungicide (Captan, Benomyl) to prevent spread of fungus. Keep plant on the dry side, in a well-ventilated area. Don't mist until fungus clears up. |
| *BRUISING:* Tips of leaves, leaf edges turn brown and die back. | Plant is being brushed against. | Cut away damaged sections of foliage, being careful to keep as much of leaf and stem intact as possible. Place plant in a location where people and pets can not get at it. |
| *CROWN- AND STEM-ROT DISEASE:* A fungus disease where the base and stems of plant become soft and mushy, and this spreads rapidly throughout the plant. | Excess humidity, overwatering, extreme temperature changes. | Remove infected portions of plant. Spray wounds with a foliar fungicide such as Captan or Benomyl. Repot in fresh soil in clay pot. For succulents and cacti, try dipping plant in hot water for 20–40 minutes before cutting away any foliage. |
| *DAMPING-OFF DISEASE:* Soil-borne fungus disease. Attacks seedling stems at base and lower portions, causing them to collapse. Leaves look pinched, die quickly. | Unsterilized growing medium; overwatering, too high humidity and temperatures. | Use sterilized medium for starting seedlings. When wilting noticed, reduce watering, humidity, temperature. Apply fungicide to control it (Captan or Benomyl). |

| PROBLEM | CAUSE | CURE |
|---|---|---|
| *DRAINAGE:* Water remains on surface of soil after watering. Wilting, slow growth, leaves turn yellow, older leaves drop off rapidly. General deterioration of plant. | Compacted soil caused by improper soil or insufficient drainage material over drainage holes. Compressed soil does not allow oxygen to get to the roots, drying process happens too quickly. | Remove all damaged foliage. Repot plant (see *Potting*), using proper soil for plant and providing proper amount of drainage material at bottom of pot. |
| Soil is constantly wet. Plant shows signs of overwatering. | Overwatering. If you have not been overwatering plant, waterlogged soil probably caused by improper drainage. | See "Watering." |
| *FERTILIZER:* Leaves pale bleached in color, or has yellow spots on leaves, yellowing of leaf beginning at edges and spreading over whole leaf. Older leaves drop off. Stems weak and limp. No flowering. | Too little fertilizing. | Fertilize more frequently, and especially during the growing season of the plant. Remove damaged foliage. |
| Yellowing of foliage at edges and over leaf. Yellow spots, crisp brown spots, scorched edges on leaves. Wilting. No flowers. Root damage. | Too much fertilizing. (Also see "*Salt Damage.*") | Flood soil with water and allow to drain, twice. Remove fertilizer salts if accumulated on pot with warm water and a stiff brush. Remove damaged foliage. Fertilize less often or use about half as much fertilizer as you have been using. |
| Dark, undersized leaves, and stunted growth. | Phosphorus deficiency. (Also see "Underwatering.") | Use superphosphate to correct this. |
| Plant yellowish green in color. Undersides of leaves often turn purple. | Nitrogen deficiency. | Use a fertilizer high in nitrogen every other feeding. |
| *HUMIDITY:* Leaf tips brown, margins of leaves yellow, no new | Too little humidity. | Place pot on bed of moist pebbles. Don't allow bottom of pot |

| PROBLEM | CAUSE | CURE |
| --- | --- | --- |
| growth or stunted growth, wilting, shriveling, buds drop off. | | to touch water. Spray-mist leaves daily. In winter, use a humidifier. |
| Promotes molds and mildews, decay and rot characteristic of overwatering, soft discolored growth. | Too much humidity. Succulents and cacti are especially vulnerable. | Lower humidity, mist plant less often and ventilate plant's growing area well (avoid drafts). Move succulents away from humidity-loving plants. |
| *LEAF-SPOT DISEASE:* Fungal or bacterial invasion. Black, brown, yellow spots, damp or blistered, usually with yellow margins. If infection severe, all foliage will be lost. | Appears following physical injury, or caused by cultural, environmental deficiencies, ie., poor air circulation, high humidity, overwatering, low light, chilling. | Remove infected areas. Spray with fungicide (Captan or Benomyl). Increase temperature, light, and improve ventilation. Let soil dry out before rewatering. Resume proper care. |
| *LIGHT:* Pale, discolored leaves, yellow foliage, tips of leaves and margins turn brown and die. No new growth, or if new growth it shrivels and dies. Older plants lose leaves from bottom up; young plants elongated, misshapen, underdeveloped leaves, inadequate branching, especially succulents and cacti. In winter, growth is soft and discolored. Variegated leaves turn solid green, yellow, drop off. Poor or no blooms. | Too little light. | Plant needs brighter exposure. (Check Dictionary.) If growing under artificial light, move closer to tubes, closer to center area of tubes, or the wattage must be increased, and lights remain on longer. |
| Scorch marks, spots on leaves that turn grayish. Plant looks bleached out. Plant might go limp, shrivel up and die if no sun is needed. Growth might be small. | Too much light. | Shield plant from light with curtain or other plants, or move it away from light source. If using artificial light, move plant farther away from center of tubes, or use lower wattage. |

| PROBLEM | CAUSE | CURE |
|---|---|---|
| *OVERWATERING:* See "Watering." | | |
| *POWDERY MILDEW:* A parasite organism. Looks like feltlike coating on foliage, gray or white in color. Leaves will curl and shrivel up due to mildew preventing light from getting through. | High humidity. | Lower humidity. Maintain good air circulation. Remove damaged foliage. Rinse undamaged foliage in warm water. |
| *BLACK SOOTY MOLDS:* Black coating on leaves. It is not a disease parasite. | Very humid conditions; attracted to honeydew secretions of insects. | Remove the mold by washing leaves with soapy water. Make sure air circulates well around plant. Check plant for insects. |
| *GRAY OR WHITE MOLD (BOTRYTIS):* Looks like bread mold. Found on soil, flowers or leaves. More common on plants growing in plastic pots where drying out of soil is reduced. | Wet soil or overuse of organic fertilizers, poor light, high humidity. The mold itself reduces ability of soil to dry out, causing other problems related to soggy soil. | Carefully scratch away mold from soil surface without injuring any roots that may be growing close to surface. Reduce watering, especially in plastic pots. Ventilate growing area. If mold persists, drench soil with diluted solution of Captan. Rinse foliage with warm water. |
| *NITROGEN DEFICIENCY:* See "Fertilizer." | | |
| *PHOSPHORUS DEFICIENCY:* See "Fertilizer." | | |
| *PH, ACID AND ALKALINE SOIL:* (Acidity and alkalinity are measure on pH scale of 0–14. 7 is neutral point.) Discolored leaves, yellowing of leaf | Too alkaline soil (iron or magnesium deficiency). Plants that prefer a more acid soil (pH 5–6.5) are: shrimp plant, camellia, century plant, gardenia, citrus, | Acid fertilizers help lower the pH for acid-loving plants. Add peat and sphagnum to soil (they are acid substances but will also absorb excess acid and alkaline |

§ 207

| PROBLEM | CAUSE | CURE |
| --- | --- | --- |
| margins, yellow top leaves, retarded growth, no root development. | palm, asparagus fern, podocarpus. | elements). Soil testers are available, but read the directions carefully in order to test accurately. |
| *POLLUTION:* Brown crisp spots, yellow spots, bleached leaves, dropping leaves, soft growth, wilting, drying of foliage from base upward. | Polluted, stagnant air. | Increase ventilation around growing area. In damp weather, keep plants on dry side. Avoid excess moisture on leaves. Remove damaged foliage. |
| *ROOT-ROT DISEASE:* A fungus which prevents root system from absorbing water. Top growth appears underwatered, lower leaves yellow; stems become soft and dark. Plant wilts, new growth dies back, and plant will eventually die. | Improper watering, bad drainage. | Remove plant from pot, and clean all soil from roots. Wash roots in warm water. Repot in fresh soil (see *Potting*). Remove damaged foliage. With first watering, drench soil with fungicide (Captan) and water only enough to keep plant from wilting, until plant resumes normal growth. |
| *RUST:* Rusty spots on leaves and stems. | Soil becomes too acid and the damage shows up on the foliage. | Repot (see *Potting*) in fresh soil. Spray plant with Captan and keep the foliage dry until problem is cleared up. |
| *SALT DAMAGE:* White salts on soil, pot side, rim. Brown crisp spots on leaves, scorched leaf edges. New growth dwarfed, thick. | Too much fertilizer. | Flood the plant with water until water pours out of drainage holes. Scrape off accumulated salts from pot's rim and sides with stiff brush and warm water. Give plant more light. Fertilize less frequently or use half the amount you have been using. |
| *TEMPERATURE:* Soft, discolored foliage, curled leaves, brown edges. | Too cool temperatures. Drafts will cause stems to rot from top down. | |

| PROBLEM | CAUSE | CURE |
| --- | --- | --- |
| Soft, discolored foliage. Lower leaves turn yellow with brown spots, edges of leaves dry and curl under. Foliage dies from base upward, older leaves drop off. Flowers have short life. Plants leggy, elongated, especially succulents. | Too warm temperatures. | |
| Yellowing leaves fall suddenly, glossy translucent plant tissue. | Sudden changes in temperature. | If plant has been severely damaged by temperature, remove from pot and check roots. If brown and soft they are rotted. Discard plant. If roots white and healthy, prune roots back to keep them in balance with the surviving top growth. Repot plant, remove damaged top growth. Keep plant away from drafts, air conditioners, radiators. |
| *UNDERWATERING:* See "Watering." | | |
| *WATERING:* Rotting, wilting, bleaching of foliage. Mass yellowing of leaves and they drop off. Leaves curl, tips turn brown die back. Weak new growth. Flowers blight. Soil always wet. | Overwatering. These symptoms also can indicate fungus diseases. but overwatering often precedes such diseases. When overwatering reaches advanced stages, diseases occur. | Remove plant from pot to check the root (see *Potting*) and also check the soil and the drainage holes to make sure they are not clogged, and check to see there is enough drainage material in the bottom of the pot. If roots white and healthy, repot plant and stir up surface soil to aerate it, or repot plant in a warm, well-ventilated area until new growth appears. Resume proper care. If roots soft, brown and mushy, discard plant. |

| PROBLEM | CAUSE | CURE |
| --- | --- | --- |
| Plant stems weak, limp, wilted. Leaves curled under, lower leaves yellow with brown spots and fall off. Brown crisp spots, scorched edges on leaves and flowers. Short flowering period, flower buds drop. Dark, undersized leaves, older leaves drop off. New growth dies, and soon whole plant dies. If plant is allowed to wilt more than a few times, it might die. Cactus and succulent leaves turn yellow and shrivel. | Improper watering or under-watering. | Thoroughly soak plant at each watering. Water over entire soil surface, slowly, until excess water drains out of drainage holes. Don't let plant sit in water for more than an hour. Let plant dry out enough to meet its proper requirements between waterings. Remove damaged foliage. Cover plant with plastic bag to speed recovery. Most plants will pick up soon after watering. |

# Index